$\mathscr{B}$IBLE DOCTRINES

A Pentecostal Perspective

William W. Menzies
and
Stanley M. Horton

Stanley M. Horton, Th.D.

General Editor

LOGION
P R E S S

Springfield, Missouri

02–0318

Originally published as *Understanding Our Doctrine* by William W. Menzies. Revised and expanded by Stanley M. Horton

8th Printing 2001

Logion Press books are published by Gospel Publishing House.

Library of Congress Cataloging-in-Publication Data
Menzies, William W.
    Bible doctrines : a Pentecostal perspective
  / William W. Menzies : Stanley M. Horton, general editor.
      p. cm.
    Rev. and expanded ed. of: Understanding our doctrine.
    Includes bibliographical references.
    ISBN 0–88243–318–0
    1. Assemblies of God—Doctrines. 2. Pentecostal churches—Doctrines. 3. Bible—Criticism, interpretation, etc. I. Menzies, William W. Understanding our doctrine. II. Horton, Stanley M. III. Title.
    BX8765.5.Z5M46   1993
    230'.994—dc20   92–43219
Printed in the United States of America

CONTENTS

Bible Doctrines: A Pentecostal Perspective

Bible Doctrines: A Pentecostal Perspective

The study of Bible doctrines is very important, especially in these days when the number of false prophets and false teachers is increasing. Too many Christians are being "tossed back and forth by the waves, and blown here and there by every wind of teaching and by the cunning and craftiness of men in their deceitful scheming" (Eph. 4:14). Unfortunately, some believers (perhaps not realizing that "doctrine" is simply another word for "teaching") object to the study of doctrine—just what the propagators of false doctrine would like a person to do. This then makes one a likely candidate for their "wind of teaching." That's why God wants Christians to grow to the point that they know the basic teachings of the Bible. Such knowledge will protect them from false teachers and false doctrine.

The book *Understanding Our Doctrine,* by Dr. William W. Menzies, was originally written as a unit in a training course entitled "Fundamentals for Sunday School Workers." Dr. Menzies, currently president of the Asia Pacific Theological Seminary (formerly Far East Advanced School of Theology) in Baguio, Republic of the Philippines, gave me his kind permission to revise and enlarge his excellent book for general use.

The chapters in the book follow the sixteen points of

the Statement of Fundamental Truths, as accepted by the Assemblies of God. Our purpose, however, is not to promote Assemblies of God doctrines, but to bring out the biblical basis and applications of these fundamental Bible truths. Thus, this study will be helpful to those who believe the Bible, whatever their denomination or background. Christians need to know where they stand with respect to Bible doctrines.

Pastors will find the book useful in the training of new converts. Sunday school teachers will find it useful either for course work or as background for their teaching. Bible college students will find it giving them a solid basis for further studies in theology.

I wish to thank Dr. G. Raymond Carlson, general superintendent of the Assemblies of God; The Assemblies of God Theological Seminary; Central Bible College; the Division of Foreign Missions of the Assemblies of God; and others who by their generosity have made this project possible. Special thanks are due also to Glen Ellard and his editorial staff for their expert help.

For easier reading, Hebrew, Aramaic, and Greek words are all transliterated with English letters.

A few abbreviations have been used:

Gk.: Greek
Heb.: Hebrew
KJV: King James Version
NASB: *New American Standard Bible*
NIV: New International Version

STANLEY M. HORTON, TH.D.
DISTINGUISHED PROFESSOR EMERITUS
OF BIBLE AND THEOLOGY
AT THE ASSEMBLIES OF GOD
THEOLOGICAL SEMINARY

INTRODUCTION

Bible Doctrines: A Pentecostal Perspective

The Assemblies of God came into being as a result of the Pentecostal revival that began early in the twentieth century. This revival came as God's mighty supernatural answer to Modernism, the antisupernatural religious liberalism that was taking over the major Christian denominations in America and around the world. Books written to defend the faith were being ignored by the seminaries that trained their ministers. The possibility of God-given miracles was denied. A spiritual vacuum was developing. As Dr. William Menzies points out:

The United States in the years between the Civil War and the close of the [nineteenth] century was in social and religious ferment. Moral, political, and economic corruption increased the stresses occasioned by urbanization, industrialization and immigration. The great denominations, successful in Christianizing the frontier, had become complacent and sophisticated, lacking the vision and vitality to meet the changing needs of a distressed populace. Varying degrees of accommodation to popular ideas, newly imported from Europe, which assaulted orthodox Evangelicalism, further weakened the great communions. Against the erosion in the church world arose the Fundamentalist and Holiness movements. It was largely out of the spiritual concern gen-

erated in this segment of the church that the yearning for a new
Pentecost was born. Prior to 1900 there were charismatic manifestations, but these were isolated and episodic in nature. But
the stage was being set for a great outpouring of the Holy Spirit
which would quickly encircle the earth, bringing a great refreshing in the Latter Days.[1]

The current Pentecostal movement traces its origin to
a revival at Bethel Bible College in Topeka, Kansas, that
began on January 1, 1901. Students, from their studies of
the Bible, concluded that speaking in tongues (Acts 2:4)
is the initial outward evidence of the baptism in the Holy
Spirit. One of the students, Agnes Ozman, said she felt "as
though rivers of living water were proceeding from [her]
innermost being."[2]

The revival became a Pentecostal explosion when, in
1906, W. J. Seymour secured an old two-story frame building at 312 Azusa Street in Los Angeles, California. For about
three years services ran almost continually, from ten in the
morning to midnight. Many of those who received the
Pentecostal baptism in the Holy Spirit there scattered to
spread the message. Many independent Pentecostal
churches sprang up. Then,

After the Pentecostal outpourings began, numerous publications
appeared advocating its teachings and serving as channels for
teaching information, and the support of missionaries overseas.
One of these publications, the *Word and Witness* edited by
Eudorus N. Bell, issued a call in 1913 for a conference of Pentecostal believers to convene in Hot Springs, Arkansas, the following year. This became the founding meeting of the General
Council of the Assemblies of God.[3]

Five basic reasons were given for calling the General
Council of April 2–12, 1914. They were "(1) to achieve

[1]William W. Menzies, *Anointed to Serve: The Story of the Assemblies
of God* (Springfield, Mo.: Gospel Publishing House, 1971), 33.

[2]Stanley H. Frodsham, *With Signs Following,* rev. ed. (Springfield,
Mo.: Gospel Publishing House, 1946), 20.

[3]Gary B. McGee, "A Brief History of the Modern Pentecostal Outpouring," *Paraclete* 18 (Spring 1984): 22.

better understanding and unity of doctrine, (2) to know how to conserve God's work at home and abroad, (3) to consult on protection of funds for missionary endeavors, (4) to explore the possibilities of chartering churches under a legal name, and (5) to consider the establishment of a Bible training school with a literary division."[4] More than three hundred attended and elected E. N. Bell as the chairman of their new Assemblies of God fellowship. Then in 1916, a "statement of truths" was prepared, primarily by Daniel Warren Kerr, of Cleveland, Ohio.[5] It was adopted with the following preamble:

This statement of Fundamental Truths is not intended as a creed for the church, nor as a basis of fellowship among Christians, but only as a basis of unity for the ministry alone (i.e., that we all speak the same thing, 1 Cor. 1:10; Acts 2:42). The human phraseology employed in such statement is not inspired nor contended for, but the truth set forth in such phraseology is held to be essential to a full Gospel ministry. No claim is made that it contains all truth in the Bible, only that it covers our present needs as to these fundamental matters.[6]

The original statement served the Assemblies of God well for many years. There was little dissatisfaction with any of the sixteen points.[7] However, since some of the doctrines were stated quite briefly, it was felt that some of them needed clarification and enlarging. In 1960, a committee worked on this and minor rewording and clarity. The work was approved and adopted by the General Council in 1961. The only significant change was in dropping

---

[4]*In the Last Days: An Early History of the Assemblies of God* (Springfield, Mo.: Assemblies of God, 1962), 11.

[5]Carl Brumback, *Like a River: The Early Years of the Assemblies of God* (Springfield, Mo.: Gospel Publishing House, 1977), 55.

[6]General Council of the Assemblies of God, General Council Minutes, October 2–7, 1916. This is slightly modified in the current statement, which is available in booklet form: *The General Council of the Assemblies of God Statement of Fundamental Truths,* rev. (Springfield, Mo.: Gospel Publishing House, 1983).

[7]There were 17 points originally. Revision combined points 2 and 13, added one on Christ's deity, and combined points 10 and 11, leaving 16 all together.

the term "entire sanctification," because it was understood in different ways by different theologians and was thus ambiguous. "The clarification of 1961 specified the belief that the imputed righteousness accorded the believer at his justification was to be exhibited in a life of holiness."[8]

The concern for the preservation of doctrinal integrity within the Movement has also resulted in a number of position papers. These papers were called for by ministers of Assemblies of God churches from time to time, as the need for further help and clarification on various subjects was felt on the field. Most of them were prepared by the Commission on Doctrinal Purity, a standing committee appointed by the Executive Presbytery of the Assemblies of God. A number of pastors, district officials, and professors of the Bible colleges and seminary have served on that committee at various times. The papers were approved by the Executive Presbytery and the General Presbytery, the leadership bodies of the Assemblies of God, and then printed. All papers up to 1989 have been collected and published under the title *Where We Stand.*[9] Their titles follow: (1) "The Inerrancy of Scripture"; (2) "Can Born-again Believers Be Demon Possessed?" (3) "Divorce and Remarriage"; (4) "The Ministry of the Body of Christ"; (5) "Divine Healing: An Integral Part of the Gospel"; (6) "The Discipleship and Submission Movement"; (7) "Transcendental Meditation"; (8) "Deacons and Trustees"; (9) "Eternal Punishment"; (10) "The Assemblies of God View of Ordination"; (11) "The Doctrine of Creation"; (12) "The Security of the Believer"; (13) "Homosexuality"; (14) "The Rapture of the Church"; (15) "The Believer and Positive Confession"; (16) "The Initial Physical Evidence of the Baptism in the Holy Spirit"; (17) "A Biblical Perspective on Gambling"; (18) "Abstinence"; (19) "A Biblical Perspective on Abortion"; and (20) "The Kingdom of God as Described in Holy Scripture." Since the publication of *Where We Stand,* another position paper has been pub-

---

[8]Menzies, *Anointed,* 318 (see pages 317–318 for further discussion on this change).

[9]*Where We Stand* (Springfield, Mo.: Gospel Publishing House, 1990). The position papers are also available individually.

lished: *The Role of Women in Ministry as Described in Holy Scripture.* Others will be prepared as the need arises. They are a valuable supplement to our understanding of Assemblies of God doctrine and practice. Where it seems appropriate, some of the material from these position papers will be discussed in this book.

We would also like to acknowledge the foundation laid by Peter Christopher Nelson in his book, *Bible Doctrines,* which in 1948 was the first written commentary on the *Statement of Fundamental Truths.*

1st

FUNDAMENTAL TRUTH

THE AUTHORITATIVE RULE

The Scriptures, both the Old and New Testaments, are verbally inspired of God and are the revelation of God to man, the infallible, authoritative rule of faith and conduct (1 Thess. 2:13; 2 Tim. 3:15–17; 2 Pet. 1:21).

The Scriptures Inspired

THE AUTHORITATIVE RULE

How can I know which is the true religion? is an important question frequently asked. It is deserving of an answer, since one's eternal welfare is at stake. The real issue is the matter of authority.

There are three basic kinds of religious authority: (1) human reason, (2) the Church, and (3) God's Word. Perhaps the most common today is human reason. We will not dispute the obvious fact that human beings have mental equipment which has produced an amazing array of breathtaking achievements, particularly in scientific fields. Nor will we brush aside the need for handling one's daily affairs in a logical fashion. The process of dealing with problems in a commonsense fashion is called rationality. It is no sin to function on this level. Rationality, however, must not be confused with rationalism. Rationalism is the belief that the highest authority is human reason. Given enough time, the rationalist contends, human genius will unlock all the secrets of the universe and lead to perfect life, peace, health, wealth, and continuing prosperity.

One form of rationalism is a scientism that believes science, with its modern methodologies and equipment, will eventually be able to analyze and solve all problems. However, such a view has severe limitations. It fails to recognize that science is not able to deal with some things. For example, it cannot work directly with the qualities of color and sound. It has to express them in quantitative terms. But qualities are not quantities. For example, people who are born blind can understand all the science and mathematics of the wave lengths of light. That does not mean they have any idea of what a beautiful sunset, a red rose, or the exquisite coloring of a butterfly's wing looks like. Those born deaf can understand all the science and mathematics of sound waves. That does not mean they have any idea of what a symphony or a congregation of people praising God and glorifying Jesus in the Holy Spirit sound like. Science cannot deal with things that cannot be weighed or measured, such as the human soul. Neither can it deal with unique occurrences. Consequently, it cannot deal with miracles, since each one is a distinct and separate manifestation of the grace and power of God and not repeatable for lab analysis.

Actually, those who take rationalism as their authority usually end up making their own reason the final authority. But as Solomon observed, "There is nothing new under the sun," for this same kind of arrogance displayed itself in ancient times. In Genesis 11 we read about those who attempted to defy God and make a name for themselves by building a city and a very high tower at Babel. Rationalists of all ages are much like that—putting their ultimate trust in their own reasoning ability. Again, repeatedly in the days of the Judges, "everyone did as he saw fit" (Judg. 17:6; 21:25). The chaos and confusion resulting from trust in human reason as the ultimate authority are vividly portrayed in the tragic stories recorded in the Book of Judges.

A second common belief is that the Church is the ultimate authority. Some contend that Christ gave His authority to Peter and that Peter laid hands on the bishops he ordained, giving them authority to lay hands on their successors. By this "apostolic succession," authority was transmitted from Christ through the twelve apostles and so down through the centuries. On this ground, certain churches hold themselves aloft as the only authorized representative of Christ, and hence its leaders are supposed to hold a special authority to judge truth.

Commonly associated with this view of apostolic succession is the assertion that the New Testament is a product of the Church, giving the Church a kind of priority over the Bible. It should be noted, however, that the theory of apostolic succession did not appear until near the end of the second century A.D. Furthermore, the Council of Carthage in A.D. 397 did not authorize the list of New Testament books that we today accept as canonical; it merely gave assent to what was already generally recognized and used in the churches of the day. The death of Christ put the new covenant into effect (Heb. 9:15–17). After His resurrection, Christ and the Holy Spirit brought the Church into being. Then, the Holy Spirit inspired the writers who gave us the New Testament books. Today, since there are disputes and quarrels among ecclesiastical bodies, the questioning heart yearns for an authority higher than an earthly church organization.

The third alternative is to trust implicitly in the authority of the Word of God. This view is based squarely on the conviction that God by nature is self-disclosing.[1] He is a speaking God; He wishes to communicate with His creatures. Hebrews 1:1–2 indicates this characteristic in God: "In the past God spoke to our forefathers through the prophets at many times and in various ways, but in these last days he has spoken to us by his Son."

God has spoken. His fullest and final declaration, as Hebrews 1:1–2 indicates, is in the person of His Son, Jesus Christ. We call this manner of speaking the Incarnation, the clothing of the divine with human flesh. It is the fullest measure by which God can communicate with us, for it is person-to-person communication. Jesus Christ, as the first chapter of John's Gospel reminds us, is "the Word," the messenger and the message of God. Now, just as Christ is

[1]The key difference between other religions and Christianity is that other religions see humanity in the dark seeking for something within themselves or beyond themselves. Christianity reveals God bringing light into the darkness as He comes down into the stream of human life and history and reaches out in love for fallen human beings.

the Living Word, so the Bible is the written Word. In the absence of the personal presence of Jesus from the time of His ascension until His second coming, the Bible is the authoritative speaking of God, which the Holy Spirit is pleased to use to direct people to Christ. The apostle Paul, in Romans 10:8–15, dramatically points out that without the proclamation of the Good News—the message of the Bible—people do not find God. It alone provides the grounds from which with the belief of the heart we confess "Jesus is Lord," bringing salvation.

THE REVELATION OF GOD TO HUMANKIND

If one grants that God does speak, is the Bible the only medium of His speaking? God also makes himself known, to an extent, to all people (1) through creation and (2) through conscience. This manner of God's speaking is usually called general, or natural, revelation. Romans 1 and 2 outline this kind of utterance God has employed. Romans 1:20 speaks of the knowledge of God that all people everywhere can gather from their acquaintance with nature: "Since the creation of the world God's invisible qualities— his eternal power and divine nature—have been clearly seen, being understood from what has been made, so that men are without excuse." In other words, people should have known, and should know, that some little tin god could not have made the universe. Nor could the many pagan gods, represented as always fighting each other, have created the consistency, order, and beauty we find in nature. Who can deny the inspired expression of Psalm 19: "The heavens declare the glory of God; the skies proclaim the work of his hands."

The Bible says God speaks through the individual's conscience: "Indeed, when Gentiles, who do not have the law, do by nature things required by the law, they are a law for themselves, even though they do not have the law, since they show that the requirements of the law are written on their hearts, their consciences also bearing witness, and their thoughts now accusing, now even defending them" (Rom. 2:14–15). The very fact that people everywhere have a conscience, an idea of right and wrong that is in line with the Bible, shows that there is authority beyond the individual and the circumstances. Even people who have rejected the Bible retain a conscience, though it will operate on the basis of what they have come to believe is the right thing for them to do.

God has spoken externally in the universe He created, and internally in the conscience of every individual. However, the tragedy recorded in Romans 1 and 2 is that mankind, given the glimmering of light available in the universe, has cursed God and rebelled against Him. Even so, there is sufficient light so that none can claim that God has been unjust. The result is that people by their own willful rejection of the light of natural revelation consign themselves to eternal punishment. It is not God who sends people to hell. It is people who demand that God leave them alone so they may go their own way and attempt to fulfill their own desires who send themselves to hell. When God sadly, reluctantly, leaves them to their own devices, perversion and destruction and hell are the grim, inevitable prospect. Therefore, natural revelation is inadequate by itself if fallen human beings are to be helped.

A special revelation, a message carried only in the Bible, is the wonderful news that God has invaded the human situation, acted to redeem us, and offered a way by which we can enter into that redemption. Nature and conscience do not disclose this. The Old Testament points ahead to the coming Redeemer; the New Testament tells of His coming and interprets its meaning.

THE VERBALLY INSPIRED WORD OF GOD

The Greek word most nearly equivalent to our word "inspiration" is found in 2 Timothy 3:16. It is *theopneustos.* It means, literally, "God-breathed." By divine breath and power the Holy Spirit moved the (human) authors of the Bible with such precision that the product accurately reflects the intention of God himself. As God spoke through prophets and apostles, the original documents they produced bear the special marks of divine inspiration. This means that the sixty-six books in the canon, which make up the Bible, in their original expression are entirely trustworthy as the voice of the Holy Spirit. (See 2 Pet. 1:17–21.)

Several points should be kept in mind regarding the manner of inspiration. Mechanical dictation holds that God spoke through human beings to the extent that their individual personalities were suppressed. Such a view is erroneous. Personalities and particular vocabularies of the various writers are obviously distinguishable; of the forty-plus writers of Scripture, a variety of walks of life are clearly observable—shepherds, statesmen, priests, fishermen, the well-educated and the relatively unlearned. The writers were not, robot-like, manipulated while in trances; God did not pick them at random and tell them to write. For example, God set Jeremiah apart to be a prophet and began preparing him while he was still in his mother's womb (Jer. 1:5). God took all the writers of Scripture through experiences, preparing them in such a way that He could use them to bring out the truth in exactly the way He wanted. In this way, the integrity of the writers as individual personalities was carefully preserved by the special acts of inspiration and guidance of the Holy Spirit. At the same time, the fruit of their writing is unmistakably the Word of God. The Holy Spirit "prompted the original thought in the mind of the writers (Amos 3:8). He then guided their choice of words to express such thoughts (Exod. 4:12,15); and, lastly, He illumines the mind of the reader of such words in a way that the reader potentially may comprehend the same truth as was originally in the mind of the writer (1 Cor. 2:12; Eph. 1:17–18). Thus both thought and language are revelatory and inspired."[2]

Another widely-held view of inspiration is known as dynamic inspiration. This view conceives of the Bible as not being intended to convey "propositional truth"[3] about God himself; advocates of this idea say this because they have concluded that God is unknowable. They say He is "totally

---

[2]*Where We Stand* (Springfield, Mo.: Gospel Publishing House, 1990), 7.

[3]By "propositional truth" we mean real, objective, rational information.

other"[4] and discloses only truth about how we ought to live.

This is also termed functional interpretation of inspiration since it says the Bible can reveal nothing about what God is, but can reveal only His work. It is at the heart of many of the modernistic, or theologically liberal, systems that deny the supernatural. It lends itself to the idea that the Bible is basically folklore, but insofar as it talks about how to live rightly, it speaks meaningfully to people. In this view, ethics supplants doctrine. It opens the door to relativism, since objective standards of truth are largely washed away. People then interpret on their own what they think is proper to accept and what they wish to reject as merely folklore (cf. Judg. 17:6).

A variation of this view is the emphasis on salvation-history. In this view, there is a clear acknowledgment that God has acted in history in saving ways. This view accepts the Bible as a record of such divine activity, but claims it is a merely human record: open to the errors of human judgment, limited by the experience and the worldview of the (human) writers, and subject to (unaided) human interpretation of divine activity. The one big point where this view is on the right track is when it accepts the Bible as a record of supernatural events in which God acts in history to redeem people. Its major failure is in not seeing that even the interpretation of such events is inspired by the Holy Spirit. If this were not so, we would still be left in the dark, since events by themselves are filled with ambiguity; there is not complete revelation until they are interpreted authoritatively.

What does the Bible itself teach about the true manner of inspiration? It emphasizes the actual inspiration of the writers. In some cases God spoke to them in an audible voice. In some cases He gave them revelation in dreams and visions. Sometimes He spoke to their hearts and minds in a way that they knew it was God. Amos 3:8 emphasized this: "The lion has roared—who will not fear? The Sovereign Lord has spoken—who can but prophesy?" Jeremiah

---

[4]That is, they say God is infinitely different from human beings and therefore unknowable.

at one point decided he would quit prophesying; it seemed no one was listening. God's word in his heart, however, became like a burning fire shut up in his bones, and he could not stop (Jer. 20:9). No wonder statements such as "this is what the Lord says" occur 3,808 times in the Old Testament alone. Second Peter 1:20–21 shows us that no writer of Scripture ever depended on his own reasoning or imagination in the writing process: "Above all, you must understand that no prophecy of Scripture came about by the prophet's own interpretation. For prophecy never had its origin in the will of man, but men spoke from God as they were carried along by the Holy Spirit." "Carried along" might sound as if they were in the midst of the stream of the Holy Spirit and were carried along. But an examination of the Scriptures shows that God taught them and led them along. (See Exod. 4:15.) And going back to 2 Timothy 3:16, one can clearly see that the inspiration of Scripture also extends to the words and to the entirety of the text of the original documents, or autographs, of these men.

Jesus accepted the full inspiration of the entire Old Testament with His sweeping declaration, "Scripture cannot be broken" (John 10:35; see also Matt. 5:18). This view we call plenary (full), verbal (extending even to the words) inspiration. Romans 3:2 is in accord with this view when it cites the Old Testament as "the very words of God." So is Hebrews 3:7–11 when it quotes Psalm 95:7–11, not giving a human author, but introducing the quotation with "as the Holy Spirit says. . . ."

One may ask, That is very well for the Old Testament, but what about the New Testament? Jesus went from village to village teaching. Undoubtedly He repeated many things as He went from place to place. Consequently, He left a body of teaching, promising His disciples, "the Holy Spirit . . . will remind you of everything I have said to you" (John 14:26). This body of teaching was passed along to the Church by the apostles (Acts 2:42). From it also the Holy Spirit directed the writers of the Gospels to select material that would be beneficial to those they wrote to. For example, Luke tells us that he "carefully investigated everything" (Luke 1:3); we can be sure he was moved by the Holy Spirit to do this. Thus, in the Apostolic Age a process of revelation was going on. Christ was the fulfillment of Old Testament prophecies. Necessary for the generations to come was the record of His virgin birth, His teachings, His death and resurrection (recorded in the Gospels); the account of the institution of the Church with patterns normative for the whole Church Age (recorded in the Book of Acts); an explanation of the meaning of the life, death, and resurrection of Jesus, with practical help for the churches (recorded in the Epistles); and a glimpse into the consummation of the age (recorded in the Book of Revelation).

That the apostles recognized the propriety of a new covenant, or testament, is borne out by such passages as 2 Peter 3:15–16: "Bear in mind that our Lord's patience means salvation, just as our dear brother Paul also wrote you with the wisdom that God gave him. He writes the same way in all his letters, speaking in them of these matters. His letters contain some things that are hard to understand, which ignorant and unstable people distort, as they do the other Scriptures, to their own destruction." Notice the expression, "the other Scriptures." Here is clear testimony to the belief of Peter in the seventh decade of the first century that Paul was writing material that was on a plane with Old Testament Scripture. Paul also declares in some places that he has a word of the Lord, that is, a saying of Jesus, to back up what he writes. (See 1 Cor. 11:23; 1 Thess. 4:1–2,15.) But even though he does not always say this, that does not mean that what he writes is any less inspired of the Holy Spirit. (Cf. 1 Cor. 7:12.)

The Bible teaches us regarding itself that the Holy Spirit so moved upon prophets and apostles that even the words themselves in the original documents are fully authoritative. If the words were not inspired, then people would be free to change them to fit their own ideas. Therefore, inspiration of the words was necessary to protect the truth. Jesus indicated the importance of every word by saying: "Until heaven and earth disappear, not the smallest letter [in Heb., the *yod*], not the least stroke of a pen, will by any means disappear from the Law until everything is accomplished" (Matt. 5:18).

CHAPTER

1
———

The
Scriptures
Inspired

THE INFALLIBLE RULE

The divine source and authority of the Scripture assure us that the Bible is also infallible, that is, incapable of error and therefore not capable of misleading, deceiving, or disappointing us. Some writers make a distinction between inerrancy ("exempt from error") and infallibility, but they are very near synonyms. "If there is any difference in the shade of meaning between the two terms, inerrancy emphasizes the truthfulness of Scripture, while infallibility emphasizes the trustworthiness of Scripture. Such inerrancy and infallibility apply to all of Scripture and include both revelational inerrancy and factual inerrancy. It is truth (2 Sam. 7:28; Ps. 119:43,160; John 17:17,19; Col. 1:5)."[5]

Humanistic unbelief is the real source of objections to the authority and infallibility of the Bible. Its arguments are not new. Ancient writers such as Irenaeus, Tertullian, and Augustine had to combat some of them and in doing so declared their own confidence in the Scriptures. The reformers Zwingli, Calvin, and Luther also accepted the full authority of Scripture.[6] Over the years unbelieving critics have made extensive lists of what they called discrepancies in the Bible, and some have claimed the Bible was indisputably in error. In 1874 J. W. Haley did a thorough study that is still worth reading.[7] He classified these alleged discrepancies and found they arose from several causes:

1. A failure to read exactly what the Bible says.

2. False interpretations of the Bible, especially those which fail to take into account ancient customs and modes of speech.

3. Wrong ideas of the Bible as a whole and a failure to recognize that the Bible on occasion records the words of Satan and of evil people. For example, God told Job's friends, "You have not spoken of me what is right" (Job 42:8). But the Bible gives a true record of what they said, even though they were wrong.

---

[5]*Where We Stand,* 7–8.

[6]Ibid., 9.

[7]John W. Haley, *Alleged Discrepancies of the Bible* (Grand Rapids: Baker Book House, 1988).

4. A failure to recognize that some accounts are condensations of what was said or done.

5. Chronological difficulties due to the fact that Babylonians, Egyptians, Greeks, and Romans all used different systems of measuring time or dating. Even Israel and Judah sometimes differed in their methods of counting kings' reigns.[8]

6. Apparent discrepancies in numbers due to the fact that some passages use round numbers, others give more exact figures, depending on the purpose of the writer.

7. In some places copyists' errors crept into certain ancient manuscripts. A comparison of manuscripts has corrected most of these errors. (In fact, most scholars agree on what was the original reading in the vast majority of the cases.[9] Furthermore, those cases where we cannot be sure do not affect the teachings of the Bible in any way.)

8. Finally, some so-called discrepancies were just a matter of a Hebrew or Greek word having more than one meaning, just as some of our English words do (e.g., compare "lead" in "lead weight" and "lead the blind").

One after another, alleged mistakes and discrepancies have been proved false. Again and again new discoveries by archaeologists and other scholars and scientists have shown that the so-called errors were errors of the critics due to their unbelief and insufficient knowledge.[10]

Some who deny the infallibility of Scripture nevertheless believe the Bible has value. That is, they say it does not matter whether the history and science of the Bible are

---

[8]For a good discussion of this, see Edwin R. Thiele, *The Mysterious Numbers of the Hebrew Kings* (Grand Rapids: Zondervan Publishing House, 1983).

[9]R. K. Harrison and others, *Biblical Criticism: Historical, Literary and Textual* (Grand Rapids: Zondervan Publishing House, 1980), 150.

[10]For example, Dr. Stanley Horton heard a Harvard professor say that sevenfold lamps were not in existence in Moses' time; therefore, the Bible was mistaken when it told of one being made and placed in the tabernacle (see Exod. 37:17–24). However, on an archaeological expedition at Dothan in 1962 with Dr. Joseph Free of Wheaton College, Dr. Horton watched workmen uncover a sevenfold lamp dating from 1400 B.C., right from the time of Moses. Stanley M. Horton, "Why the Bible is Reliable," *Pentecostal Evangel*, 14 January 1973, 8–11.

true. They say that a sinner can be saved without knowing the whole Bible or its claims to inspiration. It is true that the sinner does not need to know about the Virgin Birth, divine healing, sanctification, the baptism in the Holy Spirit, and the second coming of Christ in order to be saved. But once a person becomes a believer, such teachings will become the means of becoming mature in the faith (cf. Heb. 5:11 to 6:2).

For those who are troubled by what they consider the imprecision of the Bible in describing natural phenomena, they should realize that scientific language and terminology have developed only in modern times. Moreover, each science develops its own vocabulary. For example, the word "nucleus" means one thing to the biologist and quite another thing to the astrophysicist. Even ordinary words can be given new meanings by scientists. To the botanist, for example, the word "transpire" means "to give off moisture through pores (stomata)." Consequently, the Bible uses nontechnical, everyday language; we can expect its use of terms such as "sunrise" and "sunset" to be just like ours, even though we now know that it is the movement of the earth that is taking place, not that of the sun. Nevertheless, when the Bible does make an authoritative, propositional statement, such as "God created the heavens and the earth," we can be sure the Bible is infallible.

The Bible will not lead us astray. It is a wonderful revelation of God as our Creator and Redeemer; a personal God who loves us and is concerned about us; a God who has a plan, who sent His Son to die for us (1 Cor. 15:3), and who will continue to do His work until Satan is crushed, death destroyed, and a new heavens and earth established. The whole Bible shows that He is reliable, dependable, trustworthy, and that His very nature guarantees the authority, infallibility, and inerrancy of His Word.

THE CANON AND LATER TRANSLATIONS

Although it is asserted that the autographs were inspired by God, we no longer have them. (They were probably worn out by frequent use and repeated copying.) So how, then, can we trust the text we have in our modern Bibles?

The trustworthiness of our Bibles today is tied into canon history and the transmission and translation of the books of the Bible.

The word "canon" means "a rule, a standard, a measuring rod." Therefore, a book considered canonical is a book that has met certain criteria, or standards. By the time of Jesus and the apostles the thirty-nine Old Testament books were solidly accepted by Judaism as inspired by God. Jesus repeatedly referred to the Old Testament, recognizing that God himself was speaking (e.g., Matt. 19:4; 22:29). To attest the confidence the writers of the New Testament had in the Old, one need but consider that in the hundreds of quotations of Old Testament passages scattered throughout the New Testament, there is only one place where possibly an apocryphal (spurious or doubtful) Old Testament book is quoted. That single reference is in Jude 14–15, where there appears to be a similarity to the Book of Enoch 1:9, and even this is not difficult to attribute to a common oral tradition available both to the writer of the Book of Enoch and to Jude.

What of the New Testament canon? This is a fascinating story all its own, but let us move to the conclusion of the story, into the fourth century. In A.D. 367, the most orthodox theologian of the time, the great champion of biblical truth, Athanasius, sifted through all the books being circulated in the Mediterranean world purporting to be apostolic documents. His examination disclosed twenty-seven books, the ones we have today, to be God's Word.[11] Thirty years later, quite independently of Athanasius, a church council met in Carthage to discuss the problem of what books were genuinely Scripture.[12] They applied four tests to the documents considered: (1) Apostolicity: Was the book the product of an apostle or a close associate of an apostle? (2) Universality: Was the book widely accepted and used in the churches? (3) Contents: Did the subject matter of the book appear to be on a plane with known Scripture? (4) Inspiration: Did the book bear the special

CHAPTER 1

The Scriptures Inspired

---

[11]Everett F. Harrison, *Introduction to the New Testament* (Grand Rapids: Wm. B. Eerdmans Pub. Co., 1982), 108.
[12]Ibid.

quality that speaks of divine inspiration? Note that three of the four tests to which the books were subjected were objective, a matter of factual evidence. Only the fourth, the matter of inspiration, could be considered subjective, a matter of personal judgment. The Council of Carthage, after considering the facts, concluded that the twenty-seven books we now have in our New Testament were the only books in circulation at that time that measured up to the criteria established. For all practical purposes, the question of canon was closed until the advent of modern rationalism.

The other question remaining about the trustworthiness of the Bible is the accuracy of the transmission of the text. Inspiration extends only to the autograph; no case is made for the inspiration of any particular translation (version) of the Bible. You may ask, Just how nearly does my Bible conform to the original documents inspired by God?

Let us look first at the New Testament, which is nearer to us in time than the Old Testament text. Most remarkable is that there are over 5,300 ancient hand-written copies (manuscripts) of the New Testament in the original Greek. Some come from the third and fourth centuries. One fragment of the Gospel of John comes from about A.D. 125, within 30 years of the time it was written. This is in contrast to other ancient writings. The oldest manuscript we have of Virgil comes from about 350 years after his death. The oldest of Horace is from 900 years after his death. Most of the manuscripts of Plato come from 1,300 years after his death.[13] Sir Frederic Kenyon, noted biblical scholar, speaking of modern discoveries in biblical archaeology, said, "They have established, with a wealth of evidence which no other work of ancient literature can even approach, the substantial authenticity and integrity of the text of the Bible as we now possess it."[14]

The Old Testament text has had a dramatic breakthrough in this century. With the discovery of the Dead Sea Scrolls in 1947, manuscripts of all or part of every Old Testament

---

[13]Sir Frederic Kenyon, *The Story of the Bible,* 2d ed. (Grand Rapids: Wm. B. Eerdmans Pub. Co., 1964), 26.

[14]Sir Frederic Kenyon, *Our Bible and the Ancient Manuscripts,* 5th ed. rev. (London: Eyre & Spottiswoode, 1958), 318–319.

book except Esther have been uncovered. They come from as early as 250 B.C., taking us back 1000 years earlier than the previous best manuscripts available in the Hebrew text. In fact, probably the most important contribution of the Dead Sea Scrolls is the light cast on the text of the Old Testament books. The net result is that we are given massive reassurance of the accuracy of our Bibles. They make possible the comparison of a large number of texts that let us know the Old Testament "has remained virtually unchanged for the last two thousand years."[15] In fact, there is remarkable conformity of the Dead Sea documents to our present-known texts.

God's purpose in calling Abraham and choosing Israel as His servant (Isa. 44:1) was to prepare the way to bring blessing to all the nations of the earth (Gen. 12:3; 22:18). It was important therefore that the Bible be put into the various languages of other nations. All nations need the Bible because it is the sword of the Spirit (Eph. 6:17); it is the only means of winning spiritual victories. It is also God's hammer, His tool to break down opposition and to build God's building (Jer. 23:29). It is a lamp to light life's pathway (Ps. 119:105). Even when people are blinded by sin, and the Bible seems foolish to them, such "foolishness" still gives to preaching the wise and powerful content that the Holy Spirit uses to save those who believe (1 Cor. 1:18,21). The Bible is also necessary for the continued growth of believers. Consequently, as soon as the Church began to spread into countries where they did not speak the original Hebrew and Greek of the Bible, Christians wanted the Bible translated into their own languages.

The story of Bible versions (translations) is thrilling.[16] It actually begins before the time of Jesus. As a result of the conquests of Alexander the Great, Greek became the language of trade, commerce, and education in the Middle East. The city of Alexandria in Egypt became the great

CHAPTER
1
———
The
Scriptures
Inspired

———

[15]Geza Vermes, *The Dead Sea Scrolls in English,* 2d ed. (Harmondsworth, Middlesex, England: Penguin Books, Ltd., 1975), 12.

[16]Much of the following discussion of translations is taken from Stanley M. Horton, "Perspective on Those New Translations," *Pentecostal Evangel,* 11 July 1971, 6–8.

center of Greek language, learning, and culture. Jews living there wanted the Old Testament in Greek. Over the period of 250 to 150 B.C. they gave the world the famous Septuagint Version.[17] This version was often used by early Christians in preaching the gospel during the first generation after Pentecost. (This is indicated by New Testament usage.) At the same time the Holy Spirit directed the writers of the New Testament to write their books, not in the classical Greek used several hundred years before by the great Greek philosophers, but in the everyday Greek spoken by the common people on the street and in the marketplace.

God has always wanted His Word to be preached in the language the people actually spoke. Moses wrote the Law not in the hieroglyphics used by the scholars of Egypt but in the Hebrew spoken in the tents of Israel. Jesus preached and taught with a simplicity of language that made the common people listen to Him with delight (Mark 12:37). When the gospel spread, people naturally began to translate the Bible into their own languages. Four centuries after Christ, when neither Greek nor the old Latin was spoken any longer in the Western Roman Empire, Jerome made a new translation into the "vulgar," or "common," Latin spoken in his day. This version became known as the Vulgate.[18]

Unfortunately, the Vulgate was made the official version of Western Europe and England. Further attempts to translate the Bible were discouraged even though in time the common people did not speak Latin at all. When in A.D. 1380 Wycliffe translated the Vulgate into English, large numbers were converted to Christ. But after his death in 1384, persecution of his followers arose due to their rejection of some Roman Catholic doctrines. In 1415 a general council of the Roman Catholic Church condemned his teaching. Then in 1428 Bishop Richard Fleming had his bones dug up, burned, and the ashes thrown into a

---

[17]Gleason L. Archer, Jr., *A Survey of Old Testament Introduction*, rev. ed. (Chicago: Moody Press, 1981), 44.

[18]Ibid., 80.

stream.[19] Most of the copies of his handwritten Bible were also burned.

God, however, was working. The invention of printing made a difference. Between 1462 and 1522 at least seventeen versions and editions of the Bible appeared in German. They helped prepare the way for the Reformation under Martin Luther, which brought to the people a scriptural understanding of salvation by grace through faith. Martin Luther himself then went to the Hebrew and Greek to make a new, better translation into German. As a result of Luther's influence, William Tyndale made the first important printed translation of the New Testament into English in 1525.[20] Many copies were burned but the printing presses kept pouring out floods of Bibles. Since they could not burn all the Bibles, they arrested Tyndale and burned him at the stake. Even so, other translations soon followed. After Henry VIII broke with the Roman Catholic Church, a translation known as the Bishop's Bible became the authorized version of the English Church. It was not popular, however, and most people preferred the Geneva Bible, a version translated by English refugees who fled from Catholic persecution to Switzerland. It was this version that was brought to America by the Pilgrims and Puritans in 1620 and 1630.[21]

Many English leaders recognized the need for a better translation, so King James I appointed several groups of scholars to revise the Bishop's Bible. It was an opportune time: The English language, under the influence of Shakespeare and other literary giants, was at a new height. All the best English was poured into this revision, which was completed in 1611 and "authorized" by King James to be read in the churches of England; it ultimately became known

---

[19]Jack P. Lewis, *The English Bible/From KJV to NIV: A History and Evaluation* (Grand Rapids: Baker Book House, 1981), 19–20; K. B. McFarlane, *John Wycliffe* (London: The English Universities Press, 1952), 106.

[20]Ibid., 20–21.

[21]However, "John Alden's Bible, preserved in Pilgrim Hall at Plymouth, Massachusetts, is a KJV." Ibid., 32–33. See also Christopher Anderson, *The Annals of the English Bible,* abridged and continued by S. I. Prime. (New York: Robert Carter & Brothers, 1849), 486.

as the King James Version (KJV). It was not only beautiful English; it was the English of the day. In fact, the KJV translators took pains to make the Bible more understandable to the common people than the previous English translations were. For example, they took the Israelite expression "Let the king live!" and translated it by the corresponding phrase then used in England: "God save the King!" In the New Testament, the Greek phrase meaning "Let it not be!", or "Do not let it happen!" is very emphatic—more emphatic than a literal translation would make it, so the KJV translators substituted a phrase the people would understand: "God forbid!" They also translated the Greek word *ekklēsia,* meaning "assembly" (an assembly of free citizens), by the more common word "church," though they did translate it "assembly" in three passages (Acts 19:32,39,41).

Translating from one language to another has its own set of problems.[22] There is, for example, no one Greek word for "miracle," but two words contain that idea *(dunamis* and *sēmeion).* So the KJV translators used "miracle" for both; but for variety, and to bring out other shades of meaning, they also translated them as "powers" (Heb. 6:5), "mighty works" (Matt. 11:21–23), "strength" (Rev. 10:10), "might" (Eph. 3:16), "virtue" (Luke 6:19; 8:46), "mighty deed" (2 Cor. 12:12), "sign" (John 20:30), "wonder" (Rev. 13:13), and "token" (2 Thess. 3:17). Still another problem came from the fact that both Anglicans and Puritans practiced sprinkling for water baptism, and the Greek word *baptizō* means "plunge under," "dip," "immerse." So the KJV translators did not translate the word. Instead, they transliterated the Greek word into English letters (thereby giving us the word "baptize"). In this way they avoided a controversy that might have kept some people from read-

---

[22]One of the problems missionaries face today is that in translating from one language to another it is often difficult to find exactly equivalent words in both languages. For example, Missionary John Hall told of a problem he had while translating the Bible into the Mossi language of Africa. The Mossi people had no word for "anchor." They were an inland people who rode horses. They tied their horses to picketing pegs, so Hall translated the first part of Heb. 6:19: "Which hope we have as a 'picketing peg' for the soul which cannot be rocked loose or broken."

ing this new version of the Bible. At other times they were overliteral. For example, they took the Greek word *mono-genēs* apart, translating *mono* as "only" and *genēs* as "begotten."[23] However, the word in New Testament times had come to mean simply "only," in the sense of unique, special. Hebrews 11:17 uses it of Isaac as the special, promised son, even though Abraham had another son, Ishmael. Though we become "sons" [children] of God through Christ, Jesus is God's beloved Son in a special, unique sense that we never can be.

The richness of the Greek also is difficult to put into English. The KJV translators used one English word for a number of different Greek words. For example, they translated nine different Greek words as "abide," twelve different ones as "bear," five as "cast out," thirty-one as "come," twelve as "deliver," fifteen as "keep," nine as "mind," six as "power," six as "preach," twelve as "think." In each case, each Greek word represents fine shades of meaning. However, in English a great number of words would have to be used to describe the shade of meaning. This is one of the reasons commentaries and expanded or amplified translations are helpful.

In many cases, however, the KJV translators tried to bring out whatever shade of meaning is being emphasized in a particular passage.

GREEK WORD	TRANSLATIONS IN THE KJV
ekballō	"cast out" (John 6:37); "bring forth" (Matt. 12:25); "send forth" (Matt. 9:38); "send out" (James 2:25); "leave out" (Rev. 11:2)
apolutrōsis	"redemption" (Eph. 1:7); "deliverance" (Heb. 11:25)
hilastērion	"propitiation" (Rom. 3:25); "mercy seat" (Heb. 9:5)

---

[23]In Luke 7:12; 8:42; and 9:38, the KJV translators did use the word "only" instead of "only begotten."

GREEK WORD	TRANSLATIONS IN THE KJV
hilaskomai	"make reconciliation" (Heb. 2:17); "be merciful" (Luke 18:13)
Amen (Heb.)	"amen" (Deut. 27:15–26; Rom. 1:25); "so be it" (Jer. 11:5); "truth" (Isa. 65:16); "verily" (Matt. 5:18)
anomia	"iniquity" (Matt. 7:23); "transgression of the law" (1 John 3:4); "unrighteousness" (2 Cor. 6:14)
hikanos	"meet" (1 Cor. 15:9); "worthy" (Matt. 3:11); "sufficient" (2 Cor. 2:16); "able" (2 Tim. 2:2); "good" (Acts 18:18); "great" (Mark 10:46)
apeitheō	"disobedient" (Rom. 1:21); "unbelieving" (Acts 14:2)
agapē	"love" (John 15:9–10,13); "charity" (1 Cor. 1–13); "feast of charity" (Jude 12); "dear" (Col. 1:13)
aiōnōn	"ages" (Col. 1:26); "the beginning of the world" (Eph. 3:9)
chrisma	"anointing" (1 John 2:27); "unction" (1 John 2:20)
sōzō	"save" (Matt. 1:21); "heal" (Acts 14:9); "whole" (Matt. 9:21); "make whole" (Matt. 9:22); "preserve" (2 Tim. 4:18)
elegchō	"reprove" (John 16:8); "rebuke" (Rev. 3:19); "convict" (John 8:9); "convince" (John 8:46); "tell [his] fault"
elpizō	"hope" (1 Pet. 1:13); "trust" (Matt. 12:21)
kairos	"season" (Mark 12:2); "time" (Matt. 13:30); "opportunity" (Gal. 6:10)
makarios	"blessed" (Matt. 5:3–11); "happy" (John 13:17)
marturia	"witness" (John 1:7); "testimony" (John 3:32–33); "record" (John 1:19); "report" (1 Tim. 3:7)

GREEK WORD	TRANSLATIONS IN THE KJV
homologeō	"profess" (1 Tim. 6:12); "confess" (Matt. 10:32); "promise" (Matt. 14:7); "give thanks" (Heb. 13:15)
paraklesis	"consolation" (Rom. 15:5); "exhortation" (Acts 13:15); "comfort" (Rom. 15:4); "entreaty" (2 Cor. 8:4)

Then because the Hebrew does not contain the word "have," nor does it use many common English words, such as helping verbs or "to be" as connectives, the KJV translators added them and many other words to make the translation understandable and smooth reading in English. For example, they added the word "art" in Nathan's words to David, "Thou art the man" (2 Sam. 12:7).[24] The result was an excellent translation in the language of the people who lived in England in 1611.

At first the KJV, as a new version, was rejected by many. The clergy preached against it. One Hugh Broughton went so far as to say "that it was so poorly done that it would grieve him as long as he lived. He insisted that he would rather be tied between wild horses and torn apart than to let it go forth among the people."[25] For fifty years many continued to condemn it, but it gradually won favor because it was a superior translation. It was worthy of the place it came to have in the hearts of the people.

Unfortunately, all languages are constantly changing. We no longer speak Shakespearian English with its "thees" and "thous." In fact, meanings of some words have changed considerably: "Let" in 1611 meant "hinder." "Prevent" meant "precede." "By and by" meant "immediately." "Charger" meant "wooden platter."

---

[24]Many (though by no means all) of these added words, which are necessary in English, the KJV translators put in italics.

[25]Lewis, *English Bible,* 29; cf. Hugh Broughton, *A Censure of the Late Translation for Our Churches,* ca. 1612 (S.T.C. 3847).

Missionaries want to get the Bible into the language the people actually speak. Believers everywhere are blessed when they read an easy-to-understand version in their own language. The world, including the English-speaking world, is a mission field today. This is the reality that has called forth new versions in modern English. Admittedly, none of them are final perfection, but all, except those put out by some of the cults, have enough truth in them for the Holy Spirit to use them to make the way of salvation clear.

Some modern versions, such as the New Berkeley Version, use a high English style that seems to be aimed at college professors instead of the average reader. In contrast, the New Century Version is aimed at a third-grade reading level. Some, such as *The Good News Bible*,[26] *The Living Bible*, the Phillips translation, and the *New English Bible*, are paraphrases, which do more interpretation than strict translation. The Phillips translation seems to catch the spirit of the Greek, however, especially in Paul's epistles. The Revised Standard Version is fairly good in the New Testament, but the Old Testament is too subjective in the way it changes the Hebrew vowels and divides Hebrew words, so it is not useful as a study Bible. The New Revised Standard Version is an improvement over the earlier RSV. The *New American Standard Bible* is faithful to the original languages, but sometimes overliteral and not very readable. In between is the New International Version (NIV), which is a good translation made by Bible believers and is also very readable.[27] Whichever version you choose, it is important to seek out the full meaning of the original languages (Greek, Hebrew, Aramaic) using concordances, commentaries, Bible dictionaries, as well as comparing with other versions.

Reading a new translation may stimulate thinking. Comparing various translations also helps one to see the various shades of meaning that are in the Scripture. As Dr. Jack

---

[26]Today's English Version. Some Bible versions are published under more than one name.

[27]Several Assemblies of God scholars have been involved in some of the recent translations.

[28]Lewis, *English Bible*, 366.

Lewis points out, "The religious problems of the world are not caused by people reading different translations; the most serious problem is that many read no translation."[28]

The KJV is still a good translation and worthy of respect. Its beauty, especially in the Psalms, will probably never be surpassed. But the important thing is to get people to read the Bible. As the people read, the Holy Spirit will illuminate their hearts and minds and make the truth of God's Word real to them. In the providence of God, the inspired words of prophets and apostles of old have been preserved for us in the most remarkable of all books, the Holy Bible.

The Bible is a miracle of God's care. The Holy Spirit acted at the time of the first writing. This we call inspiration. He has preserved for us the text. Now, today, the same Holy Spirit who inspired the writers helps the reader and the hearer. The unregenerate is not promised this assistance, being blind to the truth of God (1 Cor. 2:14). But the believer is promised special assistance from the Holy Spirit (John 16:13–16; 1 Cor. 2:10). God wishes to speak to the reader—and His Spirit is pleased to shed light on the truth and its application to your life.

Study Questions

STUDY QUESTIONS

1. Why is rationalism insufficient as a basis for religious authority?

2. Why is the Bible a better basis for religious authority than the Church?

3. What does the Bible itself teach us about its inspiration?

4. How should we deal with alleged mistakes and discrepancies in the Bible?

5. What are the chief grounds for accepting the sixty-six books in our Bible as canonical and no others?

6. What are the chief reasons that over the centuries new versions (translations) of the Bible have been made?

7. Why is it important to get the Bible translated into the language the people actually speak?

8. How can we receive the illumination of the Holy Spirit in Bible study today?

2nd

FUNDAMENTAL TRUTH

THE ONE TRUE GOD

The one true God has revealed himself as the eternally self-existent "I AM," the Creator of heaven and earth and the Redeemer of mankind. He has further revealed himself as embodying the principles of relationship and association as Father, Son, and Holy Ghost (Deut. 6:4; Isa. 43:10,11; Matt. 28:19; Luke 3:22).*

*The full text of this tenet appears on pages 44–46.

CHAPTER TWO

The One True
God

In 1913 a great crowd gathered in the Arroyo Seco of South Pasadena, California, to hear Mrs. Maria Woodworth-Etter in what was called a worldwide Pentecostal camp meeting.[1] One night an immigrant from Danzig, Germany, John Scheppe, woke everyone up by shouting the name of Jesus. He had just received a vision of Jesus that made him feel Jesus needed to be given greater honor. One of the pastors, Frank J. Ewart,[2] a former Baptist minister, soon took advantage of this and said the way to give honor to Jesus was to be rebaptized in water in the name of Jesus only.[3] Soon some were declaring that those who refused this rebaptism would lose their salvation.[4] They also

---

[1]William W. Menzies, *Anointed to Serve: The Story of the Assemblies of God* (Springfield, Mo.: Gospel Publishing House, 1971), 111.

[2]Ewart was pronounced by most people then as "You-r't."

[3]Menzies, *Anointed,* 112–113. Both Scheppe and Ewart were influenced by a sermon of R. E. McAlister on water baptism in the name of Jesus Christ.

[4]This was told to Myrle M. Fisher in 1913. She was rebaptized, but later, through her own study of the Scripture, returned to a trinitarian position. She married Harry Horton and became the mother of Stanley M. Horton, who often heard her tell of this.

**CHAPTER
2**
———
The One
True
God

declared that there is only one Person in the Godhead: Jesus, who filled the offices or modes of Father, Son, and Holy Spirit as the time or occasion demanded. Those who revived this doctrine soon become known as Jesus Name, Jesus Only, or Oneness, and they referred to their doctrines as "The New Issue" (though it actually was an old heresy revived[5]).

Shortly after the Assemblies of God was formed in 1914, some began to spread this doctrine. To counteract it, the Assemblies of God in 1916[6] included a section in its Statement of Fundamental Truths entitled "The Adorable Godhead." It is currently stated as follows:

(a) Terms Defined

The terms "trinity" and "persons" as related to the Godhead, while not found in the Scriptures, are words in harmony with the Scriptures, whereby we may convey to others our immediate understanding of the doctrine of Christ respecting the Being of God, as distinguished from "gods many and lords many." We therefore may speak with propriety of the Lord our God, who is One Lord, as a trinity or as one Being of three persons, and still be absolutely scriptural (e.g., Matt. 28:19; John 14:16–17; 2 Cor. 13:14).

(b) Distinction and Relationship in the Godhead

Christ taught a distinction of Persons in the Godhead which He expressed in specific terms of relationship, as Father, Son, and Holy Ghost, but that this distinction and relationship, as to its mode is *inscrutable* and *incomprehensible,* because *unexplained* (Matt. 11:25–27; 28:19; Luke 1:35; 1 Cor. 1:24; 2 Cor. 13:14; 1 John 1:3–4).

(c) Unity of the One Being of Father, Son and Holy Ghost

Accordingly, therefore, there is *that* in the Son which consti-

---

[5]This doctrine was held by the Sabellians and Monarchians of the third century A.D., but was rejected by the majority of Christians in those days.

[6]For a discussion of this controversy see Thomas F. Harrison, *Christology* 2d. rev. ed. (Springfield, Mo.: Published by the author, 1985), 35–77.

tutes Him *the Son* and not the Father; and there is *that* in the Holy Ghost which constitutes Him *the Holy Ghost* and not either the Father or the Son. Wherefore the Father is the Begetter, the Son is the Begotten, and the Holy Ghost is the one proceeding from the Father and the Son. Therefore, because these three persons in the Godhead are in a state of unity, there is but one Lord God Almighty and His name is one (see Zech. 14:9; John 1:18; 15:26; 17:11,21).

(d) Identity and Cooperation in the Godhead

The Father, the Son and the Holy Ghost are never *identical* as to *Person;* nor *confused* as to *relation;* nor *divided* in respect to the Godhead; nor *opposed* as to *cooperation.* The Son is *in* the Father and the Father is *in* the Son as to relationship. The Son is *with* the Father and the Father is *with* the Son, as to fellowship. The Father is not *from* the Son, but the Son is *from* the Father, as to authority. The Holy Ghost is *from* the Father and the Son proceeding, as to nature, relationship, cooperation and authority. Hence, neither Person in the Godhead either exists or works separately or independently of the others (see John 5:17–30,32,37; 8:17–18).

(e) The Title, Lord Jesus Christ

The appellation, "Lord Jesus Christ," is a proper name. It is never applied, in the New Testament, either to the Father or to the Holy Ghost. It therefore belongs exclusively to the *Son of God* (see Rom. 1:1–3,7; 2 John 3).

(f) The Lord Jesus Christ, God with Us

The Lord Jesus Christ, as to His divine and eternal nature, is the proper and only Begotten of the Father, but as to His human nature, He is the proper Son of Man. He is, therefore, acknowledged to be both God and man; who because He is God and man, is "Immanuel," God with us (see Matt. 1:23; 1 John 4:2,10,14; Rev. 1:13,17).

(g) The Title, Son of God

Since the name "Immanuel" embraces both God and man in the one Person, our Lord Jesus Christ, it follows that the title, Son of God, describes His proper deity, and the title Son of Man, His proper humanity. Therefore, the title Son of God belongs to the *order of eternity,* and the title, Son of Man, to the *order of time* (see Matt. 1:21–23; Heb. 1:1–13; 7:3; 1 John 3:8; 2 John 3).

(h) Transgression of the Doctrine of Christ

Wherefore, it is a transgression of the Doctrine of Christ to say that Jesus Christ derived the title, Son of God, solely from the fact of the incarnation, or because of His relation to the economy of redemption. Therefore, to deny that the Father is a real and eternal Father, and that the Son is a real and eternal Son, is a denial of the distinction and relationship in the Being of God; a denial of the Father and the Son; and a displacement of the truth that Jesus Christ is come in the flesh. (John 1:1–2,14,18,29,49; Heb. 12:2; 1 John 2:22–23; 4:1–5; 2 John 9).

(i) Exaltation of Jesus Christ as Lord

The Son of God, our Lord Jesus Christ, having by himself purged our sins, sat down on the right hand of the Majesty on high; angels and principalities and powers having been made subject unto Him. And having been made both Lord and Christ, He sent the Holy Ghost that we, in the name of Jesus, might bow our knees and confess that Jesus Christ is Lord to the glory of God the Father until the end, when the Son shall become subject to the Father that God may be all in all (see Acts 2:32–36; Rom. 14:11; 1 Cor. 15:24–28; Heb. 1:3; 1 Pet. 3:22).

(j) Equal Honor to the Father and to the Son

Wherefore, since the Father has delivered all judgment unto the Son, it is not only the *express duty* of all in heaven and on earth to bow the knee, but it is an *unspeakable* joy in the Holy Ghost to ascribe unto the Son all the attributes of deity, and to give Him all the honor and the glory contained in all the names and titles of the Godhead except those which express relationship (see paragraphs b, c, and d), and thus honor the Son even as we honor the Father (see John 5:22–23; Phil. 2:8–9; 1 Pet. 1:8; Rev. 4:8–11; 5:6–14; 7:9–10).

THE EXISTENCE OF GOD

The Bible does not attempt to prove the existence of God. Genesis begins by recognizing that He is: "In the beginning God ... " Psalm 14:1 declares, "The fool says in his heart, 'There is no God.' " Hebrews 11:6 states emphatically that "anyone who comes to him [God] must believe that he exists." The Scriptures affirm what is universally experienced by people everywhere: There is a God. To say there is no Supreme Being—or to live that way—is to deny what is intuitively known by all (see John 1:9; Rom. 1:19). The existence of God is so fundamental to human thinking that to abandon this conception is to embark upon a wild sea of irrationality that leaves us without meaning or purpose.

Although the Bible does not attempt to argue a case for God's existence, there are implications that support such arguments. Several classical arguments have been put forth from medieval days which, although limited in themselves, together provide intellectual confirmation and support to the truth of the Bible. They serve as "pointers." The first of these pointers is the ontological argument. This argument, briefly stated, is that the conception of a Perfect Being requires that Being to have a real existence, since if the idea of a Perfect Being does not have a genuine manifestation in actuality, it is less than perfect. Therefore, to conceive of a Perfect Being, namely God, it is a contradiction in terms not to believe that He truly exists.[7]

The second classical argument is the cosmological argument. It logically flows out of the ontological argument. The universe, as you might guess, is not self-existent. All events of which we are aware are dependent on some cause beyond the events themselves. If you push the causes back far enough, you will eventually come to a First Cause, a self-existent Being not dependent on anything else at all.

The third classical argument for God's existence is the teleological argument, or the argument from design. The amazing world uncovered by scientific inquiry discloses a remarkable, breathtaking orderliness in nature. The mathematical improbability of the marvels of living and nonliving structures just having occurred by chance drives the se-

CHAPTER 2

The One True God

---

[7]For a good discussion of the value of the ontological argument see James Oliver Buswell, *A Systematic Theology of the Christian Religion,* vol. 1 (Grand Rapids: Zondervan Publishing House, 1962), 98–100.

rious thinking person to a sense of awe and wonder at the Designer responsible for this amazing display. We can join our voices to the Psalmist who said: "The heavens declare the glory of God; the skies proclaim the work of his hands" (Ps.19:1).[8]

The fourth classical argument, the moral argument, arises out of the innate sense of right and wrong with which every person is equipped. The existence of a great Lawgiver in the universe is the logical consequence of the awareness of morality. Even though standards of morality vary widely from culture to culture, there remains nonetheless the consciousness of moral values.

Similar to the preceding is the fifth classical argument, based on aesthetics, or beauty. That people have a conception of relative values regarding beauty and an appreciation of it (however widely the standards may vary) points in the direction of One who himself is the giver of beauty, and who is altogether lovely.

THE NATURE OF GOD

Romans 1:19–20 indicates that the existence of God may be known by all through general revelation.[9] However, to know the nature of God, it is necessary to turn to special revelation, to the Bible. God discloses himself in a variety of ways in the Bible. An important way of knowing something about Him is supplied through His divine names.

'El (Heb. "God"), the singular form, occurs about 250 times in the Bible and emphasizes the idea of strength (see Gen. 14:18–22). A related singular form, *'Eloah* (Heb.), is found 42 times in the Book of Job alone. But its plural, *'Elohim,* occurs over 2,000 times in the Old Testament; it is usually connected with God's creative power and providential care of the universe and humankind. Further, its implication is of plurality in the Godhead (see Gen. 1:26; 3:22).

---

[8]For a good discussion of Ps. 19 and other passages referring to general revelation in nature see Millard J. Erickson, ed., *Christian Theology* (Grand Rapids: Baker Book House, 1986), 166–171.

[9]See "The Revelation of God to Humankind" pp. 20–21.

Yahweh is translated "Lord" in many English versions.[10] It is God's covenant-keeping name (see Mal. 2:5; 3:6). This name occurs some 7,000 times in the Bible. Its meaning is "He will [actively] continue to be." It also implies He will show what kind of God He is by what He does, and is especially connected with the promise "I will be with you" (see Exod. 3:12).

Special compound names, employed with *'El* and with *Yahweh,* emphasize the nature of God and His covenantal relationships. These include *'El Shaddai,* "God Almighty" (Gen. 17:1, from a root *shadu,* meaning "mountain"); *'El Elyon,* "God Most High" (Gen. 14:18); *'El Ro'i,* "The God who sees me" (Gen. 16:13); *'El 'Olam,* "The Eternal God" (Gen. 21:33); *'El 'Elohe Yisra'el,* "God, the God of Israel" (emphasizing God's special relation with Israel, Gen. 33:20); *Yahweh-ropheka,* "The Lord your [personal] Physician" (Exod. 15:26); *Yahweh-nissi,* "The Lord my Banner" (Exod. 17:15); *Yahweh-shalom,* "The Lord is Peace" (Judg. 6:24); *Yahweh-ro'i,* "The Lord my Shepherd" (Ps. 23:1). The One who forgives is denoted by *Yahweh-tsidkenu,* "The Lord our Righteousness" (Jer. 23:6). The name of the New Jerusalem will be *Yahweh-shammah,* "The Lord is there" (Ezek. 48:35). And God's heavenly name is *Yahweh-sabaoth,* "The Lord of hosts [including angelic hosts]" (Ps. 148:2; cf. Matt. 26:53).

These are other important terms that describe the nature of God: *'Adonai (Heb.), Kurios* (Gk.), "Lord"; *'Attiq Yomin* (Aramaic), "The Ancient of Days," a title given in connection with His judging and ruling over the kingdoms of this world (Dan. 7:9,13,22); *Qedosh Yisra'el* (Heb.), "The Holy One of Israel" (used 29 times by Isaiah); *Tsur* (Heb.), "Rock"; *'Ab* (Heb.; Aramaic *'Abba;* Gk. *Ho Patēr),* "Father," or "O, Father!" (a very respectful form of address in Bible times); *Melek* (Heb.), "King" (Isa. 6:1,5); *Go'el* (Heb.), "Redeemer"; *Despotēs* (Gk.), "Lord," "Master," "Owner"; and *Rishon wa-'acharon* (Heb.; Gk. *Ho Prōtos kai Ho Es-*

---

[10]The consonants of the personal name YHWH were written in the New Latin as JHVH and combined with the vowels of the Heb. word for Lord to give the nonbiblical form "Jehovah."

chatos), "The First and the Last" (speaking of His rule over the entire course of history, Isa. 44:6; 48:12; Rev. 2:8).

Moving from names and titles used in Scripture that speak of the nature of God, let us look briefly at some of the important concepts describing the nature of God. God is by nature, first of all, infinite, without limit or limitation. He is greater than the universe, for He created it. This is a picture too big for our finite minds to capture, but it is important to our understanding of God to accept this postulate (see 1 Kings 8:27). Closely related to this is the unity of God. There is but one God (Deut. 6:5; Isa. 44:6,8).

God is at the same time both transcendent (above, beyond, and greater than the universe He has created) and immanent (present and active within the universe). Only Christian teaching about God adequately unites these two views. Transcendence preserves the distinction between God and His created universe. Not to do this causes one to fall into pantheism, in which God and the universe are hopelessly confused[11] and the idea of a supreme personal God is ruled out. The idea of immanence, which recognizes that God is present within His created universe, is necessary to preserve the loving relationship of God to the people on the earth He created (Exod. 8:22; Acts 17:24–25,27–28). "He is not far from each one of us" (Acts 17:27). Those who do not give sufficient place to God's nearness fall into the error of deism, which conceives of God merely as a great First Cause, something like the disinterested "clockmaker" who got the universe started and then went off to let it run by itself.

God is also immutable (not susceptible to change) and eternal. This means God's nature does not change, and never will (see Mal. 3:6). In the Old Testament two very important Hebrew words used to describe God are *chesed* (faithful, steadfast, covenant-keeping love) and *'emeth* (reliability, permanence, continuance, fidelity, truth). He is *'Elohe 'emeth* "the true God" (2 Chron. 15:3), and He will be true to himself. These terms occur repeatedly in Psalm

---

[11]Pantheism says that the universe with its forces and laws is all there is. Then it calls the universe God.

89, for example. They vividly depict the dependability of our God.

THE ATTRIBUTES OF GOD

In addition to the attributes that describe His inner nature, God bears special relationships to His creation. These are called communicable attributes, for they can be found (to a much lesser degree, of course) in human nature. They may be divided into two categories: natural and moral.

Among these natural attributes is God's omnipotence (the quality of being all-powerful). He enjoys freedom and power to do all that is consistent with His nature. He is sovereign over the universe. Isaiah 40:15 describes the majesty of the King of kings: "Surely the nations are like a drop in a bucket; they are regarded as dust on the scales; he weighs the islands as though they were fine dust." But if God is sovereign, one may ask, why is there sin in the world? The answer lies in the fact that God is sovereign over himself and has the power to limit himself:[12] He chose freely to create beings (people and angels) with the integrity of moral choice. God determined that He would not invade the freedom of the personal will. Ultimately, one must acknowledge that God, who allows for personal freedom, is still Lord of history, and He is in control of the destiny of nations and of the universe. The entire Book of Revelation, together with important passages in Daniel (e.g., 4:34–35; 5:20–21; 7:26–27; 8:19–25) and Ezekiel (e.g., 37:24–28; 38:3; 39:1), clearly discloses the control God has over the future of our universe. But in the interim, He has, for reasons known best to Him, permitted freedom of individual choice and the sin that this allows.

God is omnipresent, everywhere present (Ps. 139:7–10). He is not limited by space. He is present to people everywhere, and to all that He has created, in manifold and wonderful ways, loving and caring for even the sparrow that falls (Matt. 6:25–29). Although He is present every-

---

[12]One of the greatest evidences of God's ability to limit himself is seen in the coming of Jesus as a baby in the manger and in His life, ministry, and death on the cross. See Phil. 2:6–8.

where, one must remember that while He especially reveals himself and His glory in heaven, on earth He dwells only in intimate personal relationship with those who humble themselves and choose to admit Him into the sanctuary of their inmost being (Isa. 57:15; Rev. 3:20).

God is omniscient, having infinite, universal, complete knowledge and insight. He views reality from a different perspective than we do. We see things in a stream of consciousness. Life is for us a flow along a time line. For example, we look ahead to the future, which eventually becomes the present and then the past. For God, however, all reality is known to Him. All events, past, present, and future, are available to Him as present knowledge (cf. Rom. 8:27–28; 1 Cor. 3:20). Now, some may wonder how God can know who will be lost and allow them to be lost. God's foreknowledge does not predetermine individual choices, for He has chosen not to violate the individual free will. In Ephesians 1:3–14 we have the outlines of the panorama of predetermined world history, but this glimpse into the predestination of the course of the universe does not rule out the "islands of freedom" God has reserved for the personal choices of free people. God does not send people to hell; He permits them to choose their own eternal destiny.

Besides the natural attributes of God, which form an important category of His communicable attributes, there are several moral attributes. Goodness is one of them. God is truly a good God. He is disposed to looking out continually for the welfare of His creation. He does not set out to lay snares for His creatures. Evil is an enemy of both creation and God. The Bible is filled with descriptions of God's goodness, people ascribing to Him such characteristics as love (1 John 4:8), loving-kindness and faithfulness (Ps. 89:49), grace (Acts 20:24), and mercy (Eph. 2:4). The greatest act of God's love is displayed in the climax of His plan of redemption at the Cross. No one has greater love than this.

God is holy. Central to the biblical message about God's character is His holiness. "Holy" in the Bible basically means "separated, dedicated." There are two important aspects of God's holiness. (1) He is separated from and elevated above all that is transient, impermanent, finite, imperfect, as well as all that is evil, sinful, and wrong. (2) He is also separated to and dedicated to the carrying out of His great plan of redemption, the bringing in of the coming Kingdom, and, ultimately, setting up the new heavens and the new earth. This conception of God is utterly necessary for a proper understanding of worship. It is a helpful corrective to "cheap, easy believism" and superficial religious experience, which do not serve to dedicate us to doing the will of God. God evokes awe, for He is holy. (See Isa. 6:1–5.)

God is also righteous. This means He can be depended on to act with justice (see Deut. 32:4; Dan. 4:37; Rev. 15:3). More than that, it means that God is in himself essential righteousness itself (Ps. 71:19). It is His nature to be just; He will always be true to His nature (Isa. 51:4–6). It is this characteristic of God that gives moral order to the universe. Related to this lofty standard of being and behavior are the attributes of justice, truth, and anger, or wrath. God deals fairly with people (2 Chron. 19:7). That is justice. That He is the embodiment of truth is grounded in His absolutely transparent purity. It is necessary for justice and truth to be served by the exhibition of holy anger, or wrath, against those who rebel against Him (Rev. 16:1–5). Yet at the same time, God yearns to redeem broken humankind (2 Pet. 3:9). This is love. It is at the cross of Christ that God's wrath and God's love flow together (Rom. 3:22–25)!

THE TRINITY

A great mystery is before us here, for, since there is only one God, only one Trinity (or "Triunity"), we have no adequate analogies, or comparisons, to aid us in understanding the Trinity of the Godhead (the divine Being that exists in a unity of three distinct, divine Persons).[13] Difficult

---

[13] Dr. Nathan Wood, former president of Gordon College and Gordon Divinity School, believed we could see the imprint of the Trinity in nature. He suggested, for example, that three-dimensional space shows it. If the dimensions of a room are taken as equal units, the length goes through the entire room, so do the width and the height, yet each is distinct. And to get the space you do not add $1 + 1 + 1$; you multiply $1 \times 1 \times 1$, which is still one. (Like all analogies, however, this one falls short, since dimensions are not personal.)

**CHAPTER
2**

**The One
True
God**

as it may be to comprehend the truth, it is a vital and urgent doctrine. Church history contains the tragic tales of groups that failed to do justice to the concept of the Trinity.

The daily Jewish family prayer, taken from Deuteronomy 6:4, emphasizes the great truth of the unity of God. "Hear, O Israel: The LORD our God, the LORD is one."[14] Alongside this important truth is the concept of personality in God. Personality involves knowledge (or intelligence), feeling (or affection), and will. The Father, Son, and Holy Spirit each show these characteristics in their own personal way. The Holy Spirit, for example, does things that show He is not a mere power or thing (see Acts 8:29; 11:12; 13:2,4; 16:6–7; Rom. 8:27; 15:30; 1 Cor. 2:11; 12:11).

Personality also demands fellowship. But before the creation of the universe, where was the possibility of fellowship? The answer lies in the complex arrangement within the Godhead. The unity of the Godhead does not preclude compound personalities. There are three distinct personalities, each wholly deity, yet so harmoniously interrelated that they are one essence. This is quite different from saying there are three Gods.

One helpful way to disclose the distinctions of persons within the Godhead is to observe the functions especially attributed to each. For example, God the Father is principally credited with the work of creation; God the Son is the principal agent in applying the work of redemption to humanity; God the Holy Spirit is the deposit, or first installment, guaranteeing our future inheritance. This threefold distinction is sketched in Ephesians 1. Yet one must not press this distinction too far, for there is also abundant biblical testimony to the cooperation of the Son and the Spirit in the work of creation: The Father created through the Son (John 1:3); the Holy Spirit hovered gently over the earth in preparation for the six days of creation (Gen. 1:2). The Father sent the Son into the world to effect redemption (John 3:16), and the Son himself, in His ministry,

---

[14]"One" here is the Heb. *'echad,* which can represent a compound or complex unity. Although the Heb. has a word that means "one alone," "the only one," *yachid,* it is not used of God.

went "in the power of the Spirit" (Luke 4:14). The Father and the Son also share in the Holy Spirit's ministry of sanctifying the believer.

The Trinity is a harmonious fellowship within the Godhead. This fellowship is also a loving fellowship, for God is love. But His love is an outgoing love, not a self-centered love. This kind of love demands that before the creation there had to be more than one Person within the Being of God.   God talks of Himself as plural

An important term to bear in mind with respect to the doctrine of the Trinity is subordination. There is a kind of subordination in the order of relation of the persons, but not of their nature. The Son and the Spirit are said to "proceed" from the Father. This is a subordination in relationship, but not of essence. The Spirit is said to proceed from the Son and the Father. This is the orthodox statement of the western Church, adopted at the council of Nicea in A.D. 325 and embodied in the standard Christian creeds and doctrinal statements.

Two major kinds of heresies that diverged from the consensus of Church understanding of biblical teaching regarding the Trinity were Sabellianism and Arianism. About the middle of the third century A.D., Sabellius, in an attempt to avoid the possibility of teaching that there were three Gods, promoted the idea that there was but one God with one personality, but that He manifested himself in three different modes. First, there was God the Father, the Creator. Then God manifested himself as Son, the Redeemer. Now, He manifests himself as Spirit. God, for Sabellius, was just exhibiting three different "masks." A modern form of this heresy erupted in Pentecostal circles about 1915, assuming the epithet of "Jesus Only," or "Oneness."[15] It is a

---

[15]They usually point to the fact that the word "name" in Matt. 28:19 is singular and they say that that "name" is Jesus. However, in Bible times the word "name" included both names and titles (see Luke 6:13, KJV) and was used in the singular when only one name was given for each person (as in Ruth 1:2 where the "name" is singular in the Heb. when referring to the two sons). It should be noted also that in Matt. 28:19 the command was literally to baptize them "into the name," which was their way of saying into the worship and service of the Father, Son, and Holy Spirit. In Acts 2:38, however, a different form is used in the

species of Unitarianism that oversimplifies the Trinity,[16] actually dragging God down to the human level. On the human level there is only one person to one being. It does not matter what part of a person (e.g., will, emotions) acts, he must say, "I did it." But on the divine level there are the three Persons to the one Being. God has three "places" where He can say "I." And why not—surely we should expect God to be greater than we are!

Most of those who now follow this Jesus Only doctrine teach that people are not saved until they are baptized in the Holy Spirit and speak in tongues. This flows out of their confusion about divine persons, failing to distinguish the redemption wrought in Christ and the anointing and empowerment made available through the ministry of the Holy Spirit.

The other serious heresy that has periodically afflicted segments of the Church is Arianism. Arius, in A.D. 325, went to the other extreme, emphasizing so much the distinction among the persons in the Godhead that he in effect divided the Godhead into three distinct essences. The result was a subordination not only of relationship but of nature, for both the Son and the Holy Spirit. This led to the reduction of Jesus Christ, and the Spirit as well, to a position of less than full deity. Arius denied the eternal Sonship of Christ, considering Him to have come into existence at some point after the Father. Further, the Holy Spirit was said to have come into existence through the operation of the Father and the Son, making Him even less deity. There are many groups of people today who hold that neither the Son nor

---

Gk. and means "upon the Name of Jesus," which was their way of saying "upon the authority of Jesus," an authority expressed in Matt. 28:19. Luke used that terminology to distinguish Christian baptism from the baptism of John the Baptist.

[16]Some of them use an illustration like this: Dr. William Jones is addressed by his title, Dr. Jones, in his office. On the golf course his friends call him by his personal name, William or Bill. At home his children call him Daddy or Father. The problem with this is that Bill Jones on the golf course does not go to the telephone and talk to father Jones at home or Dr. Jones in the office. Yet Jesus prayed to the Father, and the Father declared, " 'You are my Son, whom I love; with you I am well pleased' " (Luke 3:22).

the Spirit is in the fullest sense deity. Such groups are in league with their spiritual ancestor Arius.[17]

Although there is no specific passage in the Bible that uses the term "trinity," there are numerous passages that allude to the Trinity. A vivid example is clearly given in the events of the baptism of Jesus at the Jordan River by John the Baptist: "As soon as Jesus was baptized, he went up out of the water. At that moment heaven was opened, and he saw the Spirit of God descending like a dove and lighting on him. And a voice from heaven said, " 'This is my Son, whom I love; with him I am well pleased' " (Matt. 3:16–17). The Trinity is admittedly a mystery, a mystery too great for human comprehension. But as with so many truths hard for the unregenerate person to accept, the Spirit of Truth helps our weakness and human inability (1 Cor. 2:13–16). We worship the Father, the Son, and the Holy Spirit, and recognize their personalities in what we see in the Bible. Therefore, we humbly acknowledge that they are One in fellowship, purpose, and substance.

STUDY QUESTIONS

1. Although unbelievers do not accept the classical arguments for the existence of God, in what sense can these arguments be helpful to believers?

2. When the Bible speaks of God's great name, the word "name" may be collective and include all that is revealed in the various names of God given in the Bible. What kind of God does the Old Testament reveal? What does the New Testament add to this?

3. How can God be both transcendent and immanent?

4. How can you relate the attributes of God to your experience of God?

5. What are the two important aspects of God's holiness and how do they relate to the holiness He wants to see in us?

6. What is the difference between holiness and righteousness?

---

[17]Some of the passages that refute such subordination are John 15:26; 16:13; 17:1,18,23. (See also 1 Cor. 12:4–6; Eph. 4:1–6; Heb. 10:7–17.)

CHAPTER
2
___

The One
True
God

7. Why is it important to recognize God as a Trinity of Persons in one Being rather than as three separate Gods?

8. What are some of the ways the Bible indicates that the Father, the Son, and the Holy Spirit are distinct Persons?

9. What are some of the ways the Bible shows that there is indeed a Trinity ("Triunity")?

3rd

rd

FUNDAMENTAL
TRUTH

THE DEITY OF THE LORD JESUS CHRIST

The Lord Jesus Christ is the eternal Son of God. The Scriptures declare:

(a) His virgin birth (Matt. 1:23; Luke 1:31,35).

(b) His sinless life (Heb. 7:26; 1 Pet. 2:22).

(c) His miracles (Acts 2:22; 10:38).

(d) His substitutionary work on the cross (1 Cor. 15:3; 2 Cor. 5:21).

(e) His bodily resurrection from the dead (Matt. 28:6; Luke 24:39; 1 Cor. 15:4).

(f) His exaltation to the right hand of God (Acts 1:9,11; 2:33; Phil. 2:9–11; Heb. 1:3).

CHAPTER THREE

The Deity of the Lord Jesus Christ

THE PERSON OF CHRIST

Jesus Christ is the eternal Son of God. John 1:18 expresses His deity in a very explicit way: "No one has ever seen God, but God the One and Only, who is at the Father's side, has made him known." His being "at the Father's side" expresses, not a distinction in essence or an inferiority in any way, but a close relationship to the Father and a sharing in the Father's authority. The opening verse of this great chapter in John identifies the "Word" as being in the beginning with the Father, a clear statement of the coexistence of the Son with the Father from eternity. It also declares "the Word was God," that is, Deity.[1]

Jesus himself acknowledged His deity, at least by implication, when He stated, " 'Anyone who has seen me has seen the Father' " (John 14:9). He also received worship from people (Matt. 2:2,11; 14:33; 28:9) and exercised

---

[1]Though the word "God" does not have the article in the Gk. here, it clearly means God with a capital "G"; just as it does in John 1:18; 3:21; and many other places where the Gk. does not have the article. It should be noted too that Thomas called Jesus literally "the Lord of me and the God of me" (Gk. *ho theos mou*). Thus he clearly meant God with a capital "G."

CHAPTER
3
___

The Deity of the Lord Jesus Christ

divine authority, forgiving sins (Mark 2:1–12). His disciples recognized Him as the Son of God (Matt. 16:16). Even "doubting Thomas" was convinced of the deity of Jesus Christ at that dramatic encounter in the Upper Room (John 20:28). And today as well, those who meet the resurrected Christ fall in adoration and worship before Him, saying, "My Lord and my God."

The deity of Christ includes His coexistence in time and eternity with the Father and the Holy Spirit. As the prologue of John indicates, the "Word" was eternally preexistent. The use of the term "Word" (Gk. *Logos*) is significant, since Jesus Christ is the chief agency of the Godhead for expressing the divine will. He is not only the one Mediator between God and mankind (1 Tim. 2:5), He was also the Mediator in creation. God spoke the universe into existence through the Son as the Living Word, and "without him [apart from Him], nothing was made [in creation] that has been made" (John 1:3). As Colossians 1:15 says, Christ is "the image of the invisible God." Hebrews 1:1–2 also proclaims the great truth that Christ is the fullest and finest revelation of God to humankind. From the beginning, the "Word," the very expression of God himself, has been actively disclosing God. And then, "when the time had fully come" (Gal. 4:4), "the Word became flesh and made his dwelling among us" (John 1:14).

Prior to that great coming of God in a new way into human history, the Word was eternally in existence, functioning as the Revealer of God. It is very probable that the theophanies (divine appearances) of the Old Testament were in reality "Christophanies," since in His preexistent state, Christ's brief encounters with people to reveal God's will would be in perfect accord with His office work as Revealer. Consider for example such passages as Genesis 21:17–20; 48:16; and Exodus 23:20. In these passages "the angel of the Lᴏʀᴅ" is clearly identified as Deity, yet distinguished from God the Father. Genesis 48:16 specifically refers to the heavenly messenger as one who "redeemed" (KJV), or "delivered" (NIV). In other passages where the angel of the Lord is both identified with God and distinguished from Him, or where the angel of the Lord receives worship (as in Judg. 13:16–22), it seems obvious that the angel was a manifestation of Christ.[2] Such Old Testament manifestations of the Second Person of the Trinity point forward to the Incarnation, when Christ would come to make His dwelling among the people of this world.

Not only is Jesus Christ fully God, He is also fully human. He was not part God and part man. He was and is 100 percent God and at the same time 100 percent human. That is, He held a full set of divine qualities and a full set of human qualities in the same Person in such a way that they did not interfere with each other. He remains the God-Man in heaven now and He will return as the "same Jesus" who ascended into heaven from the Mount of Olives (see Acts 1:11). Numerous passages teach clearly that Jesus of Nazareth had a truly human body and a rational soul. All that was characteristic of unfallen human beings (i.e., Adam and Eve) was found in Him. He was truly the Second Adam (see 1 Cor. 15:45,47). The Gospel accounts take for granted Christ's humanity. He is described as a baby in the manger and subject to human laws of growth (see Luke 2:40,52). He learned; He became hungry, thirsty, and tired (see Mark 2:15; John 4:6). He suffered anxiety and disappointment (see Mark 9:19); He suffered physical and mental pain, and succumbed to death (see Mark 14:33,37; 15:33–38). In the Book of Hebrews great care is taken to show the full identification of Jesus Christ with humanity (2:9,17; 4:15; 5:7–8; 12:2.)

The truth, then, is that in the one person of the Lord Jesus Christ dwells a fully divine nature and a fully human nature, two natures unconfused residing in one Person. He is indeed fully God and fully human, heaven and earth come together in the most wonderful of all persons.

Before leaving this very brief discussion of the person of Christ, let us look at the significance of the full title given to Him in the Bible: "the Lord Jesus Christ." This title

---

[2]Some fear that identifying the angel of the Lord with Christ would take away from the uniqueness of Christ's New Testament incarnation. However, that uniqueness involves Christ's full identification with humanity in His birth, life, ministry, death, and resurrection. No temporary preincarnate manifestation takes away from that uniqueness.

**CHAPTER
3**

**The Deity of
the Lord
Jesus Christ**

describes Him and helps us to see more clearly who He is.

The term "Lord" represents the Greek *kurios* and the Hebrew *'Adonai*[3] and *Yahweh*.[4] To the cultures of the ancient Near East, "Lord" was always an ascription of great reverence when applied to rulers. The nations around used it of their kings in the same way they used it of their gods, for most of the pagan kings claimed to be gods. The term, therefore, represented worship and obedience. *Kurios* could be used in addressing ordinary persons simply as a very polite way of saying sir. However, the Bible declares that Jesus was given the name "Lord" by the Father, thereby identifying Him as divine Lord (Phil. 2:9–11). The Christians easily adopted this term, recognizing Jesus as divine Lord and clearly intending by its use to acknowledge complete servitude and submission to the Supreme Being. A favorite title Paul used of himself was "servant" (Gk. *doulos,* "slave," that is, a love slave) of Christ Jesus (Rom. 1:1; Phil. 1:1). Absolute surrender is appropriate with respect to an Absolute Master. The practical significance of this term is staggering in its implications for daily life. All of life is to be included under the lordship of Christ. He is to be Master of everything and every moment in the life of everyone who has been born into the family of God.

This does not mean He is a tyrant. Jesus said, "The kings of the Gentiles lord it over them; and those who exercise authority over them call themselves Benefactors. But you are not to be like that. Instead, the greatest among you should be like the youngest, and the one who rules like the one who serves. For who is greater, the one who is at the table or the one who serves? Is it not the one who is at the table? But I am among you as one who serves" (Luke 22:25–27; see also Matt. 20:25–28). Jesus lived and taught servant leadership.

The personal name "Jesus" comes from the Hebrew name Joshua, meaning "the Lord [Yahweh] is salvation." It is the given name of God's Son, given before His birth by divine

---

[3]A title, "my Lord, my Master, the One I belong to."

[4]God's personal divine Name.

direction (see Matt. 1:21; Luke 1:31). This name is a reminder of the great purpose God has in the Incarnation—to bring salvation and deliverance from the bondage of sin. It is important to note that the Bible is careful to designate one particular person at a particular time in history as the embodiment of God's salvation. It is not just any person, but the One whom people called "Jesus of Nazareth," "the carpenter," "Mary's son." A unique feature of Christianity is that it is bound up in a historical personage, not relegated to the philosophical systems that are but products of human reasoning and imagination. Christianity is anchored in historic events and a historic Person.

It must be pointed out, however, that although the name "Jesus" depicts His humanity, the Bible very carefully guards the manner of His birth from mere natural procreation. He was born of a virgin. His conception was miraculous, the creative work of the Holy Spirit by the power of the Most High who overshadowed the virgin Mary (see Luke 1:34–35). This was prophesied by Isaiah over 700 years before the event (see Isa. 7:14),[5] and was fulfilled in due time according to the Gospel record (see Matt. 1:18–25). Jesus differs from us because of this unique event, having two natures but in one person. He was free from sin, protected by the Holy Spirit from the effect of Adam's fall. Yet He would enter fully into the testings we have as human beings and would represent us before the heavenly tribunal. He was fully human, but not a mere man. Zechariah 9:9 presents Him as literally "being salvation."

"Christ" (Gk. *Christos*) is the appellation that ties Jesus of Nazareth to the Old Testament prophecies about the Coming One. It translates the Hebrew *Mashiach*, "Anointed One." The term was used of God-anointed kings, but came to describe especially the prophesied Son of David who would come.[6] Jeremiah 33 and Isaiah 9 and 11 look forward

CHAPTER
3

The Deity of the Lord Jesus Christ

---

[5] In Isa. 7:14, the Heb. word for "virgin" is *'almah,* a word always used of virgins of marriageable age (see Gen. 24:16, for example).

[6] See *The New Testament Greek-English Dictionary, Sigma-Omega,* vol. 16, The Complete Biblical Library (Springfield, Mo.: The Complete Biblical Library, 1991), 524–529, for an excellent discussion of this subject.

to the Anointed One who will come to bring deliverance and who will reign.

THE OFFICES OF CHRIST

Bridging the teaching of who Christ is and what He came to do is the conception of His divine offices. Three terms designate these offices. He is God's anointed "Prophet," "Priest," and "King." Each of these terms emphasizes the mediatorship of Christ between the Father of heaven and the people of earth.

The term "prophet" comes from the Greek *prophētēs,* "one who speaks forth."[7] It became a technical term for one who speaks for God.[8] It carries with it the notion of proclamation, preaching, and informing. Isaiah 42:1–7 speaks of Christ as the anointed Servant who will enlighten the nations, and Isaiah 11:2 and 61:1 speak of the Spirit of the Lord resting upon Him. The New Testament portrays Jesus as a "preacher" as well as a teacher[9] and a healer (Matt. 9:35). He announced salvation to the poor (Luke 4:18–19). In Bible times the term "prophet" did not necessarily include the ability to look into the future. Prophets were simply speakers for God, and if God foretold the future to confirm or clarify their message, it was God, not the prophet, who saw the future and revealed it. The prophet was just a mouth for God to use. The prophets were also called seers because God let them see His message, sometimes in their minds, sometimes with dreams or visions.

Jesus, however, fulfilled the ministry of a prophet in the highest sense. He said, " 'These words you hear are not my own; they belong to the Father who sent me' " (John 14:24). Particularly in the closing year of His public ministry, Jesus taught His disciples much about the events yet to come. Entire chapters of discourse in the Gospels, Matthew 24,

---

[7]In the Old Testament it most often translates the Heb. *navi',* which comes from an old word for "speaker."

[8]Or a god or goddess. There were prophets of the false god Baal and his consort, Asherah (1 Kings 18:19).

[9]"Teacher" (Gk. *didaskalos*) is usually translated "Master," KJV, meaning schoolmaster.

for example, are futuristic prophecy. Clearly Jesus fulfilled the office of prophet. In the earliest days of His ministry, Jesus came proclaiming that what the Old Testament prophets had foreseen was being fulfilled in Him (see Luke 4:16–21). The Kingdom was already near in His person and ministry (see Matt. 4:17). The prophetic message was coupled with a call for repentance, and, as in the case of the Old Testament prophets, that call flowed out of a heart of love for the people and a desire to see the blessing of God on them.

Jesus Christ also fulfilled the office of priest. A priest is a specially consecrated individual who represents God to people, and people to God. Old Testament priests offered sacrifices for themselves and for the people to secure divine forgiveness and divine favor, and to celebrate their relationship with the Lord (see Heb. 8:3). In Christ, as the Book of Hebrews so beautifully elaborates the theme, one finds the Great High Priest, a perfect representative from among the people. Furthermore, He did not need to cleanse himself as the ordinary priests did, nor did He need to offer a sacrifice for himself. He himself became the perfect, pure, sinless sacrifice. He offered himself to God the Father as the atonement sufficient to cover, pay for, and forgive the sins of the whole world.

The office of king is appropriate to Christ as well. He is our Priest and our Atonement. He is our Lord and Master. But more than these, He is the One who has broken the forces of death, hell, and the grave, and is the Triumphant One. He will reign in majesty for the eternities unending! The Old Testament prophecies foretold a coming one who would unite in himself the functions of prophet, priest, and king. David was promised that there would be a kingdom without an end (2 Sam. 7:16). Isaiah looked through the lenses of prophetic vision and foresaw one who would bear the emblems of authority on His shoulder (Isa. 9:6) and who would make the throne of David eternal (Isa. 9:7). The Book of Revelation pictures the Lamb of God in the final triumph reigning as King of kings (Rev. 5:6–13; 11:15). And now, in the interim, He sits at the right hand of the Father in the heavenly realms and reigns as Head of the Church (Eph. 1:22–23).

CHAPTER

3

The Deity of
the Lord
Jesus Christ

THE WORK OF CHRIST

Jesus Christ came to live a sinless life, to be an example of perfect righteousness, a model by which His disciples could gauge their own behavior. He was not only born sinless, but He lived without sinning (see Heb. 4:15). An important term in this connection is "kenosis," Jesus' "self-emptying." During His earthly sojourn, Jesus "emptied" (Gk. *ekenōsen*), or divested, himself of the glory and privileges He enjoyed with the Father in past eternity (Phil. 2:7). Although there were fleeting occasions when His heavenly glory shone through, such as the spectacular Transfiguration on the mountain in Galilee (Matt. 17:1–13), much of His earthly ministry was accomplished in and by the power of the Holy Spirit (see Acts 10:38). He prayed that the glory would be restored (see John 17:5), and it was indeed restored after His ascension (see Acts 26:13). The great doctrine of the kenosis is given its fullest expression in Philippians 2:1–11.

Although Jesus came in a miraculous manner into this world, and although He lived a miraculous life, the central reason for His Incarnation is wrapped up in His death. First Corinthians 15:3 states it succinctly: "Christ died for our sins according to the Scriptures." Jesus came primarily to die. In a sense, the shadow of the Cross was over Him from the time of His birth (see Simeon's prophecy to Mary in Luke 2:34–35). The Cross is the central event of all history. It is that which distinguishes Christianity from all other religious systems. Christianity is given its fullest significance not by the life and teachings of its founder, important as they are, but by His death. The four Gospels are not biographies in the ordinary sense. They rush through the life and teachings of Jesus to get to the events leading up to His death. For example, John gets to the last week, the Passion Week,[10] in chapter 12, only halfway through his book. This shows the significance the Holy Spirit, through the Gospel writers, attached to this awesome spectacle.

---

[10]The term "passion" comes from the Low Latin *passio,* meaning "suffering." "Christ's passion" is a term for His sufferings between the Last Supper and His death on the Cross.

The Epistles are saturated with references to the Cross and to the meaning of the death of Christ. (A subsequent chapter will deal more specifically with the doctrine of Atonement).

When Jesus said, "It is finished," and died, His work for our redemption was complete. Only one thing more needed to be done: He was raised for our justification (see Rom. 4:25). The resurrection of Christ is the bold proclamation to the universe that the death of Christ was efficacious: that indeed the hosts of darkness had been conquered and that in triumph the victorious Christ had risen from the grave, making His resurrection the guarantee of ours. The great resurrection chapter of the Bible, 1 Corinthians 15, concludes with the ecstatic announcement: " 'Death has been swallowed up in victory.' 'Where, O death, is your victory? Where, O death, is your sting?' The sting of death is sin, and the power of sin is the law. But thanks be to God! He gives us the victory through our Lord Jesus Christ!" (vv. 54–57).

It is important to emphasize that the resurrection of Jesus was a genuine bodily resurrection out of a real death. It is the cardinal miracle of the Bible upon which our faith and salvation rest. Those who categorically rule out the possibility of miracles in the universe try desperately to explain away the resurrection of Jesus. Some deny that He actually died, claiming that He merely "swooned" and recovered in the cool tomb. But a half-dead Jesus crawling out of the tomb could hardly have inspired the apostles to risk their lives proclaiming the gospel. Others claim that only His spirit was resurrected. But the disciples were able to touch Him (see John 20:27); He was not just a spirit, or ghost (see Luke 24:37–39). Still others say that Peter fell asleep on board the ship, dreamed he saw Jesus on the shore, and—still dreaming—he jumped overboard and walked in his sleep to the shore. When he came to, he saw the ashes of yesterday's campfire someone had left, and it all seemed so real that he began telling people he had seen Jesus. This caused others to have mass hallucinations where they merely thought they saw the resurrected Jesus. But those who say this need a great deal of faith to believe Peter would not wake up when he hit the water, or that

CHAPTER
3

The Deity of the Lord Jesus Christ

such mass hallucinations would convince all the disciples
and the others who saw Jesus. Still others imply that the
disciples in their enthusiasm lied about the facts. But, again,
they would hardly have died for the gospel if they had
known in their hearts they had lied.

Several unmistakable points must be borne in mind regarding the proof of a real resurrection of our Lord. The
stone was rolled away from the tomb. But who would roll
away the stone? The Jews and the Romans set a guard; they
would not have done so. Certainly the soldiers knew the
penalty would be death if they did. As for the disciples,
they were afraid and in hiding. And the women who came
did not have the strength to do so. The Bible's answer that
angels were responsible is the only sensible explanation.[11]

The abundance of testimony from more than five hundred
witnesses covering no less than ten recorded appearances
of the postresurrection Lord is powerful confirmation of
the actual event; when the Gospel accounts were written,
any contemporaries who wished to take exception to their
testimony could easily have done so (1 Cor. 15:6). There
is no evidence that any were able to dispute the disciples.
Further, apart from a genuine resurrection, one cannot
adequately account for the dramatic change in the
disciples. It would take more than mass hallucination to
cause them to obey the Lord and stay in Jerusalem, waiting
for the promised Holy Spirit. Again, the Jews failed to produce the body of the Lord—a favorite argument having
been that the disciples stole the body and lied about the
event. But it is not easy to get rid of a body, and there is
no indication that the Jewish leaders commissioned anyone
to search for it. On the contrary, they gave money to soldiers to lie about what had happened (see Matt. 28:11–
15). When everything is objectively examined, there is
simply no adequate explanation that accounts for the tiny
Jerusalem church's survival, growth, and impact on world
civilization—apart from the empty tomb.

The resurrection body of Jesus had several remarkable
characteristics. The full understanding of what took place

---

[11]Frank Morrison, *Who Moved the Stone?* (London: Faber & Faber,
1930). The entire monograph is worth reading.

in the body of Jesus remains shrouded in a mystery that the Lord has not seen fit to unveil this side of eternity (see 1 Cor. 15:35–44). There are, however, some things that are told us. The Gospels disclose that the resurrection body of Jesus was real; it was the same body that had been entombed. He still had the ability to engage in physical activities appropriate to the human body. For instance, He ate food (see Luke 24:39–44). However, in addition to normal human capabilities, the resurrection body of our Lord was changed and had some unusual properties. Some of the usual limitations of the human body were gone. Peter saw the burial head cloth intertwined like a turban[12] and the linen wrapping still in place in the tomb, but apparently he did not understand at first. Then when John entered the tomb, "He saw and believed" (John 20:8). That is, he recognized that Jesus rose right through the wrappings, and consequently he believed (see John 20:6–8). Jesus also passed through locked doors to be with His disciples, and He vanished from the sight of the two who walked with Him on the road to Emmaus. Perhaps the brief glimpses of Christ's resurrection body are indicative of the state of the glorified bodies which will be ours at the time of the final resurrection of the believers, when we shall all be changed (see 1 Cor. 15:51).

Forty days of appearances to the disciples following the Resurrection were ended with the ascension of Jesus. There on the Mount of Olives, opposite the city of Jerusalem, Jesus was taken up bodily while a great company of His disciples watched (see Acts 1:9,11). This final dramatic moment closed the period of the Incarnation in which the God-Man, Christ Jesus, participated in physical presence with people on earth. When the cloud hid Him from their sight, Jesus entered into heaven (see Heb. 4:14; 1 Pet. 3:22), where He took up a new phase of His ministry. The work of redemption had been successfully discharged: He had instructed His disciples carefully in the program He had initiated for them, the Church. They were also to wait for

---

[12]The Gk. word *entetuligmenon* is in the perfect tense, indicating it had been and still was in the same shape as when it was wrapped around His head.

CHAPTER
3

The Deity of
the Lord
Jesus Christ

the promise of the Father, the Holy Spirit, who would continue Christ's work on earth through them. Now, with the phase of His work associated with humiliation and death over, His ascension inaugurated the beginning of a reign of exaltation.

We as believers receive several important benefits from the ascension and exaltation of Christ. The exalted Lord is now our friend and advocate at the right hand of the Father, engaging in the ministry of intercession on our behalf (see Rom. 8:34; Heb. 7:25; 1 John 2:1). He has entered into a new phase of His priestly ministry. With the atonement achieved, our Great High Priest now has sat down, which is evidence of His completed work, and pleads our cause in heaven. We have the assurance that "if we confess our sins, he is faithful and just and will forgive us our sins and purify us from all unrighteousness" (1 John 1:9). Further, He is our pledge, being already in heaven, that a place is being prepared for us there and that He will see to it that there will be rooms enough for everyone (see John 14:1–3).[13] And lastly, His exaltation is accompanied by His sending of the Holy Spirit to be "another Counselor" or Helper (Gk. *paraklētos,* "helper," "intercessor"[14]) to us (see John 14:16–26). Consequently, today, even though the Lord is separated from us physically, we can enjoy genuine union with Him through the ministry of the Holy Spirit, given to take the things of Christ and apply them to our hearts. In this very important sense, then, Jesus Christ is available to everyone today, no longer limited by the restrictions of physical appearance by which He operated during the time of His earthly ministry. These indeed are marvelous blessings available to us because of Christ's ascension and exaltation.

---

[13]The word "rooms" comes from the Gk. *monai* and is derived from *menō,* which means to "remain," "stay," "dwell," "continue," "be permanent." It indicates that though our stay on earth is temporary, our stay with the Lord will be permanent (cf. 1 Thess. 4:17). "Many" also indicates that God has not put a limit on the number of people who can come.

[14]"Another" means "another of the same kind," One just like himself. See Stanley M. Horton, "Paraclete," *Paraclete* 1 (Winter 1967), 5–8.

STUDY QUESTIONS

1. What are some of the ways the Bible declares, recognizes, or reveals the deity of our Lord Jesus Christ?

2. How does the Bible show that Jesus during His life and ministry on earth was fully human as well as fully divine?

3. How could Jesus be Lord and Servant at the same time?

4. What is the importance of the Virgin Birth?

5. How did Jesus fulfill the offices of the anointed Prophet, Priest, and King during His ministry? How is He fulfilling them now? How will He fulfill them when He comes again?

6. In what sense did Jesus "empty himself" when He came to earth and took human form?

7. What are the evidences for a real bodily resurrection of Jesus?

8. In view of 1 John 3:2, what does the resurrection body of Christ indicate about the nature of our resurrection bodies?

9. What benefits for us result from the ascension and exaltation of Jesus?

CHAPTER

3

The Deity of
the Lord
Jesus Christ

4th

th

FUNDAMENTAL
TRUTH

THE FALL OF MAN

Man was created good and upright; for God said, "Let us make man in our image, after our likeness" [Gen. 1:26, KJV]. However, man by voluntary transgression fell and thereby incurred not only physical death but also spiritual death, which is separation from God (Gen. 1:26–27; 2:17; 3:6; Rom. 5:12–19).

CHAPTER FOUR

The Fall of Man

THE ORIGIN OF HUMANKIND

What are we as human beings? This is a question that has been asked by thoughtful people through the centuries. It is an important question, since without its proper answer, life's meaning remains uncertain. Much of the unrest among youth may be attributable to this urgent quest.

A good beginning point for our discussion might be to reflect on two passages from the Book of Psalms. "What is man that you are mindful of him, the son of man that you care for him? You made him a little lower than the heavenly beings and crowned him with glory and honor. You made him ruler over the works of your hands; you put everything under his feet" (Ps. 8:4–5). In this passage the words "heavenly beings" translate the Hebrew 'Elohim, which is a general word for "God," "gods," or "angels," depending on the context. The writer of the Book of Hebrews, inspired by the Spirit, incorporates this Old Testament text in his New Testament work (2:5–9; applying the psalmist's verses to Jesus as our representative and as the one through whom we can achieve the destiny that was blocked by sin). In doing so, he translated 'Elohim into the Greek word *angelous*—"angels"—and in this way provided a clarification

**CHAPTER
4**

**The Fall of
Man**

of the original Hebrew. The important point, however, is that the perspective of the Psalmist with regard to human beings is from above, from their relation to heaven. A sharp distinction between human beings and the rest of creation is evident here.

Another psalm begins: "O LORD, what is man that you care for him, the son of man that you think of him? Man is like a breath; his days are like a fleeting shadow" (144:3–4). This view of human beings discloses our plight. We are, after all, but frail creatures. Apart from our Creator, we are in peril. Between these two important views of human-kind—one that sees us as a special object of God's creative interest, the other that sees us dependent on God's sustaining power—the realistic Bible account of humanity is cast. All nonbiblical views of humanity are either too high or too low. The Bible depicts us as we are in reality.

Where did human beings originate? The Bible does not give us a detailed, precise account of creation, such as modern scientists might produce. Scientific language as we know it was not developed until modern times. The Bible uses everyday language, and in that sense is prescientific in its categories and language; but it is not untrue or mythical. It is a common sense reporting of events and information in language appropriate to the people of the ancient Near East. And, remarkably, in spite of the span of millennia, in spite of our sophisticated, scientifically-oriented culture, the language of Genesis still conveys the essential information we need. After all, science is but a system of classifying empirical data. And though scientists can speculate about origins, they have no way to go back and be sure of them. We have assurance of our origin, however, through the facts given by revelation in God's Word. True science and the Bible are not at odds.

Very simple, yet utterly profound is the assertion in Genesis 1:26–28 regarding the origin of human beings:

> Then God said, "Let us make man in our image, in our likeness, and let them rule over the fish of the sea and the birds of the air, over the livestock, over all the earth, and over all the creatures that move along the ground." So God created man in his own image, in the image of God he created him; male and female he created them. God blessed them and said to them, "Be fruitful

and increase in number; fill the earth and subdue it. Rule over the fish of the sea and the birds of the air and over every living creature that moves on the ground."

It should be noted that this passage does not imply exploitation of the natural world, but care and proper use. Subduing the earth means bringing its resources under proper control and use. It was the go-ahead for a physical science that would help people learn about the earth and how to use it properly. Ruling the animal world included proper care and respect for its creatures. It was the go-ahead for a biological science that would help people learn about all living organisms and how to treat them. Unfortunately, as Romans 1 indicates, people took God off the throne, put self on the throne, and fell into all kinds of idolatry, sin, and perversion. Then, as long as they believed in many gods—none of whom were in complete control, and many fighting each other—they could not believe in any consistency in nature or in natural laws. It was not until the latter part of the Middle Ages, when Christian theologians said that God had a plan and that He was faithful and consistent, that people began to realize there was a consistency in nature. In effect, Christian theologians gave the impetus to scientific research, and science began to make progress.

Several crucial and far-reaching implications may be derived from the Genesis record. First of all, Adam and Eve were products of special creation by God. The Bible explicitly demands a creationist viewpoint, in sharp distinction to evolutionism, which teaches an organic development from the lower animals to human beings. Although the biblical record does not specify the time of creation, saying only "In the beginning,"[1] it does clearly differentiate

CHAPTER
4

The Fall of Man

---

[1]The Bible gives no total for the years from Adam to Abraham. Some have tried to add up genealogies and have come out with dates of creation anywhere from 3900 B.C. to 9000 B.C., depending on how they added them up. The ancient church historians Eusebius and Augustine accepted a date of 5202 B.C. Later the Archbishop of Dublin came up with 4004 B.C. But when we look at the genealogies in the Bible we see that the Bible never intended to mention every person in the line. Matt. 1:8, for example, leaves out three people found in the Books of 2 Kings and 2 Chron. Other genealogies do the same. God never intended us to add them up.

between the creation of all other living organisms and the special creation of Adam and Eve. The various theories of biological evolution, which blur the distinction between human beings and animals, require a view of Scripture other than that held by the apostles. For Paul, there was a literal Adam, and he makes a theological point on the fact that Adam was the first man (Rom. 5:12–21). And if there was a literal Adam, evolution is hard-pressed to account for some way that Adam could have evolved into Eve. Usually, evolutionists propose that a female was first in the human line.

Evolutionary views are of two basic types: theistic and atheistic. We may rule out atheistic evolution as obviously out of bounds by definition, though the majority of evolutionists today believe evolution has taken place by the same natural processes we see going on today and that in themselves they are a sufficient explanation. Therefore, they see no need for divine intervention. Yet even some of them are having a hard time explaining the origin of many of the complex structures in nature.[2]

There are numerous sincere Christians, however, who feel that they must accommodate the teaching of the Bible to various so-called facts of science, choosing therefore to adopt a position known as theistic evolution. Although the motives for taking such a position are commendable, it requires a type of biblical hermeneutics that raises more questions than it resolves. It forces a mythical, or at least a figurative or allegorical, interpretation on part of Genesis. None of these views corresponds to that of the apostle Paul. It appears further that the capitulation of theistic evolutionists to the demands of certain scientific theories may be premature. The theory of biological evolution, due to recent scientific inquiry, is under more serious question by many today than it was a generation ago. The Bible does not deny that there is change and development. God created one man and one woman. Today we have all the variety seen in the various races. Even so, we all are still human beings, much more alike than we are different. God

---

[2]A number of books dealing with this subject have been published. Christian book stores should carry them.

in creation seems to have made provision for additional variety to develop. But the development and changes are seen within the "kinds" that God created. Fossil records show also that all the major groups of animals go back in straight lines to the earliest fossils (found in the Cambrian period). For example, an echinoderm (starfish family) in the Cambrian was just as much an echinoderm as one is today; an arrow worm in the Cambrian was as much an arrow worm as one is today. Most of the so-called proofs of evolution are taken from changes and development within the various kinds.[3]

Actually the theory of evolution has become more of a philosophy than a scientific theory. As Bible believers we can rest assured that the facts really do dovetail with the legitimate demands of Scripture.[4] God does speak in nature. But the Bible is God's eternal Word. What science discovers is often interpreted in various ways, but there are thousands of people today working in science or who have scientific training who believe that there is no real conflict between science and the Bible. The Bible-believing person need not fear truth.[5]

THE NATURE OF HUMANKIND

Several important implications regarding the nature of human beings flow out of the Genesis account of special creation. One is that all people have a common ancestry: Adam and Eve. This testifies to the unity of mankind. Basically there is only one race, the human race. The teaching in Romans 5:12–21, regarding the Fall, is based squarely on the solidarity, the unity, of the human race. Through this unity, the tendency toward sin occasioned by Adam's

---

[3]The word "kind" in Gen. 1, the Heb. *min,* is a broad term, broader than "species." It is used in Lev. 11 even of superfamilies (of animals).

[4]For further research in this area, see Duane T. Gish, *Evolution: The Fossils Say No!* 2d ed. (San Diego: ICR Publishing Co., 1973); and Pattle T. T. Pun, *Evolution, Nature and Scripture in Conflict?* (Grand Rapids: Zondervan Publishing House, 1982).

[5]Several Christian organizations exist whose members have scientific training. One example is the American Scientific Affiliation with over 2,500 members.

fall reaches throughout the entire race. Likewise, the redemption that is ours through Christ, the second Adam, has a similar potential (Rom. 5:18).

When God created Adam, He first formed the body from the moist dust of the ground. Then He breathed into him the breath of life[6] and he "became a living being."[7] The Bible speaks later of the material body, an immaterial soul, and an immaterial spirit. Those who emphasize these three categories are called trichotomists. There is justification in this threefold distinction in such passages as 1 Thessalonians 5:23: "May God himself, the God of peace, sanctify you through and through. May your whole spirit, soul and body be kept blameless at the coming of our Lord Jesus Christ." Others take the statements of 2 Corinthians 4 and 5 to indicate there are basically two categories, the body and the inner person. Those who emphasize this dual aspect, material and immaterial, without giving special consideration to the distinction between soul and spirit, are called dichotomists.[8]

Regardless of which camp one may class oneself on this issue, it is clear that there are three functions of the human nature, indicated by the three categories. The body is the world-conscious aspect of our being. The sensory apparatus God has given us—sight, touch, hearing, smell, and taste—furnishes us an awareness of our physical surroundings. It is chiefly through this kind of avenue that we communicate with our environment. Our bodily appetites are part of our physiological and psychological makeup.

Nowhere in the Bible are such bodily appetites considered evil in themselves. This is very important. The Greeks, as well as other pagans in the early centuries, looked on

---

[6]The Heb. *chayyim* is plural. Some interpret this to mean God gave Adam both spiritual and physical life at the same time.

[7]The Heb. *nephesh,* translated "soul" in the KJV here, but "creature" in Gen. 1:20,24. It is also translated "person," KJV, Num. 5:6; 31:19; 35:11,15,30; Prov. 28:17; and many other places; also "life" in Gen. 9:4–5; 19:17,19; 32:30; Lev. 17:14; Job 2:4; and many other places. The emphasis in Gen. 2:7 is that Adam became a real, live person.

[8]Some dichotomists see the inner nature as having two aspects: soul in its relation to the world around and spirit in its relation to God.

the body as a "prison house." Not so the biblical writers. God created the body good. It is intended to be the habitation of the Holy Spirit. Someday it will be resurrected. We will need a body for the full expression of our nature even in our risen, glorified state, for we will always be finite beings. This understanding of the human body and the value God places on it is of utmost significance for proper ethical behavior. If the body were in and of itself evil, we could argue that we are victims of hopeless circumstance when we are solicited by our appetites to sin, and in despair give ourselves over to indulgence. As Christians we are not to permit natural bodily appetites to govern our behavior, but by exercise of proper discipline we must make our bodies become useful instruments for doing the bidding of God (Rom. 6:13; 1 Cor. 9:27).

The two facets of our immaterial nature, soul and spirit, are intimately linked and virtually inseparable; nevertheless, they are used in sufficiently distinct ways that we can note the difference. One may say that generally the term "soul" is used theologically to denote the self, particularly with respect to conscious life here and now (Rev. 6:9). The human soul provides for self-consciousness. It is that which makes the individual a genuine personality, having characteristics unique to that person. Faculties of the soul are commonly held to be intellect, emotions, and will. Together these compose the real person. They give an internal awareness of selfhood. It is that which links the spirit and the body; it governs the total personality.

We also have a spirit. God is by His nature spirit (John 4:24). On the other hand, the Bible speaks of the human spirit as being *within* oneself (1 Cor. 2:11); that is, the human being is not spirit, but houses spirit. Our spirit is that aspect which bears relationship to the unseen spiritual world, whether good or evil. It is that capability in us which is God-conscious. Paul, in Ephesians 2:1–10, describes the state of the unregenerate as being dead in "transgressions and sins." The unregenerate have bodies, just like their Christian contemporaries. They also enjoy a similar psychological ability, with power to reason, to will, to have feelings. However, they are "dead" with respect to God. They are separated from Him and are spiritually inert. When the Holy Spirit quickens the unregenerate, bringing new life to the individual, that capacity to relate to God is restored.

THE IMAGE OF GOD

Genesis 1:26–27 speaks of man (including both male and female) being created in the image and likeness of God. "Image" (Heb. *tselem*) is used of statues and working models. It implies a reflection in the human being of something of the nature of God. "Likeness" (Heb. *demuth*) is used of patterns, forms, or shapes that are something like what they portray. The word implies there is something like God about us. Both Hebrew words imply that further development of the human being is possible. In other words, Adam and Eve were not created all they could become: Although there was a perfection in their creation, it was the perfection of the bud, rather than of the flower or the fruit. However, we will never be totally like God, for we will always be finite beings, dependent on God. Jesus declared in John 5:26, "As the Father has life in himself, so he has granted the Son to have life in himself," that is, by His own right and nature. God has never done that for anyone else. We have eternal life only as long as Christ's life is in us through living union with Him (see John 15:1–6).

The image of God in us consists of both a natural and a moral image—not a physical one. Our bodies were made from the dust. Jesus did not have the outward form of a man before the Incarnation (see Phil. 2:5–7). God warned Israel not to make images because He by His nature does not have the kind of form one can make an image of (Deut. 4:15–19). Consequently, no image can be like God, and worshiping any image is worshiping something other than God. What Moses and Israel saw was glory (Exod. 33:18,22). The natural image includes those elements of personality or selfhood that are appropriate to all persons, whether human or divine, and are found in all of us as well as in God. Intellect, sensibility, will—such are categories that compose true personality and form a clear line of separation between human beings and animals. The vast natural capabilities of humankind, the potential for what one calls culture and civilization, lies in this accord we have with our Creator.

The moral image includes the will and the sphere of freedom in which we can exercise our powers of self-determination. It is the part of the image that makes possible fellowship with God and communication with Him.[9] God is love (1 John 4:8), and we are capable of love and are responsible for its exercise, first toward God (Deut. 6:5), responding to His love (1 John 4:19), and then toward our neighbor, including the foreigner (see Lev. 19:18,33–34; Deut. 10:19; Matt. 5:43–44; Luke 10:27–37). Our intellect informs our will, and for this, too, we bear a responsibility. The moral image in mankind is also the quality of our personality that relates to the rightness or wrongness of the use of our powers. This gives us a moral nature and furnishes the awful potential for great evil or for true goodness, righteousness, and holiness. In the beginning Adam and Eve were created with real holiness of heart, not mere innocence. They had a genuine inclination toward God and wanted to walk and talk with Him. With the Fall, this inclination toward God was ruined, becoming a strong disinclination instead. But God through Christ has provided us with a "new self, created to be like God in true righteousness and holiness" (Eph. 4:24). This shows God is especially concerned about the moral image and wants to see it restored. Its restoration is necessary if we are to have fellowship with Him.

THE ORIGIN OF SIN

A question philosophers have been working on and reasoning about since the time of the ancient Greeks has been how to account for the entrance of evil into the world. A

---

[9]Animals act largely through instinct. They do what is their nature to do; therefore, they are amoral. They are not able to have fellowship with people. A dog may be loyal to its master and even whine on his master's grave, but he cannot enter into the dreams, plans, and aspirations of his master. On the other hand, we can understand and enter into the plan and purposes of God as we exercise the qualities of the moral image. In this way we can have true fellowship with Him.

wide variety of nonbiblical notions have been put forth through the years. One such view is called dualism. Held by ancient Zoroastrians, later by Gnostics (who troubled the Early Church), and by heretics called Manicheans, this view has a long history. Dualists contend that there is an eternal principle of evil in perpetual conflict with good. Usually such a view looks on matter, or the physical universe, as inherently evil. The result is that the body is considered evil by nature, and either repression of its desires or gross indulgence out of sheer resignation is the result. The consequence for theology is also severe, for it conceives God to be less than absolute and infinite, or it conceives two gods, one good and one bad. For example, some dualists believe a bad god created the universe while the good god was not looking. Some believe only spirit is good, and therefore they suppose that the physical body of Jesus was only an illusion. Others say the Christ spirit was far below God, separated enough from Him so as not to contaminate Him, and that the Christ spirit came on Jesus either at his birth or his baptism—and some even say the Christ spirit left Him just before His crucifixion.

Another conception regarding evil's origin is that it is simply part of man's finiteness. Sin is but a "negation of being." This belief tends toward pantheism, since being and morality are confused. If creatureliness carries with it automatically the conception of sinning, then it removes human beings from moral responsibility. Sin would thus be purely a result of ignorance and weakness, with the environment more to blame than the individual. People have been trying to shift the blame for their sin ever since the Fall (see Gen. 3:12–13).

A variation on the foregoing theme is that sin is chiefly, if not wholly, corporate evil. Reinhold Neibuhr wrote a famous book called *Moral Man and Immoral Society.*[10] In this volume he attempted to show that the evil a man might not have the courage to do alone he would participate in if he were part of a group, such as a mob or a corporation, where his individuality would be blended with others who

---

[10]Reinhold Niebuhr, *Moral Man and Immoral Society* (New York: Charles Scribner's Sons, 1932).

would then corporately share the responsibility. Although Niebuhr acknowledged personal sin, others have sought to go far beyond his position: emphasizing the social aspect of sin to the total neglect of personal responsibility. For example, in a generation previous to Niebuhr's, Karl Marx was teaching that sin is nothing more than social injustice.

A common misunderstanding is a regarding of sin as having the nature of a substance. But if sin were a substance, or a thing, it would have to have been created by God and would therefore in its essence be good. Christian teachers over the years, in view of God's hatred of sin in the Bible as a whole, have rejected the idea that sin has its origin in God. Even though sin is not a substance or a thing, that does not mean it doesn't have reality. It acts in the realm of reality. Darkness is the absence of light. Although sin and evil are sometimes compared to darkness, they are more than the absence of good. Sin is also more than defect. It is a force that is active, pernicious, and destructive.

What does the Bible teach on this important subject? The biblical view is that sin originated in an abuse of the freedom given to created beings equipped with a will. God did not create evil. Evil is a matter of relationship, not a thing. Basically, it disregards the glory of God, the will of God, and the Word of God. It breaks away from a relation of obedience to and faith in God and makes a decision to fail Him. God did permit, however, for reasons known best to Him, the possibility of moral failure.[11] Freedom of the will is an important corollary of rational personality. Moral action is what determines character. And this involves a terrible risk, the risk of failure. God, in providing for truly free moral decisions in the angels and human beings He created, had to allow for the possibility of failure in some of His creatures. Without that possibility there would not

---

[11]There are some things God has not revealed to us. Speculative theology tries to search out these things by human reason. An example is the Scholasticism that dominated the thinking of Western Europe from the ninth to the seventeenth centuries. It combined religious teachings with human philosophies, primarily those of Augustine and Aristotle, and attempted to say more than God intended to reveal.

be genuine freedom or true personality.[12] The marvelous thing is that God at the same time provided a remedy for those who had fallen.

Sin, then, originated in the free choice of God's creatures. When the serpent[13] tempted Eve, he began with a question (as Satan so often does), "Did God really say, 'You must not eat from any tree in the garden'?" He implied, "Can it be that a good God would keep something from you that you might want?" Then he followed the question with a denial, "You will not surely die ... for God knows that when you eat of it, your eyes will be opened, and you will be like God, knowing good and evil." Satan was implying here that God says He created you in His image and He wants you to become like Him; but He has forbidden the one thing that will make you like Him. Then, by letting Satan focus Eve's attention on the forbidden thing, her mind began to reason that the fruit would indeed be good for her. Satan, therefore, did not have to pick the fruit or force it on her. She kept looking at it—and she made the choice. She took it, ate it, and gave it to her husband, probably conducting him through the same reasoning that led to her sin. When our first parents succumbed to temptation and sinned, several results issued from that act. They entered into a state of guilt. Not only did they become aware of their evil deed and the alienation from God which it incurred, but they became actually subject to penalty, for they were condemned by the command God had given, a command with a penalty attached.[14]

God could not be holy and ignore the disruption of divine law. For this reason, God must look upon sin with

---

[12]See Clark H. Pinnock, *The Grace of God and the Will of Man* (Grand Rapids: Zondervan Publishing House, 1989), for a good discussion of the Arminian view of sin and the sovereignty of God.

[13]See Rev. 12:9, which speaks of "that ancient serpent called the devil, or Satan."

[14]Some today confuse guilt-feelings with actual guilt. These are Christians who have accepted the forgiveness of Christ, but still retain nagging feelings of guilt. Guilt *feelings* are the result of a pained conscience. Guilt itself is the legal responsibility for wrongdoing in the sight of God, which incurs penalty.

wrath and judgment (see Rom. 1:18; Heb. 10:31; 12:29; 2 Pet. 2:9; 3:7).

Adam and Eve brought upon themselves, then, the personal consequences of sin (see Gen. 3:16–19). In addition, the entire human race was infected by sin. Ever after, children brought into this world would be naturally blighted by the inclination to sin. This disease of the human nature, upon a child's reaching the age of moral responsibility,[15] inevitably issues in personal acts of sinning, for which the individual falls under the wrath of God. The effect of Adam's sin on the human race is often called original sin. Original sin, though not itself the reason sinners are condemned by God, consequently leads one into overt personal sin, so that the apostle Paul can say with sadness, "All have sinned and fall short of the glory of God" (Rom. 3:23). Out of Adam's sin, then, innocence was lost, the divine image in humankind was distorted and weakened, people became enslaved to sin (see Rom. 6), and discord and death entered the world.

An obvious consequence of sin has been the fracturing of the relationships that prevailed in the Garden of Eden. First, Adam and Eve were estranged from God. Their consciences, instead of helping them, caused them to hide from God among the trees of the Garden and make themselves a covering of fig leaves. Then, when God faced them with their sin, they tried to shift the blame (something people have been doing ever since). But God did not accept that. He placed the responsibility back on them.

Sin, then, originated in the free choice of God's creatures. Instead of believing and trusting God, responding to His wonderful love and provision, they dethroned Him and enthroned self. Unbelief and the desire to exalt self were the key elements in their sin. Isaiah 14 shows to what extremes this can go. In that prophecy against Tiglath Pileser, who took the title "King of Babylon,"[16] is recorded the extravagant claims he made for himself. Like most of

CHAPTER 4

The Fall of Man

---

[15]The Bible gives no specific age of accountability. Some children come to a point where they understand sooner than others.

[16]See Jack Finegan, *Light from the Ancient Past,* 2d ed. (Princeton, N.J.: Princeton University Press, 1959), 206.

**CHAPTER
4**
___

**The Fall of
Man**

the ancient kings, he tried to exalt himself above all gods
and above the true God. Two years later the prophecy was
fulfilled and people who saw his corpse said, " 'Is this the
man[17] who shook the earth?' " (Isa. 14:16–20).[18] The essence of sin, then, is the substitution of the satisfying of
self for the original and highest objective in life—seeking
God and His righteousness. The result is all kinds of sins,
corruption, and perversion.[19]

Negatively, sin may be described as a transgressing of
God's laws (see 1 John 3:4). A variety of terms are used in
both Old and New Testaments, each supplying shades of
meaning that center in this basic understanding of sin as
the exaltation of self and the transgression of divine law.
The most common Hebrew word for sin is *chatta'th*, which
basically means "missing the mark," either by willfully fall-
ing short or deliberately going to one side or the other
(see Isa. 53:6; Rom. 3:9–12,23).[20] Another word, *resha'*, is
used of angry flaring up against God (Ezek. 21:24). *Pesha'*
is deliberate, premeditated rebellion (Jer. 5:6). Other words
speak of twisted, deviant behavior, which is contrary to
God's intention for us. But it all basically goes back to an
unbelief that fails to trust and obey God (see See Heb. 3:19;
4:1).

The animosity that erupted between Cain and Abel is
the first recorded example of the strained relationships that
have marred society since the Fall. Wars and fighting have
caused untold heartache down through the long history of
our fallen race—something that will continue until Jesus,
the Prince of Peace, comes back to establish His kingdom
on earth (see Matt. 24:6–8). Further, every sinner inter-

---

[17]Heb. *ha'ish*, the ordinary man, the individual male human being.

[18]Some see a parallel between the self-exaltation of Tiglath-Pileser
(also called Pul) and the self-exaltation and fall of Satan. No doubt, Satan
was behind him and encouraged his pride, a pride like that of the later
Sennacherib (see Isa. 36:18–20; 37:12–13,23–24).

[19]See Rom. 1:18–32, where the Bible shows how much suffering is
in the world because of sin, and how much, therefore, the world needs
the gospel.

[20]The same word is used in Judg. 20:16 of left-handed soldiers who
could sling a stone at a hair and not "miss."

nally is seething with discord (see Rom. 7). The conflict of mind that tears fallen man apart is a direct consequence of sin. "What a wretched man I am! Who will rescue me from this body of death?" cries the person torn by internal disharmony (Rom. 7:24).

Even nature suffered in the Fall. The very soil was cursed (Gen. 3:14–24). Not only had moral evil become a dark cloud over the world, but the Fall occasioned natural evil, too. The pestilences, diseases, and drought that have plagued mankind—causing his toil indeed to be "by the sweat of his brow"—are a result of the initial rebellion against God in the Garden.

Then sin brought death. God warned that the eating of the forbidden fruit would result in certain death (see Gen. 2:17). "Death" in the Bible often means separation. So the first effect was spiritual death; sin separated Adam and Eve from God. Their rebellion then brought physical death into the world. As a result, mankind "is destined to die once, and after that to face judgment" (Heb. 9:27). More than this, unrepentant sinners are also subject to the second death (see Rev. 2:11; 20:15), which is eternal separation from the source of life, God himself, in the lake of fire.

That the wages of all sin is death (Rom. 6:23) draws attention also to the serious nature of sin. Paul points out that sin could even use a good thing like the Law for evil purposes. God allows this in order that "sin might become utterly sinful" (Rom. 7:13). This means there is no way we can minimize even the slightest sin. No sin is too small for us to overlook and fail to seek forgiveness for. James reminds us also that "God cannot be tempted by evil, nor does he tempt anyone; but each one is tempted when, by his own evil desire, he is dragged away and enticed. Then, after desire has conceived, it gives birth to sin; and sin, when it is full-grown, gives birth to death" (James 1:13–15). In other words, if we continue to let our minds dwell on some temptation or wrong desire, it will issue in an act of sin, and if we make sin a habit or a way of life, it will bring spiritual and eternal death, that is, final separation from God. No wonder the Bible says, "whatever is true, whatever is noble, whatever is right, whatever is pure,

CHAPTER
4

The Fall of Man

whatever is lovely, whatever is admirable—if anything is excellent or praiseworthy—think about such things" (Phil. 4:8). We do not have to accept or revel in evil thoughts or desires that come to our minds. In themselves they are not sin; they can be interjected into our thoughts by the world around us. But we can reject those thoughts. It is only as we hold onto them and allow them to incubate that they lead to sin. For example, when Jesus said, " 'I tell you that anyone who looks at a woman lustfully has already committed adultery with her in his heart' " (Matt. 5:28), the Greek word for "looks" is a participle which means "keeps on looking." The fact that a passing thought enters the mind does not mean one is guilty and might as well commit the sin. Not at all. By the help of the Holy Spirit the thought can be rejected and a victory won to the glory of God.

From all this it might seem there is no such thing as a minor sin. However, the Bible does make distinctions in judging sin; but it's on a different basis—not, for example, whether murder is worse than stealing. In the Old Testament the distinction is between sins that are unintentional, for which a sin offering could be made (see Lev. 4:1 to 5:13), and sins that are deliberate and defiant, for which the death penalty was prescribed (see Num. 15:30–31). The New Testament adds, "If we deliberately keep on sinning after we have received the knowledge of the truth, no sacrifice for sins is left, but only a fearful expectation of judgment and of raging fire that will consume the enemies of God. Anyone who rejected the law of Moses died without mercy on the testimony of two or three witnesses. How much more severely do you think a man deserves to be punished who has trampled the Son of God under foot, who has treated as an unholy thing the blood of the covenant that sanctified him, and who has insulted the Spirit of grace?" (Heb. 10:26–29). The Bible thus warns us never to take a light or careless attitude toward sin. Truly the world needs the gospel. Truly everyone needs the salvation God has provided. Thank God we can walk in the light, have fellowship with God, and have the blood of Jesus his Son purify us from all sin (1 John 1:7).

STUDY QUESTIONS

1. Genesis 1 gives a step-by-step account of creation with the emphasis on the Creator. Genesis 2 takes part of the sixth day and gives additional details in a topical way in relation to the creation of mankind. Taking the two chapters together, what can be said about the nature of the man and woman God created?

2. Taking just the first two chapters of Genesis by themselves, what do you learn about the Creator?

3. How are the terms "body," "soul," and "spirit" best defined?

4. What is included of "the image of God" in human beings?

5. What is wrong with dualism and pantheism?

6. What does the Bible teach about the nature of sin and evil?

7. What were the steps in Satan's temptation of Eve? Has Satan changed his tactics today? If so, in what way? If not, why not?

8. What happened to Adam and Eve as a result of their sin?

9. What effects did their sin have on the human race?

10. What is meant by spiritual death?

5th

FUNDAMENTAL
TRUTH

THE SALVATION OF MAN

Man's only hope of redemption is through the shed blood of Jesus Christ the Son of God.

(a) Conditions to Salvation

Salvation is received through repentance toward God and faith toward the Lord Jesus Christ. By the washing of regeneration and renewing of the Holy Ghost, being justified by grace through faith, man becomes an heir of God, according to the hope of eternal life (Luke 24:47; John 3:3; Rom. 10:13–15; Eph. 2:8; Titus 2:11; 3:5–7).

(b) The Evidences of Salvation

The inward evidence of salvation is the direct witness of the Spirit (Rom. 8:16). The outward evidence to all men is a life of righteousness and true holiness (Eph. 4:24; Titus 2:12).

CHAPTER FIVE

The Salvation of Man

Built into God's program before the creation was an arrangement for the redemption of the fallen human race. That is, the death of Jesus Christ for the sins of the world was neither a plan B for, nor a patchwork on, a creation gone awry. He is "the Lamb that was slain from the creation of the world" (Rev. 13:8). Provision was decreed by the wisdom of God's foreknowledge, even before the fall in the Garden (see Eph. 1:4). Christianity is not a latecomer among the religions of the world; it was instituted in the mind of God before the dawn of time.

THE CONCEPT OF SACRIFICE

Essential to our understanding of the connection between the death of Christ on the cross and our salvation is the concept of sacrifice. God ordained this institution which would look forward to the better sacrifice to come (see Heb. 10:1–14) and also provide a perpetual lesson for everyone regarding sin, holiness, guilt, and the penalty for sin. It is an interesting anthropological fact that sacrifice is a nearly universal practice throughout the cultures of the

97

world.[1] Even in modern society people feel a need to make up, or atone, for their sins in some way, sometimes through various psychological devices—which is a form of sacrifice as well. As early as Genesis 3:21, the practice of sacrifice is recorded in human history.

Under the law of Moses, God arranged a way for the Israelites to have true forgiveness of sins by the institution of blood-sacrifice under the management of the Levitical priesthood. This priestly program is rich in typology and symbolism that point ahead to Christ. At the same time, it did provide a way of taking care of sin and guilt in the pre-Christian era. By faith, Abraham, Moses, and their spiritual descendants accepted what God by His grace provided, offered sacrifices to God, and were forgiven by a gracious and merciful God (see Rom. 4).

The shedding of blood was an important part of those sacrifices, for "the wages of sin is death" (Rom. 6:23), and the blood represents the life poured out in death (Lev. 17:11). Therefore, the Law of Moses required "that nearly everything be cleansed with blood, and without the shedding of blood there is no forgiveness" (Heb. 9:27).[2] The blood of bulls and goats was a good but temporary institution, lacking in perfection as witnessed to by the necessity of constant repetition (Heb. 10:11). In fact, the blood of animal sacrifices could not really take away sin (Heb. 10:4). The reason God could accept them and give real forgiveness was because Christ was going to die, and His death and the shedding of His blood would be sufficient for the sins of the whole world. And so, in the fullness of time, Jesus offered himself as the perfect, sinless sacrifice, doing away once for all with the need for oft repeated animal sacrifices (see Heb. 9:11–14).

---

[1]John Rogerson and Philip Davies, *The Old Testament World* (Englewood Cliffs, N.J.: Prentice-Hall, 1989), 255.

[2]The Gk. of this verse is not as absolute as the English. It does not rule out God's acceptance of a couple of handfuls of fine flour as a sin offering from the very poor (see Lev. 5:11–13). God's grace did not depend on how much people could give.

THE ATONEMENT

The concept of sacrifice is grounded in the necessity of atonement. "Atonement" is the translation of the Hebrew *kippur,* an intensive form that means "covering with a price." Sin alienates the sinner from a holy God: At the same time that we turn our backs on Him, He the Holy One cannot look with favor upon sin. The Atonement is the act of God whereby sins are covered by the price of shed blood, showing that the wages of sin have been paid, and God can once again look upon us with favor.[3] How did the Atonement occur? God is not only holy; He is loving. In His great love He was willing to bear the penalty of our sin, the suffering this breach of God's law produced. The holiness of God and the love of God converge in the cross of Christ. There the holiness of God is satisfied, and the love of God is emblazoned before the universe. God the Son, the perfect sacrifice, bore the wrath of an offended God in His own person so that sinful people might not have to endure an infinite punishment. Eternal punishment in the lake of fire is the logical corollary of finite people sinning against an infinite, holy God.

In the Atonement, there are several terms that need exploration. For example, it was a vicarious sacrifice. "Vicarious" means "in the place of another." Jesus did not die for His own sin, for He was sinless (see John 8:46; 1 Pet. 2:22). As Isaiah prophesied, "He was pierced for *our* transgression" (Isa. 53:5), so Paul pointed out, "Christ died for *our* sins according to the Scripture" (1 Cor. 15:3). It is for this reason that evangelicals speak of the substitu-

[3]The annual Day of Atonement under the Law called for two goats as a sin offering. The first was slain and its blood sprinkled on the Mercy Seat, the solid gold cover of the ark of the covenant. Under the Mercy Seat were the Ten Commandments written on tablets of stone. The Law that had been broken demanded death and judgment. But when the blood was sprinkled, God no longer looked at the broken law, but at the death of the spotless animal that the blood represented. With the spotless life having been given, there was grounds for mercy, grace, and forgiveness. The second goat as a scapegoat, literally "a goat for removal," was sent off into the desert to indicate that the sins were not only forgiven, they were gone. All of this pointed ahead to the death of Christ, by which we receive forgiveness and our guilt is gone.

tionary atonement. Christ died in place of us, instead of us. "Greater love has no one than this, that he lay down his life for his friends" (John 15:13). "God demonstrates his own love for us in this: While we were still sinners Christ died for us" (Rom. 5:8).

The atonement of Christ on the cross was satisfaction. It satisfied the claims of God's law and justice. It provided a standing before God, who is enabled to look upon us as righteous. "This righteousness from God comes through faith in Jesus Christ to all who believe. There is no difference, for all have sinned and fall short of the glory of God, and are justified freely by his grace through the redemption that came by Christ Jesus. God presented him as a sacrifice of atonement [Gk. *hilastērion,* "Mercy Seat," translated "atonement cover" in Heb. 9:5], through faith in his blood. He did this to demonstrate his justice, because in his forbearance he had left the sins committed beforehand unpunished—he did it to demonstrate his justice at the present time, so as to be just and the one who justifies those who have faith in Jesus" (Rom. 3:22–25). That is, the Old Testament sacrifices showed God's forbearance but could not show His justice, because the death of an animal cannot be a sufficient substitute for the life of a human being. It took the blood of Jesus, whose life and person are infinitely valuable, to be sufficient sacrifice for both the Old Testament saints and those who now believe in Jesus, thereby showing that God is indeed just. That is, the sacrifice of Christ is effective for the Old Testament people who believed in God as well as for us who now believe in Jesus. The implication also is that upon the appeasement of His wrath, God can once again turn His face with favor toward those who are forgiven and whose sins are covered with Christ's blood as a sufficient price and forever removed.

RESULTS OF THE WORK OF CHRIST AT CALVARY

Growing out of this concept of atonement sacrifice is the thought of reconciliation. As the atonement is the cause, reconciliation is the effect. We are reconciled to God because of the cross of Christ (Rom. 5:10; 2 Cor. 5:18–19).

The atonement provided by Christ carries with it also

the idea of redemption. The death of Christ is represented as the payment of a ransom, a price supplied to set free another who is in bondage, or slavery. Matthew 20:28 and Mark 10:45 depict Christ as coming "to give his life as a ransom for many." (The "many" includes all who believe.) The work of Christ is also spoken of as being a redemption (see Luke 1:68; 2:38; Heb. 9:12). To whom is this ransom paid? Surely not to Satan, although some ancient theologians so taught. We do not owe Satan anything. The ransom, the price, the debt, is to none other than God's attribute of justice. It is God we have offended by our sin. But when we could not pay, God the Son paid the full price God's character required. We have a beautiful illustration of this in Hosea 3, where God sent Hosea to buy back his wife who had deserted him to serve false gods and was being put on the block to be sold as a slave. There was no way she could redeem herself. So Hosea, at a great cost to himself, redeemed her and restored her to himself in a loving way. For God to redeem us the great cost to himself was the death of His one and only Son (John 3:16).

What are some of the results of this wonderful work of Christ at Calvary? There is pardon of transgressions and sins. By His atoning work, the debt for offending God, which we could not hope to pay, has been paid in full. The blot of past sins has been wiped away forever. The penalty has no more claim on the one who reaches out in faith to receive the free pardon furnished by our Savior (see John 1:29; Eph. 1:7; Heb. 9:22–28; Rev. 1:5).

There is also deliverance from the dominion of sin. Not only is the guilt totally removed so that believers become just as if they had never sinned, the Atonement also breaks the power of sin that enchained them as unbelievers. This is the great theme of Romans 6 through 8. Though we may sin after we have received Christ as our Savior and Lord, for we are still creatures of choice, yet we have been freed, and we can have the help of the Holy Spirit to make us able to not sin. Paul shudders at the thought of one delivered out of the slavery of sin even considering a return to that darkness, although the possibility of failure is ever present (see Rom. 6:1).

Another great triumph available through the atoning

CHAPTER

5

The
Salvation of
Man

death of Christ is deliverance from death. Christ "suffered death, so that by the grace of God he might taste death for everyone" (Heb. 2:9). Therefore, those who avail themselves of the provisions He has made need no longer fear spiritual death. Physical death is that last enemy to be conquered and destroyed by the victorious Christ (see 1 Cor. 15:26). Although the devil is a defeated antagonist and his judgment certain, he still operates in our world, and physical death is everyone's destiny until the return of Jesus (see 1 Cor. 15:26; 1 Thess. 4:16–18). But physical death notwithstanding, believers, whose lives are hid with Christ in God, will not be subject to spiritual death, the "second death," that eternal separation from God in the lake of fire (cf. Heb. 2:14–15; Rev. 2:11; 20:14–15). Their portion is the gift of eternal life (John 3:16).

One additional word is necessary here. Christ died for everyone, not just for a few. Redemption embraces the whole creation—potentially. It is the desire of God that everyone be saved (see 1 Tim. 2:4; 2 Pet. 3:9). Even so, redemption's application extends only to those who respond to the loving invitation of a gracious God. And this response brings salvation.

CONVERSION TO GOD

All that anyone must do to be saved from the wrath that must come on sin is to look to Christ and live. (Cf. Num. 21:4–9; John 3:14–15; 12:31–32.) Salvation is not a complicated series of elaborate rites and religious forms or a set of mystical steps. It occurs instantaneously in the life of the genuine seeker after God the moment he or she truly believes. However, even if there is no apparent or chronological order of events, there is a logical sequence, which an examination of the Bible discloses.

Several crucial terms are vitally related to the wonderful experience of salvation. We must first of all begin with the ministry of conviction. Jesus said, " 'No one can come to me unless the Father who sent me draws him, and I will raise him up at the last day' " (John 6:44). This gracious wooing of God, although in this passage attributed to the Father, is principally done by the Father through the Holy

Spirit. The Holy Spirit is the executor of the Godhead who applies the merits of redemption to those who believe. " 'When he [the Counselor, the Helper, the Holy Spirit] comes, he will convict [and convince] the world of guilt in regard to sin and righteousness and judgment: In regard to sin, because men do not believe in me; in regard to righteousness, because I am going to the Father, where you can see me no longer; and in regard to judgment, because the prince of this world now stands condemned' " (John 16:8–11). The chief instrument the Holy Spirit uses in this work is the Word of God. "Faith comes from hearing the message, and the message is heard through the word of Christ" (Rom. 10:17). The Holy Spirit does not force His attentions on the individual, but He does call sinners to come to Christ. Sometimes it is called the doctrine of vocation, or calling. Arminians and Calvinists alike are agreed that God takes the first step in the salvation of sinners. He issues the invitation.

"Conversion" means "to turn around." The Scripture makes many appeals to people to "turn themselves" to God. (Prov. 1:23; Isa. 31:6; Ezek. 14:6; Joel 2:12; Matt. 18:3; Acts 3:19). Conversion is the response of the sinner to the conviction of the Holy Spirit. This act of turning is composed of two elements: repentance and faith.

Repentance may be viewed as the negative side of "turning around." It is focused on that from which one turns; it is the forsaking of sin. There is an intellectual element in repentance. The Greek word for repentance, *metanoia*, means "a change of mind"—not a superficial or temporary change, but a fundamental change in attitudes. A change of view with regard to sin occurs. No longer is sin overlooked, excused, or called an alternate life-style. The repentant sinner acknowledges being a sinner indeed and guilty before God. There is also a change in attitude toward God and righteousness, from rebellion or indifference to love and concern. There is an emotional element in repentance. Genuine sorrow for sin is implied in this (evident in such passages as Ps. 51:1; Matt. 21:29–30; 2 Cor. 7:8; and Heb. 7:21). There is, further, a volitional element in repentance—a definite act of the will to take and receive what God offers. Again, the Greek word *metanoia* suggests

CHAPTER
5

The
Salvation of
Man

strongly that one plunges beyond the mere intellectual awareness of sinfulness, beyond the mere sorrow for sin, all the way to such a revulsion of sin that one exercises an act of will to reject sin and follow Christ, deeply desiring to learn more of Him (see Matt. 3:8; Acts 5:31; 20:21; Rom. 2:4; 2 Cor. 7:9–10; 2 Pet. 3:9).

The positive side to conversion needs to be emphasized even more. The sinner must not only "turn from" but "turn toward." We turn from sin and turn toward God. The turning toward God is an act of faith. It is entering into a positive relation to God. It is utterly central to Christian experience to emphasize the importance of faith. "Without faith it is impossible to please God, because anyone who comes to him must believe that he [the God revealed in the Bible] exists and that he rewards those who earnestly seek him" (Heb. 11:6). All our relationships to God are anchored in faith.

But what does "faith" mean? It too, like repentance, may be seen at three levels. First, there is the intellectual element. Faith is built on information. We are not asked to believe nothing. The facts of the gospel message are presented to the intellect of the person, first of all (see Rom. 10:17). We need to know the basic facts of the gospel before we can be expected to believe it. And there is an emotional element in saving faith. Jesus' explanation of the Parable of the Sower (Matt. 13:20–21) vividly pictures this level of faith—the seed that fell on rocky places and grew up quickly but perished in the heat of the day. Just so, there are many who appear to be sorry for sin (an emotional level of repentance) and ecstatic over their religious experience (an emotional level of faith), but who do not seem to get established solidly on a faith-basis with God. As soon as adversity, trouble, or persecution come, such shallow experiences are easily washed away. Many so-called backsliders may never have progressed beyond an emotional level of saving faith. There is, however, a level of faith that reaches to the core of the personality, the seat of the will. Volitional faith goes beyond mere intellectual assent, beyond the feeling of being religious, all the way to a decisive commitment of the whole self to the grace of God. We cannot take Jesus as our Savior without taking

Him as our Lord. There is a complete surrender of the will to the lordship of Jesus Christ. The words in both the Hebrew and the Greek for "believe" convey the idea of total submission, the complete surrender of the will, and continued, faithful obedience. In the Old Testament, faith could well be translated "faithfulness." In the New Testament it could be translated "faith-obedience," for there is no faith apart from obedience.

"Believe" is an active word that is always linked to its object. "Abraham believed the LORD"—not just the promise of the Lord (Gen. 15:6). Related to the Hebrew word for believe, *'aman*, are other words that can help us understand the root meaning. One is *'omeneth*, used of a faithful nurse who can be trusted not to drop the baby that is put in her arms. Another is the word *'amna*, which is used of a solid foundation that will not collapse even under the heaviest weight.[4] Consequently, believers may trust fully and completely in God: that is to say, genuine belief is a relationship. In the Bible, there is no such thing as "faith in faith"; it is always faith in God, a commitment in totality to Him (see John 1:12; 5:24; 6:53–54).[5]

One of the most glorious words in the Bible is "justification," a judicial term meaning "to declare one righteous." The guilty sinner stands before the great tribunal of a holy God, the righteous Judge. Justification is the breathtaking announcement that the sinner is not guilty. In God's eyes the sins are gone, removed from us "as far as the east is from the west"—which is an infinite distance (see Ps. 103:12). Micah 7:18–19 says it beautifully, "Who is a God like you, who pardons sin and forgives the transgression of the remnant of his inheritance? You do not stay angry forever but delight to show mercy. You will again have

---

[4]These words are not used in the Bible; however, other related words (*'emunah 'omen*) are used in Isa. 25:1 of God's perfect faithfulness and reliability.

[5]Mark 11:22 has been translated by a few writers as "Have the faith of God." God, however, does not need faith. He knows. Furthermore, the Gk. undoubtedly focuses the faith in God, so that the correct translation is indeed, "Have faith *in* God," as the vast majority of Bible versions have it.

compassion on us; you will tread our sins underfoot and hurl all our iniquities into the depths of the sea."

Three facets of blessing flow from the wonderful declaration that we are not guilty. First, the sinner has sins' penalty remitted. The penalty for sin is death—physical and spiritual (see Gen. 2:16–17; Rom. 5:12–14; 6:23). This penalty was removed by the death of Christ, who bore the punishment due us in His own body on the Cross (see Isa. 53:5–6; 1 Pet. 2:24). Further, justification speaks of restoration to divine favor. Not only had sinners incurred the penalty appropriate to sin, they also had lost God's favor. God could not enter into fellowship with sin (see John 3:36; Rom. 1:18). By faith in Christ we again are restored to divine fellowship (see Gal. 3:26; 1 John 1:3). Finally, justification carries with it the imputation of righteousness. Just as the penalty of sin had been "charged to our account," so in the act of justification the righteousness of Christ has been charged to our account (cf. Phil. 3:9 and Gen. 15:6). We have been wrapped about with the purity of Christ. He has become our wedding garment (see Matt. 22:11–12).

How is one justified before God? Again and again the Scriptures stress that it is the gift of God, it is of His grace, it is secured through simple faith in the atoning death of Christ (see Mark 10:17–22; Rom. 3:24; 4:1–5; Gal. 3:24; Eph. 2:5,8).

Conversion is turning from sin to God; justification is the declaration that the believing sinner is righteous before God; but regeneration is the actual impartation of divine (Christ's) life to the new convert.[6] As conversion is primarily human response, regeneration is God's response, the work of His Holy Spirit in the heart of the new believer. It is the impartation of spiritual life (see John 3:5; 10:10;

---

[6]It should be noted that eternal life is Christ's life in us, flowing from Him like the life of the vine flows into the branches (see John 15:1–8). " 'For as the Father has life in himself, so he has granted the Son to have life in himself,' " that is, by His own right and nature (cf. John 5:26). But God has not given that to anyone else. We have eternal life only as we maintain living contact and fellowship with Christ by active faith-obedience.

1 John 5:11–12). It is being born again—literally, "born from above" (John 3:3): the impartation of a new nature (cf. Jer. 24:7; 2 Pet. 1:4). Regeneration is a creative act of God (see 2 Cor. 5:17; Eph. 2:10; 4:24). The depravity in which the sinner is enslaved before conversion is exchanged for a clean nature, so that one is brought into the family of God (see Eph. 2:19). This is new life in Christ. It is "Christ in you, the hope of glory" (Col. 1:27).

"Adoption" is another judicial term, similar to justification in that it carries the connotation of the courtroom. As regeneration is the actual impartation of divine life to the convert, so adoption is the marvelous declaration that the "child" in the divine family has been fully accepted as an adult member of the family—eligible for all the privileges appropriate to that legal standing in the divine family.[7] "Adoption" means, literally, "placing as a son." The great passage that teaches this truth is Galatians 4:1–5, in which Paul powerfully declares the position provided for the children of God through the merits of Christ. Paul tells us that in the mind of God, adoption was provided for believers before time began (see Eph. 1:5). In actuality, the first phase becomes true personally at the time the individual accepts Jesus Christ as Lord and Savior (see Gal. 3:26).

Adoption also is the work of the Holy Spirit, for He works in believers as the Spirit of adoption (possessed by those who are children of God, heirs of God and joint heirs with Christ [see Rom. 8:15]) in contrast to the spirit of slavery, the spirit possessed by slaves. However, what we receive now is just the first installment. When Jesus returns and we are changed, we will receive the fullness of all that is included in our salvation and adoption; we will be given new bodies that are incorruptible and immortal, no longer subject to decay, disease, or death. At that time we will receive our full inheritance (see Rom. 8:23; 1 Cor. 15:42–44, 52–54). What a full salvation God has provided through

---

[7]In those days, children were adopted as they are today; however, they (even of wealthy, important families) had their lives regulated with strict enforcement, often under the tutorship of a slave. It was when they reached maturity that they were given adoption, receiving then the full privileges and status of belonging to the family.

Christ: We are saved, we are being saved, and we shall be saved. How wonderful to have new life in Christ!

STUDY QUESTIONS

1. What did the sacrifices of the Law do for Old Testament believers in the one true God? What could they not do?

2. What is the meaning of the word "atonement"?

3. What is involved in the atonement Jesus accomplished on the Cross?

4. Why does the Atonement involve redemption and ransom?

5. What is the evidence that Christ died for everyone?

6. What is involved in conversion to Christ?

7. What is included in the faith that saves?

8. What is the difference between "justification" and "adoption"?

6*th*

FUNDAMENTAL
TRUTH

ORDINANCES OF THE CHURCH

(a) Baptism in Water

The ordinance of baptism by immersion is commanded in the Scriptures. All who repent and believe on Christ as Savior and Lord are to be baptized. Thus they declare to the world that they have died with Christ and that they also have been raised with Him to walk in newness of life (Matt. 28:19; Mark 16:16; Acts 10:47–48; Rom. 6:4).

(b) Holy Communion

The Lord's Supper, consisting of the elements—bread and the fruit of the vine—is the symbol expressing our sharing the divine nature of our Lord Jesus Christ (2 Pet. 1:4); a memorial of His suffering and death (1 Cor. 11:26); and a prophecy of His second coming (1 Cor. 11:26); and is enjoined on all believers "till He come!"

CHAPTER SIX

Ordinances of the Church

Biblical Christianity is not ritualistic or sacramental. Sacramentalism is the belief that special grace is bestowed on participants who engage in certain prescribed rituals. It is usually held by sacramental churches that the grace is received whether or not the participant has any active faith—all one has to do is go through the form. Although obedience to two ordinances is prescribed in the New Testament, no special merit is attached to such obedience.[1] These two ceremonies, which the Lord instituted and commanded, are to be understood as occasions of memorial. There is no saving power in the mechanical performance of these acts; the blessing that one may receive is a matter of the heart.

WATER BAPTISM

Water baptism is a ceremony that symbolizes the beginning of the spiritual life. It is a public declaration of our

---

[1]As time went on, the Catholic Church added other sacraments. For a discussion of the seven traditional sacraments of the Roman church— the Eucharistic Sacrifice of Christ's Body and Blood, Baptism, Confirmation, Penance (now called Reconciliation), Anointing of the Sick (formerly called Extreme Unction), Holy Orders or Ordination, and Marriage—as currently held, see Arthur P. Flannery, ed. *The Documents of Vatican II*, rev. ed. (Grand Rapids: Wm. B. Eerdmans, 1984).

identification with Jesus in His death and resurrection, for they made possible our new life in Him (see Rom. 6:1–4). Peter makes a comparison with Noah and his family going through the Flood in the ark:

> In it only a few people, eight in all, were saved through water, and this water symbolizes baptism that now saves you also—not the removal of dirt from the body but the pledge of a good conscience toward God. It saves you by the resurrection of Jesus Christ, who has gone into heaven and is at God's right hand—with angels, authorities and powers in submission to him (1 Pet. 3:20–21).

The water of the Flood brought judgment on a world that was corrupt and full of violence (see Gen. 6:5,11). So the water of baptism symbolizes judgment that Jesus in His death took upon himself for all people of all times. The water of the Flood did not cleanse Noah. Rather, the fact he and his family came through the Flood and were saved from its judgment was a testimony to the faith they had before the Flood—faith that caused them to believe and obey God and build the ark. So the water of baptism does not cleanse us, but is a testimony to our faith in the risen Lord Jesus Christ, a faith we must have before we go into the water of baptism. Therefore, it is not the water itself that saves us, but what coming through the water represents: the resurrection of Jesus Christ, the resurrection that showed God had accepted Christ's sacrifice on our behalf and in our place. The New Testament clearly shows it is the blood of Jesus, not the water of baptism, that brings us cleansing and forgiveness: By His blood we are justified (Rom. 5:9), our consciences are cleansed (Heb. 9:14), we are redeemed (1 Pet. 1:19).

When Peter spoke of baptism "for the forgiveness of your sins" (Acts 2:38), he used the same Greek construction where John the Baptist said, "I baptize you in water for repentance" (Matt. 3:11). John's baptism did not produce repentance. In fact, he refused to baptize the Pharisees and Sadducees until they showed the fruit of repentance, that is, until they showed they had already repented (see Matt. 3:7–8). "For repentance" means "because of repentance" or "as a testimony of repentance." So also "for the forgiveness of sins" means "because of the forgiveness of sins" or "as a testimony to the fact that sins have been forgiven." Unless a person has first believed and been cleansed by the blood of Christ, water baptism means nothing. But for the one who is truly born again (cleansed by His blood and justified), baptism becomes not only a testimony but also the pledge that we will continue to live a new life in the power of the risen Christ.

Who then is eligible for water baptism? The New Testament teaches that water baptism is for believers only. In line with Peter's illustration, Noah believed God before going through the Flood (see Heb. 11:7). Jesus commanded His disciples to make disciples and then to baptize them (see Matt. 28:19). In Mark 16:16, believing precedes baptism. When the deacon Philip went to Samaria, his preaching and miracles "brought great joy in that city" (Acts 8:8). "When they believed Philip as he preached the good news of the kingdom of God and the name of Jesus Christ, they were baptized, both men and women" (Acts 8:12). Their baptism came after they believed. At the house of Cornelius, they not only believed, they were baptized in the Holy Spirit, spoke in tongues, and praised God before they were baptized in water. At Philippi, Paul told the jailer, " 'Believe in the Lord Jesus and you will be saved—you and your household' " (Acts 16:31). Then all heard the word of the Lord, all were baptized, and the jailer "was filled with joy because he had come to believe in God—he and his whole family" (Acts 16:34). It is clear therefore that water baptism is intended to be a public ceremony in which open witness is made to the community that the believer has accepted Jesus Christ as Savior and Lord.

The foregoing leaves no grounds for infant baptism. Nevertheless, those who argue for infant baptism sometimes take baptism as a substitute for circumcision, which was done when Israelite boy babies were eight days old. However, when the New Testament deals with circumcision it does not say, "Neither circumcision nor uncircumcision means anything; what counts is water baptism." It says, "what counts is a new creation" (Gal. 6:15). We are a new creation when we are "in Christ," by faith (see 2 Cor. 5:17).

**CHAPTER
6**

Ordinances
of the
Church

**CHAPTER
6**

**Ordinances
of the
Church**

Because the promise is "for you and your children" (Acts 2:39) and because Paul baptized the household of Stephanas (1 Cor. 1:16), some take this to point to infant baptism. But in those days, children were not considered full members of the household until the time of their "adoption."[2] Furthermore, Peter commanded the people to "repent and be baptized" (Acts 2:38). Infants are incapable of repentance, faith, and public testimony to salvation. In fact, they have no sins of which to repent. This means that infants and children who die before the age of accountability are still saved through the redemption that is by Christ Jesus. "Jesus called the children to him and said, 'Let the little children come to me, and do not hinder them, for the kingdom of God belongs to such as these' " (Luke 18:16). Because of this, we believe the dedication of infants to God is not out of order. It is, however, primarily a challenge to the parents and to the local church to make provision for the spiritual training of the child so that upon reaching an age of responsibility the child will be prepared to accept Jesus as Savior and Lord.

Immersion is the mode that conveys the full significance of such passages as Romans 6:1–4, in which the going down into the water pictures death to sin and rising up out of the water, new life in Christ. Some denominations take Ezekiel 36:25, which speaks of God sprinkling clean water on Israel as a restored nation, as grounds for baptism by sprinkling. However, the Greek word *baptizō* clearly means "to dip under," "immerse." It was used in ancient non-Christian literature to mean "plunge," "sink into," "drench," "overwhelm." Furthermore, note the following: John the Baptist was baptizing at Aenon "because there was plenty of water" (John 3:23). When Jesus was baptized, He came "up out of the water" (see Mark 1:10). When Philip baptized the Ethiopian Eunuch, both of them went "down into" and came "up out of " the water (see Acts 8:38–39). All these things point conclusively to immersion.[3]

---

[2]See chap. 5, note 5.

[3]Recently, archaeologists have found in the earliest church buildings (from the second century A.D.) baptismal tanks for immersion. In Jerusalem also there were several large pools where it would have been easy for the 120 to baptize the 3,000 who were converted on the Day of Pentecost.

The baptismal formula is supplied in Matthew 28:19— " 'baptizing them in the name of the Father and of the Son and of the Holy Spirit.' " The word "name" in the Greek also means "title."[4] It is singular here because it is used distributively and there is only one "name" or title each.[5] "In the name" here is literally "into the name," a phrase that was commonly used in those days to mean "into the worship and service." In Acts 2:38, where we read of baptism "in the name of Jesus Christ," the expression is a little different. It is literally "upon the name of Jesus Christ." "Upon the name" was their way of saying "upon the authority." Peter, in effect, was appealing to the Great Commission, in which Jesus on His authority told the disciples how to baptize (Matt. 28:19). In other words, those in the Book of Acts, on the authority of Jesus Christ, did baptize "into the name [the worship and service] of the Father and of the Son and of the Holy Spirit." Church history confirms that baptism continued to be done in the Triune Name.

THE LORD'S SUPPER

The Lord's Supper was instituted by the Lord Jesus Christ on the occasion of His last Passover meal with the disciples (often called the Last Supper), just hours before He died on the cross.[6] For us it takes the place of the Passover of the Old Testament, "for Christ, our Passover lamb, has been sacrificed" (1 Cor. 5:7). The Lord's Supper, which Jesus commanded to be repeated at frequent intervals until His Second Coming,[7] has several values in relation to the past,

CHAPTER
6

Ordinances
of the
Church

---

[4]See Walter Bauer, William F. Arndt, and F. Wilbur Gingrich, eds., *A Greek Lexicon of the New Testament,* trans. Frederick W. Danker (Chicago: The University of Chicago Press, 1971), 576.

[5]The same distributive (rather than collective) use is seen in Ruth 1:2, where the "name" (singular in the Heb.) of the two sons were Mahlon and Kilion. If "name" had been in the plural, the Bible would have had to give more than one name for each of the sons.

[6]See Matt. 26:26–29; Mark 14:22–25; Luke 22:15–20; and 1 Cor. 11:23–26.

[7]Some churches observe the Lord's Supper every service, some once a week, but most assemblies observe it once a month. All Jesus said was " '*Whenever* you eat this bread and drink this cup, you proclaim the Lord's death until he comes' " (1 Cor. 11:26).

the present, and the future: It is commemorative, instructive, and inspirational; it promotes thanksgiving and fellowship; it proclaims the new covenant; and it carries a responsibility.

First, it is commemorative: "Do this in *remembrance* of me" (Luke 22:19). It is a solemn occasion for pondering deeply the significance of the atoning death of Christ, the focal point of all history. It confronts us again with the cost of our redemption from sin and its penalty. It is also instructive, symbolizing by means of a sacred object lesson the incarnation of Christ (the physical elements of bread and wine[8]) and the Atonement (the consuming of the physical elements). When Jesus said, "This is my body" and "this cup is the new covenant in my blood," He meant that the bread and wine represented His body given in death and His blood poured out as a sacrifice on the cross.[9] The Lord's Supper is also inspirational, since we are reminded that by faith we may enter into the benefits of His death and resurrection. By partaking on a regular basis, we are repeatedly identifying ourselves with Him in His death, reminded that He died and rose again so that we might have victory over sin and avoid every kind of evil (see 1 Thess. 5:22).

The Lord's Supper calls for thanksgiving, which is *eucharistia* in the Greek (see 1 Cor. 10:16) and thus the source of the term "Eucharist," used by some churches. It is an opportunity to thank God for all the blessings that

---

[8]There is good evidence that the wine, the juice of the vine, was unfermented at the Lord's Supper. See "Wine in New Testament Times" in *The Full Life Study Bible* Donald C. Stamps, ed. (Grand Rapids: Zondervan Bible Publishers, 1990), 126.

[9]Roman Catholics teach transubstantiation, the belief that the bread and wine by a miracle become the actual body and blood of Jesus, keeping only the appearance of bread and wine—so they adore the bread and the wine. Lutherans and many Anglicans (Episcopalians) teach consubstantiation, the belief that Jesus is actually present in a substantial way with the bread and wine. However, "this is my body" and "in my blood" are metaphors. Jesus was present with the disciples when He said this of the bread and the wine. See also 1 Cor. 5:8, where Paul speaks of "the bread of sincerity and truth."

are ours because Jesus died on the cross.[10] It is an opportunity for fellowship (Gk. *koinonia*)—first of all, with the
Father and His Son, Jesus Christ (see 1 John 1:3), and,
second, with other believers who share the faith (see Titus
1:4; Jude 3), the grace of God (see Phil. 1:7; Col. 1:6), and
the indwelling of the Holy Spirit (see Rom. 8:9,11). Jesus
was the host at the Last Supper. As our risen Lord, He is
present, for He promised, "Where two or three come together in my name, there am I with them" (Matt. 18:20).
Therefore, He is the unseen host at every celebration of
the Lord's Supper.

The Lord's Supper recognizes and proclaims the new
covenant (Gk. *hē kainē diathēkē*). By partaking of the
Lord's Supper we declare our purpose to make Jesus Lord,
do His will, take up our cross daily to follow Him, and
fulfill His Great Commission. The Lord's Supper also looks
forward to the future kingdom of God, where Jesus promised to "drink it [the fruit of the vine] anew" (Mark 14:25).
This probably refers to "the Marriage Supper of the Lamb"
(cf. Matt. 8:11; 22:1–14; Luke 13:29; Rev. 19:7).

Finally, the Lord's Supper carries a responsibility. Paul
reminds us in 1 Corinthians 11:27–34 that one must guard
against participating "in an unworthy manner." What does
it mean to participate in an unworthy manner? Surely it
does not mean that one must be worthy as a person, since
none of us is able to stand in this relationship to God apart
from Christ. It refers, rather, to unworthiness of attitude
and behavior. We are all sinners, but those who have been
"made new in the attitude of your minds" and "put on the
new self, created to be like God in true righteousness and
holiness," and who are "all members of one body" (Eph.
4:23–25) are eligible for participation in the Lord's Table.
Those who harbor sin, whether it be gross and carnal or
subtle and personal, are in need first of cleansing (1 John
1:7,9).

Since the warning is so strong (see 1 Cor. 11:27,29–30),
it is important that we examine ourselves before we eat
of the bread and drink of the cup (1 Cor. 11:28). As we

CHAPTER
6
—
Ordinances
of the
Church

---

[10]See Matt. 26:27–28; Mark 14:23–24; Luke 22:19–20; and 1 Cor.
11:24–26.

eat and drink, we must recognize "the body of the Lord." The "body" we must recognize, or "discern" (KJV), is the spiritual body of Christ, the assembly of believers. "Is not the bread that we break a participation in the body of Christ? Because there is one loaf, we, who are many, are one body, for we all partake of the one loaf" (1 Cor. 10:16-17). The context shows that the Corinthians were allowing divisions and quarrels among themselves. "One...says, 'I follow Paul'; another, 'I follow Apollos'; another, 'I follow Cephas'; still another, 'I follow Christ'" (1 Cor. 1:12). This party spirit had spilled over into the celebration of the Lord's Supper (which was originally celebrated in connection with a meal). So they showed no love for each other, and they did not recognize each other as members of the body of Christ. Consequently, they did not recognize the Body in each other. (See 1 Cor. 12:12-13.) Instead, they partook in a self-centered spirit that was indifferent to each other.

Notice, however, the Bible does not tell those who were taking the Lord's Supper in an unworthy manner to stop taking it. Rather, we are to "examine" ourselves, "judge ourselves," and "wait for each other" (1 Cor. 11:28,31,33). That is, we are to wait until we can recognize the body of Christ in each other and partake of the Lord's Supper in unity of love and faith, honoring Christ and God's Word.

The warning of First Corinthians 11:29-31 is not intended to make people afraid of partaking of the Lord's Supper. Rather it is meant to encourage judging ourselves—which implies confessing any sin that might be a barrier between us and the Lord and cleansing our hearts and minds of any grudge, pride, or prejudice that would keep us from loving fellowship with the members of the local Body of Christ. This is why we need to "wait for each other."

Nor do we need to wait long. "If we walk in the light, as he is in the light, we have fellowship with one another and the blood of Jesus, his Son, purifies us from *all* sin" and "if we confess our sins, he is faithful and just and will forgive us our sins and purify us from *all* unrighteousness" (1 John 1:7,9). The moment we confess, the blood covers.

Because the Lord's Supper is a solemn time for remembering the focal point of Christ's work on our behalf, it can become a time for great spiritual blessing, provided the participants come in the proper frame of mind and allow it to be an opportunity for worship and fellowship with the risen Christ and with each other.

STUDY QUESTIONS

1. Why do most Protestants accept only two ordinances instead of observing seven sacraments?

2. What does water baptism do and what does it not do?

3. What is the biblical evidence that water baptism is for believers only?

4. Why is it important that we be baptized by immersion?

5. In what sense does the Lord's Supper have a backward look, an upward look, and a forward look? Explain.

6. What attitudes does the Lord's Supper call for on our part?

7. What does it mean to partake in a worthy manner?

7th

th

FUNDAMENTAL
TRUTH

THE BAPTISM IN THE HOLY GHOST

All believers are entitled to and should ardently expect and earnestly seek the promise of the Father, the baptism in the Holy Ghost and fire, according to the command of our Lord Jesus Christ. This was the normal experience of all in the early Christian church. With it comes the enduement of power for life and service, the bestowment of the gifts and their uses in the work of the ministry (Luke 24:49; Acts 1:4,8; 1 Cor. 12:1–31). This experience is distinct from and subsequent to the experience of the new birth (Acts 8:12–17; 10:44–46; 11:14–16; 15:7–9). With the baptism in the Holy Ghost come such experiences as an overflowing fullness of the Spirit (John 7:37–39; Acts 4:8), a deepened reverence for God (Acts 2:43; Heb. 12:28), an intensified consecration to God and dedication to His work (Acts 2:42), and a more active love for Christ, for His Word and for the lost (Mark 16:20).

CHAPTER SEVEN

The Baptism in the Holy Ghost

WHAT THE FATHER HAD PROMISED

The ministry of the Holy Spirit in the life of the believer is rich and varied. Though deeply personal and internal, one aspect of the work of the Spirit is, nonetheless, primarily concerned with the expression of the Christian life, and in this sense is external in purpose. The baptism in the Holy Spirit is not primarily for the development of holiness in the individual (although this may be and should be enhanced by the baptism in the Spirit); it is empowering for service. Jesus told the men and women gathered in the Upper Room, " 'I am going to send you what my Father has promised; but stay in the city until you have been clothed with power from on high' " (Luke 24:49). On another occasion "while he was eating with them, he gave them this command: 'Do not leave Jerusalem, but wait for the gift my Father promised, which you have heard me speak about. For John baptized with [in] water, but in a few days you will be baptized with [in] the Holy Spirit' " (Acts 1:4–5). Then just before He ascended, He said, "You will receive power when the Holy Spirit comes on you; and you will be my witnesses in Jerusalem, and in all Judea and Samaria, and to the ends of the earth' " (Acts 1:8).

Notice that this promise was given to disciples already in close communion with Christ. Their names were already written in heaven (Luke 10:20). "They were clean before God, having had a spiritual bath through Christ's Word (John 13:10; 15:3)."[1] From the time of Christ's resurrection, they were also a new covenant body, the Church, the old covenant having been abolished at Calvary (Eph. 2:15). According to Hebrews 9:15–17, the death of Christ put the new covenant into effect. The emphasis of Acts 1:8 is power for service, not regeneration, not sanctification. So we conclude that one may be regenerated, may be a saint, and yet not enjoy the baptism in the Spirit and its anointing for service, which Jesus promised believers.

Some have treated the baptism in the Holy Spirit as primarily a matter of sanctification. Some have even made the chief object of the Christian life the perfecting of oneself. We must avoid this idea. We actually achieve more growth while in service for our Lord. The saint, that is, the person who is dedicated and consecrated to the worship and service of the Lord, is not the one who spends all his or her time in study, prayer, and devotion, important as that is. The saint is the one who not only separates from evil but is separated and anointed for the Master's service. This was symbolized in the Old Testament by the fact the blood was first applied in the act of cleansing and the oil was then applied over the blood (Lev. 14:14,17). That is, cleansing was followed by a symbolic anointing that represented the Spirit's work in preparing for service. So we too are anointed, as were the prophets, kings, and priests of old (2 Cor. 1:21; 1 John 2:20).

The means and power for service come through the gifts of the Spirit. But the gifts of the Spirit need to be distinguished from the gift of the Spirit. The baptism in the Spirit was necessary before the first disciples were to leave Jerusalem or even begin to fulfill the Great Commission. They needed power, and the

---

[1]See Stanley M. Horton, *What the Bible Says About the Holy Spirit* (Springfield, Mo.: Gospel Publishing House, 1976), 132.

very name Holy Spirit is connected with power.[3] He came as the Gift and as the Power. He himself is the firstfruits of the final harvest, come to begin a work that will bring some from every kindred, tongue, people, and nation together around the throne (Rev. 5:9). The same baptism in the Spirit was experienced by others on at least four other occasions in Acts . . . as well as by still others later on, according to Titus 3:5.

---

[3]E. W. Bullinger, *The Giver and His Gifts* (London: The Lamp Press, 1953), 26, 27.[2]

BIBLICAL TERMINOLOGY FOR THE BAPTISM

The baptism in the Holy Spirit is also called by other terms. We must remember that the Holy Spirit is a person. "Baptism" describes only one aspect of the experience of His Person. It is also called a filling: "All of them were filled with the Holy Spirit" (Acts 2:4). As Joel prophesied (2:28–29), the Spirit was "poured out" upon them (Acts 2:33; 10:45). They "received" (actively took) the gift (Acts 2:38; 8:17). The Spirit "came on" them (Acts 10:44; 11:15; 19:16). Some modern writers suppose that baptism in the Spirit refers to something different from filling, or that the Pentecostal experience was limited to the Day of Pentecost. But with the use of all these terms in the Bible, it is clear that what happened on the Day of Pentecost was repeated.

Peter saw, too, that the "last days" bring opportunity for times of refreshing. Acts 3:19 could be translated, "Repent therefore and turn to [God for] the blotting out of your sins so that times of refreshing (or revival) may come from the presence of the Lord and He may send Jesus Christ who was appointed for you (or, appointed as your Messiah)."

The way Peter looked at Joel's prophecy shows he expected a continuing fulfillment of the prophecy to the end of the "last days." This means also that Joel's outpouring is available to the end of this age. As long as God keeps calling people to salvation, He wants to pour out the Spirit upon them: "The promise [that is, the Old Testament prophecy in Joel] is for you and your

---

[2]Ibid., 258–259. (See also p. 250.)

children and for all who are far off—for all whom the Lord our
God will call" (Acts 2:39).[3]

From this we see that the Spirit's baptizing work does
continue,[4] and we today have available to us the fulfillment
of Joel's prophecy, which Jesus also called the promise of
the Father.

THE PURPOSE OF THE BAPTISM IN THE HOLY SPIRIT

In addition to the power for service through which the
individual becomes a potential channel of great witness to
the world, the baptism in the Spirit becomes the entrance
into a mode of worship that blesses the assembled saints
of God. The baptism is the gateway into the manifold ministries in the Spirit called gifts of the Spirit, including many
spiritual ministries.[5]

Those who were converted, baptized in water, and baptized in the Spirit on the Day of Pentecost showed further
evidence of the work of the Spirit in their lives as "they
devoted themselves to the apostles' teaching [now found
in the New Testament] and to the fellowship, to the breaking of bread and to prayer.... Every day they continued
to meet together in the temple courts [at the morning and

---

[3]Ibid., 146–147.

[4]This is seen also in Acts 19:1–7. The twelve men undoubtedly pro-
fessed to be followers of Jesus, but Paul sensed something missing, so
he asked them (literally), "Having believed, did you receive the Holy
Spirit?" "Having believed" (Gk. *pisteusantes)* is an aorist participle, a
form that normally indicates action prior to the main verb, in this case,
prior to the receiving. Similar grammatical constructions occur in passages such as these (translated literally): "Having married a wife, he
died" (Matt. 22:25); "Having carried her [Sapphira] out, they buried
her" (Acts 5:10); "Having shaken the dust off their feet, they came to
Iconium" (Acts 13:51); "Having received this order, he threw them into
the inner prison" (Acts 16:24). It is clear also that Paul baptized the
believers in water before he placed his hands on them and the Holy
Spirit came on them. See Horton, *What the Bible Says,* 159–162; and
Donald C. Stamps, ed., *The Full Life Study Bible* (Grand Rapids: Zondervan Bible Publishers, 1990), 269.

[5]Since these gifts are intended for the corporate body of the local
church and its edification, we will discuss them in more detail in chap.
10, dealing with the Church.

evening hours of prayer]. They broke bread in their homes and ate together with glad and sincere hearts, praising God and enjoying the favor of all the people. And the Lord added to their number daily those who were being saved" (Acts 2:42,46–47). Herein is described a continuing work of the Spirit that deepened their experience and their love for God, for His Word, for one another, and for the lost.

In fact, it should always be kept in mind that the baptism in the Spirit is not a climactic experience. As Pentecost itself was only the beginning of the harvest and brought men [and women] into a fellowship of worship, teaching, and service, so the baptism in the Holy Spirit is only a door into a growing relationship with the Spirit and with other believers. It leads to a life of service where the gifts of the Spirit provide power and wisdom for the spread of the gospel and the growth of the Church. This is evidenced by the rapid spread of the gospel in many areas of the world today. New fillings, new directions of service are to be expected as new needs arise, and as God in His sovereign will carries out His plan.[6]

Some have pointed out that Paul's epistles do not say much about the baptism in the Holy Spirit. There is good reason for this: The baptism in the Holy Spirit was the normal experience of all first-century believers. All the people to whom he was writing were already filled with the Holy Spirit. So that was not a question. However, some things he does say are important; for example, "Now it is God who makes both us and you stand firm in Christ. He anointed us, set his seal of ownership on us, and put his Spirit in our hearts as a deposit, guaranteeing what is to come" (2 Cor. 1:21–22; see also 5:5). Ephesians 1:13 makes this even more emphatic: "Having believed, you were marked in him with a seal, the promised Holy Spirit." Ephesians 4:30 adds, "Do not grieve the Holy Spirit of God, with whom you were sealed for the day of redemption."

The word "deposit" (2 Cor. 1:22) really means a first

---

[6]Horton, *What the Bible Says,* 261.

installment. The firstfruits are an actual part of the harvest (see Rom. 8:23). In the same way the Holy Spirit as a "deposit" is

an actual part of the inheritance, and is the guarantee of what we shall receive in larger measure later.[13] Our inheritance is more than a hope. Now, in the midst of the corruption, decay, and death of the present age, we enjoy in and through the Holy Spirit the actual beginning of our inheritance.[14] . . .

Some have taken "seal" to mean protection, safety, or security. But the seal is a present acknowledgment that we are the Lord's. Of itself, it does not mean we cannot lose our salvation. Nor does the Greek imply here the kind of sealing that is done when food is sealed in a jar or tin can to protect it from contamination. [We indeed "through faith are shielded by God's power until the coming of the salvation that is ready to be revealed in the last time" (1 Pet. 1:5)], but this is not automatic. The faith must be maintained. . . .

The seal in the New Testament also has the idea of a designation of ownership, a trademark indicating we are His workmanship (Eph. 2:10).[15] . . . The seal is also a mark of recognition that we are indeed sons, and an evidence that God has indeed accepted our faith.

---

[13]René Pache, *The Person and Work of the Holy Spirit*, rev. ed. (Chicago: Moody Bible Institute, 1966), 25.

[14]George Eldon Ladd, *The Pattern of New Testament Truth* (Grand Rapids: Wm. B. Eerdmans Pub. Co., 1968), 101–102.

[15]William Barclay, *The Promise of the Spirit* (Philadelphia: The Westminster Press, 1960), 15.[7]

Ephesians 1:13 indicates further that the sealing is after the believing. This does not meant God's ownership is dependent on the sealing. We are made His through the blood of Jesus and through our response of faith to God's grace. Therefore, the seal is a recognition of ownership; it does not produce the ownership. Then, since the seal was always something visible or tangible that others could recognize, the baptism in the Holy Spirit with its outward

---

[7]Ibid., 237–238.

evidence of speaking in other tongues fits the New Testament idea of sealing.[8]

Another important passage is 1 Corinthians 12:13: "We were all baptized by one Spirit into one body—whether Jews or Greeks, slave or free—and were all given the one Spirit to drink." The preposition "by" (Gk. *en*) clearly means "by" in all the other verses where it is linked with the Holy Spirit in this chapter. John the Baptist declared that Jesus is the One who baptizes in the Holy Spirit (Matt. 3:11; Mark 1:8; Luke 3:16; John 1:33). Paul makes it clear that the Holy Spirit is the One who baptizes us into Christ, that is, into the body of Christ (1 Cor. 12:13; Gal. 3:27). The two baptisms are clearly distinct. The Holy Spirit first baptizes us into the body of Christ, then Jesus baptizes us into the Holy Spirit.[9]

Paul further emphasizes the importance of living in the Spirit. This means we will be careful not to grieve the Holy Spirit by such things as rage, anger, brawling, slander, or any kind of malice. Instead we will be kind and compassionate to one another, forgiving each other, just as in Christ God forgave us (Eph. 4:30–32). We will not have anything to do with the fruitless deeds of darkness (Eph. 5:11), nor will we be drunk with wine, but instead will be filled (the Gk. means "keep on being filled") with the Spirit (Eph. 5:18).

The Spirit is the source of the love, zeal, and state of heart that enables us to serve the Lord acceptably, with "spiritual fervor" (Rom. 12:11), a fervor that is boiling, burning, aglow with the Holy Spirit.[10] In fact, we must be careful not to put out the Spirit's fire by rejecting or

---

[8]"Most commentators forget also that the baptism in the Holy Spirit was the normal experience of all believers in New Testament times. Therefore, in Paul's mind he is not drawing a line between sealed believers and those who do not have that privilege. He sees all believers as having had the experience and as therefore included" (Ibid., 239).

[9]Anthony D. Palma, "Baptism *by* the Spirit," *Advance* (June 1980), 16. See also Horton, *What the Bible Says*, 214–216.

[10]Horton, *What the Bible Says*, 194.

**CHAPTER
7**

The Baptism
in the Holy
Ghost

demeaning the Spirit's supernatural manifestations (1 Thess. 5:19–20).[11]

RECEIVING THE BAPTISM IN THE HOLY SPIRIT

One final question deserves special attention: "How may one receive the baptism in the Holy Spirit?" The experience is described as a gift (Acts 10:45), and is therefore not in any way deserved or earned. It is received by faith—active, obedient faith. God has promised to pour out His Holy Spirit on hungry seekers who open their hearts to Him and ask. "If you then, though you are evil [in contrast to God who is totally righteous and completely holy and good], know how to give good gifts to your children, how much more will your Father in heaven give the Holy Spirit to those who ask him!" (Luke 11:13). We note too that the 120 who received the Holy Spirit on the Day of Pentecost worshiped Jesus and spent much time praising God (Luke 24:52–53). Joyful praise and expectation prepare our hearts to receive. We note also that when they were filled with the Spirit they all "began to speak in other tongues as the Spirit enabled them" (Acts 2:4). That is, they did not hold back, but in obedient faith used their tongues, lips, and voices to speak out what the Spirit gave them.

STUDY QUESTIONS

1. What is the evidence that the disciples were already saved and were members of the Church before they were baptized in the Holy Spirit on the Day of Pentecost?
2. What is the primary purpose of the baptism in the Holy Spirit?
3. Some today say that after the Day of Pentecost people were filled with the Holy Spirit but not baptized. What is the evidence that the term "baptism in the Holy Spirit" is

---

[11]See *Full Life Study Bible,* 442. The fire of zeal is connected with the Holy Spirit. This is in contrast to the fire of judgment. For a discussion of the meaning of "the baptism of the Holy Ghost and fire," where John the Baptist may have been offering a choice between the baptism in the Spirit and a baptism in the fire of judgment, see Horton, *What the Bible Says,* 84–89.

not limited to the experience of those who were baptized on the Day of Pentecost?

4. What effects followed in Acts 2 after the 120 were baptized in the Holy Spirit?

5. What is the meaning of the word "seal" in relation to the baptism in the Holy Spirit?

6. What is the meaning of the word "deposit" ("earnest," KJV) in relation to the baptism in the Holy Spirit?

7. What are the evidences that the baptism in the Holy Spirit is a distinct experience that should follow that of conversion?

8th

FUNDAMENTAL
TRUTH

THE INITIAL PHYSICAL EVIDENCE OF THE BAPTISM IN THE HOLY GHOST

The baptism of believers in the Holy Ghost is witnessed by the initial physical sign of speaking with other tongues as the Spirit of God gives them utterance (Acts 2:4). The speaking in tongues in this instance is the same in essence as the gift of tongues (1 Cor. 12:4–10,28), but different in purpose and use.

The Initial Physical Evidence of the Baptism in the Holy Ghost

An important question is how one may know when one has been baptized in the Holy Spirit. To be sure, there should be many evidences along the roadway of life to indicate a life empowered by the Holy Spirit. However, the real question is not the long-range result of the baptism in the Spirit, but the immediate indication that one may point to as witness of the experience itself. Has God provided such an indicator? If one concludes that the Book of Acts is not only a descriptive history, but also has a theological purpose, and that the experience of the Apostolic Church, which it records, is indeed normative[1] for the Church of all ages, then one can answer the question with a resounding yes.

SIGNS OF THE OUTPOURING

On the Day of Pentecost two signs preceded the outpouring of the Holy Spirit. They heard "a sound like the blowing of a violent wind" and they "saw what seemed to

---

[1]For a good discussion of this, see Roger Stronstad, *The Charismatic Theology of St. Luke* (Peabody, Mass.: Hendrickson Publishers, 1984).

**CHAPTER
8**

The Initial
Physical
Evidence of
the Baptism
in the Holy
Ghost

be tongues of fire that separated and came to rest on each of them" (Acts 2:2–3). These particular signs were not repeated on later occasions when people were baptized in the Spirit. One sign, however, was actually a part of the Pentecostal baptism. All who were filled with the Holy Spirit "began to speak in other tongues as the Spirit enabled them" (Acts 2:4). These "tongues" were languages they had never learned, given apart from the individual's understanding. Some present who understood the languages recognized that they were "declaring the wonders [the mighty, magnificent sublime deeds] of God" (Acts 2:11). This remarkable sign was the most spectacular phenomenon evident on the Day of Pentecost. But it was repeated again at various times, two of which are recorded in the Book of Acts (10:46; 19:6).

Special interest attaches to the episode at the house of a Roman centurion, Cornelius. There, because of the ingrained prejudice of the Jews against the Gentiles, a convincing evidence was needed. Only one evidence was given to show that these Gentiles had received "the gift of the Holy Spirit." The astonished Jewish believers "heard them speaking in tongues and praising God" (Acts 10:46), exactly as the 120 had done on the Day of Pentecost (Acts 2:4,11). Later when Peter was criticized for going to the house of a Gentile and eating with them, having table fellowship, Peter explained that " 'the Holy Spirit came on them as he had come on us at the beginning [that is, as on the Day of Pentecost]. Then I remembered what the Lord had said: "John baptized with [in] water, but you will be baptized with [in] the Holy Spirit." So if God gave them the same gift [Gk. *tēn isēn dorean,* meaning "the identical gift"] as he gave us, who believed in the Lord Jesus Christ, who was I to think that I could oppose God?' " (Acts 11:15–17). The next verse shows that apostles and the other Jewish believers accepted the sign of speaking in tongues as the convincing evidence of the baptism in the Holy Spirit: "When they heard this, they had no further objections and praised God, saying, 'So then, God has granted even the Gentiles repentance unto life.' " Surely in a day when many think, hope, believe, and then wonder whether they have the baptism in the Spirit, a convincing evidence is still needed.

Some years later, at Ephesus, the Gentiles there likewise received the Pentecostal experience and "they spoke in tongues and prophesied" (Acts 19:6). This again shows they had received the full experience of the baptism in the Holy Spirit. The Greek normally implies also that they continued to speak in tongues and prophesy. "Speaking in tongues . . . continues to bring enrichment to the individual believer in personal devotions, and to the congregation when accompanied by the interpretation of tongues."[2]

With the death of Stephen, persecution began, scattering the believers (except the apostles) and spreading the flame of the gospel in many directions (Acts 8:1). Representative of the gospel's advance is Philip's preaching at Samaria to people who had been under the influence of Simon the sorcerer. They believed and were baptized in water, but the Holy Spirit did not come upon any of them. Perhaps because they now realized they had been wrong about Simon the sorcerer, as well as about many of their Samaritan doctrines, they found it hard to take the next step of faith and receive the baptism in the Spirit.[3] But when Peter and John came, prayed for them, and placed their hands on them, they received the Holy Spirit (Acts 8:15–17). At that point Simon the sorcerer fell back into his old ways and offered money for the authority to place his hands on people so that they might receive the Holy Spirit. Obviously, there was something supernaturally evident in the receiving of the Spirit. Simon had already seen Philip's miracles. Prophecy would have been in their own language and not obviously supernatural. Speaking in tongues must have been the evidence that Simon recognized. Luke, however, at this point focuses attention on Simon's wrong attitude and thus does not mention the tongues.

There is one other episode in the Book of Acts which has at least the implication of tongues. When Paul was

CHAPTER 8

The Initial Physical Evidence of the Baptism in the Holy Ghost

[2]*Where We Stand* (Springfield, Mo.: Gospel Publishing House, 1990), 147.

[3]Stanley M. Horton, *What the Bible Says About the Holy Spirit* (Springfield, Mo.: Gospel Publishing House, 1976), 154.

CHAPTER

8

The Initial
Physical
Evidence of
the Baptism
in the Holy
Ghost

arrested by Jesus on the road to Damascus, he was blinded by the glory, led into Damascus to the house of Judas on Straight Street, and given a vision that a man named Ananias would come and place his hands on him to restore his sight. That good disciple then came and told Paul that the Lord had sent him so Paul might see again and be filled with the Holy Spirit (Acts 9:17). Tongues is not mentioned specifically on that occasion, but later Paul testified: "I thank God that I speak in tongues more than all of you" (1 Cor. 14:18). From what happened on the other occasions where people were baptized in the Spirit, we can infer that Paul's initial experience of speaking in tongues was on that occasion when Ananias came to him, as mentioned in the Book of Acts.

If all the references to Pentecostal enduement in the Book of Acts are put together, the overwhelming evidence is that tongues was the initial, physical sign or evidence of receiving the experience. Since we do acknowledge the historical description in Acts as having a theological purpose[4] and holding a pattern for the Church today, there is strong ground for our conviction that those who would be filled with the Spirit should expect to have the witness of speaking in other tongues as the Spirit enables them.[5]

FUNCTIONS OF SPEAKING IN TONGUES

It may be asked if speaking in tongues is only for the evidence of the baptism in the Holy Spirit. The answer is

---

[4]Some writers claim that doctrine must be based on declarative statements in the Epistles, not on the history in the Book of Acts. However, the Holy Spirit inspired Paul to write, "All Scripture is God-breathed and is useful for teaching [doctrine, KJV]" (2 Tim. 3:16). Furthermore, "everything that was written in the past was written to teach us" (Rom. 15:4). When the Bible wants to develop the doctrine of justification by faith in Romans 4, it goes back to a historical passage in Genesis and talks about Abraham. When it wants to show how grace comes in, it goes back to a historical passage and talks about David.

[5]"The word translated 'tongues' in Acts is the same word used in 1 Cor. and refers to actual languages of men or angels (1 Cor. 13:1). There is no justification for interpreting the word as strange or ecstatic sounds. In New Testament times, as in our own, there were people who heard and understood the speaking with tongues" (*Where We Stand*, 147).

no, the phenomenon of tongues has at least two other important functions.[6] Personal tongues, that is, the gift of utterance in unknown languages in private devotions, has the very worthwhile value of edifying the one engaged in prayer. To pray in an unknown tongue is to engage in a lofty form of worship (1 Cor. 14:4). Praying in tongues is a useful practice; it should be cultivated in the believer's daily life, for by it one is built up in faith and in spiritual life. Paul seems to take for granted in his epistles that believers normally went on to the baptism in the Holy Spirit and that tongues was a common part of their daily experience. He himself spoke in tongues more than the Corinthian believers, but in private (1 Cor. 14:18–19).

There is another use for tongues. Although the same in essence, the gift of tongues employed in public services is for a distinctly different purpose. The tongues mentioned in Acts are evidential and private, the tongues mentioned in the Epistles are public and intended for general edification. Private tongues need not be interpreted since the individual is edified even if his understanding is not fruitful. However, the disciplines regarding the employment of tongues in public gatherings emphasize the need for interpretation of the tongues so that the whole gathering may be blessed (1 Cor. 14:2–20).

CHAPTER 8

The Initial Physical Evidence of the Baptism in the Holy Ghost

QUESTIONS ON SPEAKING IN TONGUES

There are a number of questions that have arisen concerning speaking in tongues. Some of them are worth considering here:[7]

1. Can doctrine be based on less than declarative statements?

---

[6]A person may receive tongues as the evidence of the baptism in the Holy Spirit and only later receive the gift of tongues which may be manifested in personal devotions or in public services. See Smith Wigglesworth, *Ever Increasing Faith,* rev. ed. (Springfield, Mo.: Gospel Publishing House, 1971), 114; Frank M. Boyd, *The Spirit Works Today* (Springfield, Mo.: Gospel Publishing House, 1970), 83–86.

[7]The following material is adapted from *Where We Stand,* 150–154.

CHAPTER
8

The Initial
Physical
Evidence of
the Baptism
in the Holy
Ghost

Although doctrine should not be based on isolated fragments of Scripture, it can be based on substantial, implied truth. The doctrine of the Trinity is based not on a declarative statement, but on a comparison of Scripture passages relating to the Godhead. Like the doctrine of the Trinity, the doctrine of tongues as evidence of the baptism in the Holy Spirit is based on substantial portions of Scripture relating to this subject.

2. Is speaking in tongues a phenomenon that belonged only to the apostolic period?

There is nothing in Scripture to indicate that speaking with tongues would be in effect only during the apostolic period or until the New Testament canon had been completed. When Paul made the statement that tongues would cease (1 Cor. 13:8), he also indicated when this would happen: He wrote, "When perfection comes, the imperfect disappears" (1 Cor. 13:10).[8] He also indicated that at the time tongues shall cease, knowledge will pass away and prophecies will cease (1 Cor. 13:8). The context of Paul's statement makes it clear that the time when tongues shall cease is future, and other things such as knowledge and prophecy will change in significance at the same time. Until that time the words of Jesus apply, "These signs will accompany those who believe: ... they will speak in new tongues" (Mark 16:17).[9]

3. When Paul wrote, "Do all speak in tongues?" (1 Cor. 12:30), was it not a rhetorical question which required a negative response?

To understand Paul's question it is necessary to recognize the various functions of speaking in tongues. Speaking in tongues serves as the initial evidence of the baptism in the Spirit (Acts 10:46; 11:15). Speaking or praying in tongues in private is for personal edification (1 Cor. 14:2,4). And speaking in tongues in the congregation—accompanied by

---

[8]"Perfection" here must refer to the time of the return of Christ. Compare 1 John 3:2.

[9]See Donald F. Stamps, ed., *Full Life Study Bible* (Grand Rapids: Zondervan Bible Publishers, 1990), 106, 232.

interpretation of tongues—is for the edification of the church (1 Cor. 14:5).

There is no contradiction between Paul's desire that all speak in tongues (1 Cor. 14:5) and the rhetorical question asking whether all speak in tongues. All believers at the time of their baptism in the Spirit begin speaking in tongues and may continue on in personal prayer for personal edification. All, however, are not the agents through which the Holy Spirit manifests himself through tongues and interpretation in the congregation. In the congregation the Holy Spirit distributes the manifestations as He determines (1 Cor. 12:11). Rather than contradiction in these two statements of Paul, there is complementary truth.

4. Why were there periods in church history when the phenomenon seemed to be absent?

The possibility exists that any biblical doctrine can suffer from neglect. In fact, great spiritual renewals have often been the revival of doctrine. For example, the doctrine of justification by faith was almost completely lost until the time of the Reformation, when Martin Luther and others reemphasized the biblical truth. The doctrine of sanctification had suffered neglect until the time of the Wesleyan revival, when it was again brought to the attention of the Church. Although the truth of the baptism in the Holy Spirit and speaking in tongues appeared in a number of revivals throughout church history, it did not have the emphasis it has received in the present revival.[10]

5. Is there a danger that people will seek for tongues rather than the actual baptism in the Holy Spirit?

Unfortunately this is a possibility, but the abuse of a doctrine does not invalidate the doctrine. Abuse and counterfeits, rather than disproving a doctrine, help to establish the genuine.[11]

CHAPTER 8

The Initial Physical Evidence of the Baptism in the Holy Ghost

---

[10]R. P. Spittler, "Glossalalia," in *Dictionary of Pentecostal and Charismatic Movements,* Regency Reference Library, S. M. Burgess and G. B. McGee eds. (Grand Rapids: Zondervan Publishing House, 1988), 339–340.

[11]See *Full Life Study Bible,* 232, 254. This is a good discussion dealing with false speaking in tongues and testing for genuine baptism in the Spirit.

**CHAPTER
8**

The Initial
Physical
Evidence of
the Baptism
in the Holy
Ghost

6. If people speak in tongues, will there not be temptation to spiritual pride?

When people truly understand the baptism in the Holy Spirit, it will result in humility instead of pride. Believers are baptized in the Spirit not because of personal worthiness, but to empower them for humble service and a more meaningful life.

7. What about truly born-again people who have accomplished great things for the Lord but do not speak in tongues?

There can be no question that dedicated believers who do not speak in tongues are indwelt by the Spirit and have accomplished great things for God. In considering the question, however, every student of God's Word must determine whether he will base doctrine on God's Word or on experiences of even the most devout believers. Because the Bible indicates that all may speak in tongues in personal devotions if not in the congregation, every believer must determine whether to accept or reject this provision of God's grace. Scripture makes it clear that believers must recognize their personal accountability to God and not evaluate Christian experience on the basis of human comparison. Paul wrote: "We do not dare to classify or compare ourselves with some who commend themselves. When they measure themselves by themselves and compare themselves with themselves, they are not wise" (2 Cor. 10:12).

STUDY QUESTIONS

1. One Bible version refers to tongues as "strange sounds." Why is that translation inadequate?

2. What is the evidence that speaking in other tongues is the initial physical, or outward, evidence of the baptism in the Holy Spirit?

3. Why is it probable that those who were baptized in the Holy Spirit at Samaria spoke in other tongues?

4. Why can we infer that the apostle Paul spoke in other tongues when He was baptized in the Holy Spirit?

5. What is the value of continuing to speak in tongues as the Spirit enables us?

6. What are some of the reasons we should expect the baptism in the Holy Spirit with the evidence of speaking in other tongues to be the normal experience of believers today?

7. What information did you find helpful in the section "Questions on Speaking in Tongues"?

8. What other questions about the evidence of the baptism in the Holy Spirit have you heard? How would you answer them?

CHAPTER 8

The Initial Physical Evidence of the Baptism in the Holy Ghost

9th

th

FUNDAMENTAL
TRUTH

SANCTIFICATION

Sanctification is an act of separation from that which is evil, and of dedication unto God (Rom. 12:1–2; 1 Thess. 5:23; Heb. 13:12). Scriptures teach a life of "holiness without which no man shall see the Lord" (Heb. 12:14 [KJV]). By the power of the Holy Ghost we are able to obey the command: "Be ye holy, for I am holy" (1 Pet. 1:15–16).

Sanctification is realized in the believer by recognizing his identification with Christ in His death and resurrection, and by faith reckoning daily upon the fact of that union, and by offering every faculty continually to the dominion of the Holy Spirit (Rom. 6:1–11,13; 8:1–2,13; Gal. 2:20; Phil. 2:12–13; 1 Pet. 1:5).

CHAPTER NINE

Sanctification

When we are converted, born again, we are delivered from the tyranny of sin. But what about the Christian life after this crisis event? Can a Christian sin? What are the possibilities of genuine victorious living? These intensely practical questions come under the doctrinal topic of sanctification (Gk. *hagiasmos*). Let us look at this strategic topic with some care, for indeed God is concerned that His people be holy (Gk. *hagios*):

Prepare your minds for action; be self-controlled; set your hope fully on the grace to be given you when Jesus Christ is revealed. As obedient children, do not conform to the evil desires you had when you lived in ignorance. But just as he who called you is holy, so be holy in all you do; for it is written: "Be holy, because I am holy" (1 Pet. 1:13–16; cf. Lev. 20:7).

The Bible shows that sanctification is in one aspect positional and instantaneous; in another aspect, practical and progressive.[1] The chief aspect, however, is the progressive work of the Holy Spirit in the life of the believer.

---

[1]Stanley M. Horton, "The Pentecostal Perspective," in Melvin E. Dieter, *Five Views On Sanctification* (Grand Rapids: Zondervan Publishing House, 1987), 113.

CHAPTER
9

Sanctification

As regeneration is the impartation of new life to the new convert, so sanctification is the development of that new spiritual life.

DEFINING TERMS

Before we undertake our analysis of the threefold aspect of the doctrine of sanctification (positional, actual, and final holiness), several terms should be carefully noted.

The Greek and Hebrew words for "sanctification," "saint," "dedication," "consecration," and "holiness" are all related to the idea of separation. In fact, the core concept of the term "sanctification" is separation.[2] To be sanctified is to be set apart—set apart from sin in order to be set apart to God and to the reverent and joyful worship and service of God. Rich in typological imagery is the Levitical priesthood of the Old Testament and the ceremonies associated with the tabernacle and, later, the temple. That which was offered to God was to be set apart in a special way, emphasizing the holiness of the One receiving such worship. That positive dedication to God is always the chief emphasis. For example, the holy vessels used in the tabernacle and the temple were separated from ordinary use. One could not take them into an Israelite home and use them. But that is not what made them holy. They were not holy until they were taken into the tabernacle or the temple and actually used in the worship of the Lord.

Throughout the ages God has separated unto himself those He wishes to be His own. He wants to use them all in His service. He intends that those He has redeemed shall be fashioned into Godlike people:

The grace of God that brings salvation has appeared to all men. It teaches us to say "No" to ungodliness and worldly passions, and to live self-controlled, upright and godly lives in this present age, while we wait for the blessed hope—the glorious appearing of our great God and Savior, Jesus Christ, who gave himself for us to redeem us from all wickedness and to purify for himself a

---

[2]See "Spiritual Separation for Believers" in *The Full Life Study Bible,* Donald Stamps, ed. (Grand Rapids: Zondervan Bible Publishers, 1990), 371.

people that are his very own, eager to do what is good (Titus 2:11–14).

Therefore, involved in this concept of separation is a strong positive emphasis on dedication, which is separation to God and to His worship and service.

Righteousness is conformity to divine law, usually seen within the covenant relationship. Holiness is conformity to the divine nature. The terms "purification" and "consecration" relate to the latter. God is concerned not only with outward obedience to the divine will, He is concerned with an inward wellspring of motivation that is cleansed and pure (cf. Mark 7:6; Luke 6:45). As the believer submits to the gracious ministry of the Holy Spirit and the Word of God, the heart is washed and renewed progressively (see 1 Pet. 1:22 to 2:5). As the light of God's Spirit and Word floods the heart and mind, the believer is expected to respond, cooperating with God by removing himself from defilement (2 Cor. 7:1; Heb. 12:13–15). In this sense, then, as we respond to the challenges of God, we can participate in the process of purification and can engage in acts of consecration. Always, however, let it be borne in mind that the practical steps we may take in separating ourselves from evil and turning toward God are always a response to the wooing and whispering of a gracious God. Let us remember also that to neglect sanctification is to court disaster. Hebrews 12:14 reminds us to "make every effort . . . to be holy; without holiness no one will see the Lord." "Sanctification is not optional for believers in Christ."[3]

THREE FACETS OF SANCTIFICATION

Since sanctification is not optional, we examine it closely, noting three of its facets. We begin with positional holiness. In other words, to get holiness, we start with holiness: We must be declared to be holy at the outset of our Christian lives. This declaration by God is called positional holiness. It is another way of expressing the great doctrine of justification, or is at least simultaneous with it.[4] Through the

[3]Ibid., 526.

[4]Myer Pearlman, *Knowing the Doctrines of the Bible* (Springfield, Mo.: Gospel Publishing House, 1945), 220.

crowning work of the atonement, Christ has made it possible for a holy God to see us—not as we are in and of ourselves, but wrapped about with the robes of Christ's righteousness (Phil. 3:9). This aspect of our sanctification occurs by faith in Christ instantaneously, at the moment of our conversion.[5] In a very real sense, then, we are sanctified at the moment we are saved. For this reason Paul could address the Christians of the various churches to whom he wrote, some of whom sorely needed correction, as "saints" (Gk. *hagioi,* meaning "holy ones").[6] We all begin in Christ, then, as saints.[7] "We have been made holy through the sacrifice of the body of Jesus Christ once for all" (Heb. 10:10). "We are thus made partakers of the fruits of His obedience. We are set free to do God's will."[8] We have turned our backs on sin and evil and have committed ourselves to follow Christ. We are saints not because we are superior, not because we have reached final perfection, but because we are headed in the right direction.

However, what is declared instantaneously and legally about the believer is not realized in actual holiness, the second facet of sanctification, for some time, a lifetime anyway. A great biblical truth is that God begins with us where we are. How wonderful it would be if older, mature Christians were as patient with new converts as God himself is. That which marks the true perfection of a child of God is not his arrival at absolute sinless perfection, but his upward aspiration. The apostle Paul did not consider himself to have "attained," or "arrived," but he did acknowledge that he was yearning with an intense longing to be more pleasing to God day by day (Phil. 3:13–14). What was good enough for yesterday is not adequate for today

---

[5]Ralph W. Harris, *Our Faith and Fellowship* (Springfield, Mo.: Gospel Publishing House, 1963; revision by G. Raymond Carlson, 1977), 74 (page reference is to revised edition).

[6]Horton, "Pentecostal Perspective," 115.

[7]The word "saint" has been spoiled by some churches that reserve the word for people they put on a pedestal, people whom they suppose have extra merit that others can draw from. Actually, Christ is the only one whose merits are available to us. No one else has any extra merit.

[8]Horton, "Pentecostal Perspective," 116.

in the life of the believer, for growth enlarges one's capacity for the things of God. Although we may begin with "milk," we are expected to grow up to the point where we can digest "solid food" (see Heb. 5:12–14; 1 Pet. 2:1–3). This is accomplished through a daily renewal of our consecration and dedication to God. We must seek to become "more and more conformed to the image of Christ."[9] By prayer and through the Word and the Holy Spirit we draw near to Jesus and experience His love. "We, who with unveiled faces all reflect the Lord's glory, are being transformed into his likeness, with ever-increasing glory [from one degree of glory to another], which comes from the Lord, who is the Spirit" (2 Cor. 3:18).

Important to this growing stage of holiness is the ministry of the Holy Spirit.[10] Romans 7 pictures the "divided mind" of the one who is caught in the internal struggle between good and evil.[11] He knows to do good but finds himself unable in his own strength to do what is right. What is the source of Christian victory? Romans 8 and Galatians 5 supply the answer. Romans 8:13 shows us that we, by the Holy Spirit, can "put to death the misdeeds of the body," and 8:37 says that "we are more than conquerors through him who loved us." Galatians 5:16–18 points out that if we "live by the Spirit," we won't "gratify the desires of the sinful nature. For the sinful nature desires what is contrary to the Spirit, and the Spirit what is contrary to the sinful nature. They are in conflict with each other." Consequently, we are in a struggle against temptation, always soliciting us to sin. But the struggle for believers is not a contest between the "higher nature" and the "lower nature." Rather, it is a mighty contest between the indwelling Spirit of God and the old sinful nature, which still survives and wishes to express itself. The old nature is not "rooted out" as the Wesleyan doctrine of "eradication" would say. That doctrine is predicated on an understanding

---

[9]Ibid., 114.

[10]See Zenas Bicket, "The Holy Spirit—Our Sanctifier," *Paraclete* 2 (Summer 1968), 4–5.

[11]J. Dalton Utsey, "Romans 7 and Sanctification," *Paraclete* 18 (Spring 1984), 4.

of sin as a "something" rather than as a relationship. A relationship is not a "thing," subject to being "rooted out," or, as some say, "cut out root and branch." But in the proportion that we as believers are yielding to the work of the Holy Spirit, which is an act of faith, we can be assured of continuing victory over the invasions of sinful temptations (1 Cor. 10:13).

We also have the responsibility of taking an active part in the battle against sin and in experiencing the positive side of sanctification. However, the whole responsibility for progressive sanctification is not on us, for God has His part, and the Holy Spirit enables us by purifying our souls in obedience to the truth (1 Pet. 1:2,22). Our part is to actively and in faith "put to death, therefore, whatever belongs to ... [the] earthly nature: sexual immorality, impurity, lust, evil desires and greed" (Col. 3:5). Addressing the believers at Colosse, Paul observed (and we attend):

> You used to walk in these ways, in the life you once lived. But now you must rid yourselves of all such things as these: anger, rage, malice, slander, and filthy language from your lips. Do not lie to each other, since you have taken off your old self with its practices and have put on the new self, which is being renewed in knowledge in the image of its Creator. Here there is no Greek or Jew, circumcised or uncircumcised, barbarian, Scythian, slave or free, but Christ is all, and is in all. Therefore, as God's chosen people, holy and dearly loved, clothe yourselves with compassion, kindness, humility, gentleness and patience. Bear with each other and forgive whatever grievances you may have against one another. Forgive as the Lord forgave you. And over all these virtues put on love, which binds them all together in perfect unity (Col. 3:7–14).

There is victory in the Christian life. One need not be continually defeated. Even though we never come to the place in this life where we are not able to sin, we can have help so that we are able not to sin.[12] The solution lies in

---

[12]Not only do we need the continual cleansing of the blood (1 John 1:7), we never come to the place in this life where we no longer need it. This is the point of 1 John 1:10: "If we claim we have not sinned, we make him [God] out to be a liar and his word has no place in our lives."

giving place to the indwelling Holy Spirit. And, as we live in the Spirit day by day, our capacities for spiritual things develop. We grow in grace. There are failures along the way, but when we stumble and commit sin, we are not cast out. We have an advocate with the Father, a Friend in court, even Jesus Christ (1 John 1:9; 2:1). There is cleansing along the way, for "if we walk in the light, as he [God] is in the light, we have fellowship with one another, and the blood of Jesus, his Son, purifies us from all sin" (1 John 1:7). But we must confess our sins. Utterly urgent is our immediate response when we are checked or convicted by the Holy Spirit. If there is immediate repentance, we can arise with a cleansed conscience and the sure knowledge of forgiveness from God; we do not need to agonize over our failures.

There are, however, solemn warnings, which lace the Book of Hebrews, pointing out that persistent, determined rejection of the conviction of the Holy Spirit is a backsliding that can eventually lead to a hardened, settled rebellion against God, resulting in the final loss of one's salvation (cf. Gal. 5:21; Heb. 6 and 10). This is apostasy. But Paul in Romans 6:1–2 shouts aloud, "What shall we say then? Shall we go on sinning so that grace may increase? By no means! We died to sin; how can we live in it any longer?" He wonders how any who have tasted of the joy of sins forgiven could possibly want to return to the quagmire of sin—although the possibility is clear and unmistakable.

We are initially, at conversion, sanctified in Christ Jesus. During the course of our lives we are given the means to "grow in grace," to become in actuality what we are declared to be positionally and to reach a maturity of holiness (Eph. 4:7–13). There is yet a third dimension to sanctification. In Philippians 3:11, Paul expresses the wistful desire of the soldier of the Cross, looking ahead to the time when

---

The phrase "have not sinned" is in the Gk. perfect tense. This normally defines an action in the past that has continuing present results. Therefore, it might better be translated, "If we say we have come to a place, or have had an experience, where we cannot or do not sin any more"— we make God a liar, for He has provided the continuous cleansing of the blood (with the clear implication that we need it), and we are saying we do not need it.

CHAPTER
9
Sanctification

this period of probation will end and there will be a final state of holiness. This anticipation of perfection is called the doctrine of glorification. Upon life's end, believers who have kept true to Christ will be in a permanent relationship with God that will not be subject to failure. We will have a settled character of holiness. Then at Christ's second coming, "We will all be changed—in a flash, in the twinkling of an eye, at the last trumpet. For the trumpet will sound, the dead will be raised imperishable, and we will be changed" (1 Cor. 15:51–52). What a wonderful hope for the believer! "I consider that our present sufferings are not worth comparing with the glory that will be revealed in us" (Rom. 8:18).

In view of this hope, may we all maintain "unbroken communion with Christ through the resources of prayer and the Word, seeking divine guidance from the Holy Spirit and striving to 'reach unity in the faith and in the knowledge of the Son of God and become mature, attaining to the whole measure of the fullness of Christ' (Eph. 4:13)."[13]

STUDY QUESTIONS

1. What is the basic meaning of sanctification?
2. In what sense does sanctification take place at the time of our conversion?
3. What is the relationship between sanctification and justification?
4. What is involved in the ongoing work of the Holy Spirit in sanctification?
5. How can we become "more and more conformed to the image of Christ"?
6. How can we have daily victory over the old sinful nature?
7. What positive steps are necessary in addition to putting to death whatever belongs to one's earthly nature?
8. What should we do when we fail?
9. What are the causes and results of apostasy?
10. What is included in our future glorification?

---

[13]Albert L. Hoy, "Sanctification," *Paraclete,* 15 (Fall 1981), 7.

10th

FUNDAMENTAL
TRUTH

THE CHURCH AND ITS MISSION

The Church is the Body of Christ, the habitation of God through the Spirit, with divine appointments for the fulfillment of her Great Commission. Each believer, born of the Spirit, is an integral part of the General Assembly and Church of the Firstborn, which are written in heaven (Eph. 1:22–23; 2:22; Heb. 12:23).

Since God's purpose concerning man is to seek and to save that which is lost, to be worshiped by man, and to build a body of believers in the image of His Son, the priority reason-for-being of the Assemblies of God as part of the Church is:

a. To be an agency of God for evangelizing the world (Matt. 28:19–20; Mark 16:15–16; Acts 1:8).

b. To be a corporate body in which man may worship God (1 Cor. 12:13).

c. To be a channel of God's purpose to build a body of saints being perfected in the image of His Son (1 Cor. 12:28; 14:12; Eph. 4:11–16).

The Assemblies of God exists expressly to give continuing emphasis to this reason-for-being in the New Testament apostolic pattern by teaching and encouraging believers to be baptized in the Holy Spirit. This experience:

a. Enables them to evangelize in the power of the Spirit with accompanying supernatural signs (Mark 16:15–20; Acts 4:29–31; Heb. 2:3–4).

b. Adds a necessary dimension to a worshipful relationship with God (1 Cor. 2:10–16; 12–14).

c. Enables them to respond to the full working of the Holy Spirit in expression of fruit and gifts and ministries as in New Testament times for the edifying of the body of Christ (1 Cor. 12:28; 14:12; Gal. 5:22–26; Eph. 4:11–12; Col. 1:29).

CHAPTER TEN

The Church and Its Mission

WHAT IS THE CHURCH?

The word "church" translates the Greek word *ekklēsia*.[1] *Ekklēsia* was commonly used in the ancient Near East to describe an assembly of citizens, sometimes one meeting officially, sometimes one just rushing together as a mob (Acts 19:32,39,41). In the Septuagint (Gk.) version of the Old Testament this Greek word was used of the assembly, or congregation, of Israel, particularly when the people were gathered before the Lord for religious occasions (e.g., Deut. 9:10; 18:16; 23:1,3). By New Testament times, however, the Jews preferred the term "synagogue" to designate both the building and the congregation meeting there. Therefore, to distinguish themselves from the Jews and to declare themselves as the true people of God, both Jesus and the early Christians used the term *ekklēsia*.[2] It is the

---

[1]The word is derived from *ek*, "out of," and *kaleō*, "call." However, in the Bible it is used of any assembly. Usage, not derivation, determines meaning. Bible usage shows it had lost the meaning of "called-out ones." "Assembly" is the best translation.

[2]See *The New Testament Greek-English Dictionary, Delta-Epsilon*, The Complete Biblical Library (Springfield, Mo.: The Complete Biblical Library, 1990), 336.

spiritual family of God, a fellowship created by the Holy Spirit, based upon the atoning work of Christ.

The word "church" is used variously today by many people. It is sometimes used to denote a physical structure, a building used by a local congregation. It is sometimes used of a denomination. However, there are only two valid biblical uses for the term "church" (assembly). There is the local church (assembly), by which is meant not the building, but the assembled saints who worship together in a given location. In a real sense, all the attributes of the whole church are expected to characterize that local assemblage; it is the body of Christ localized. Consequently, Paul could refer to the church (assembly) of God in Corinth (1 Cor. 1:2). At the same time, there is a broader use of that term as well: Based on the context, "church" may refer to all saints, throughout history as well as throughout the world. And only to the extent that they are composed of genuine believers may denominations be said to be a part of that grand, universal Church.

There are several highly descriptive figures of speech that the Bible writers have used to help us understand the mystery of the Church. Perhaps the most important is the term "body of Christ." Christ was visibly present on earth during the time of the Incarnation. When He was preparing to depart, He took special pains to train a group of disciples whom He had commissioned to found and be the Church, the assembly of citizens of heaven (Matt. 16:18–19; 18:17–20; Eph. 2:19; Phil. 3:20). After His resurrection, Jesus breathed on the disciples and others who were in the Upper Room, imparting a measure of the Holy Spirit to them. Their names were already written in heaven (Luke 10:20); they were already clean before God, having had a spiritual bath through Christ's Word (John 13:10; 15:3). The old covenant had been abolished at Calvary (Eph. 2:15); the death of Jesus put the new covenant into effect (Heb. 9:15–17). Consequently, they were already a new covenant body, and Jesus imparted to them the new covenant life through this impartation of the Holy Spirit—the same life all believers receive when they believe that God raised Jesus from the dead and are born again (Rom. 10:9–

10).[3] At the same time, Jesus commissioned them and gave them authority. Thus, from Christ's resurrection day they were in a new relationship with Him: They were already the Church, the *ekklēsia.* Jesus instituted not an organization, but an organism. At the time of the Ascension, Christ exhorted the disciples to stay in the city of Jerusalem until they would be clothed with power from on high (Luke 24:49; Acts 1:4). On the Day of Pentecost the 120 assembled believers, who were praising God (Luke 24:53), individually received the promise of the Father, the baptism in the Holy Spirit. The Holy Spirit came to energize the community of believers, to make the resurrected Christ available everywhere through Spirit-filled disciples.

To emphasize and visualize the living relationship of the believers with Christ, the Bible talks about Christ as the "head" of the Church and the Church as His "body" (1 Cor. 12:27; Eph. 1:22–23; Col. 1:18). There are several reasons for this beautiful analogy of the Church as the body of Christ. The Church is the physical, visible manifestation of Christ in the world, doing His work, such as calling sinners to repentance, proclaiming the truth of God to the nations, and preparing for the ages to come. The Church also is like a body in that it is composed of a complex arrangement of diverse parts, each discrete, each receiving from the Head, each with its own gifts and ministry, yet all necessary for the work of God to proceed (Rom. 12:4–8; 1 Cor. 6:15; 10:16,17; 12:12–27; Eph. 4:15–16).

Another significant metaphor used to describe the Church is the "temple of God" and of the Holy Spirit (1 Cor. 3:16–17; 2 Cor. 6:14–7:1; Eph. 2:11–22; 1 Pet. 2:4–10). "Temple" (Gk. *naos*) refers to the inner sanctuary, the most holy place, where God manifested His glory in a special, localized way.[4] God is omnipresent, it is true, but in a special sense His dwelling is among His people (Exod. 25:8; 1 Kings 8:27). The word "temple" is used in 1 Corinthians 3:16 of the entire local assembly. Together each assembly

---

[3]Stanley M. Horton, *What the Bible Says About the Holy Spirit* (Springfield, Mo.: Gospel Publishing House, 1976), 128–133.

[4]The Gk. has another word, *hieron,* for the whole temple precinct with all its buildings and courts.

is the temple, for God, Christ, and the Holy Spirit is in their midst. Then in 1 Corinthians 6:19, the body of the individual is also the temple of the Holy Spirit. Even in Old Testament times, though the glory[5] was manifest in the inner room—the Most Holy Place—God's presence was not limited to His manifestation of himself in the midst of His people. "For this is what the high and lofty One says—he who lives forever, whose name is holy: 'I live in a high and holy place, but also with him who is contrite and lowly in spirit, to revive the spirit of the lowly and to revive the heart of the contrite' " (Isa. 57:15).

In Ephesians 2:20–22 Paul enlarges the figure of the temple to include all believers of all times:

> You are ... built on the foundation of the apostles and prophets, with Christ Jesus himself as the chief cornerstone. In him the whole building is joined together and rises to become a holy temple in the Lord. And in him you too are being built together to become a dwelling in which God lives by his Spirit.

Peter then combines the figures of the temple and the priesthood:

> As you come to him, the living Stone[6]—rejected by men but chosen by God and precious to him—you also, like living stones, are being built into a spiritual house to be a holy priesthood, offering spiritual sacrifices acceptable to God through Jesus Christ. ... You are a chosen people, a royal priesthood, a holy nation, a people belonging to God, that you may declare the praises of him who called you out of darkness into his wonderful light (1 Pet. 2:4–5,9).

We are not only the temple, we also offer spiritual ministry among ourselves as priests of God in this sanctuary.[7]

───

[5]Later, rabbis called this glory the *shekinah,* a term derived from the Heb. *shakan,* "dwell, stay."

[6]Notice that Christ is the One to whom we come. He, not Peter, is the "Rock" on which the Church is built (Matt. 16:18). Note also that in 1 Pet. 2:8 the word "stone" (Gk. *lithos*) is parallel to "rock" (Gk. *petra*), the word used in Matt. 16:18.

[7]Peter can mix these metaphors because in the Bible the church is always "people."

Another vivid figure used with respect to the Church is "the bride of Christ." This figure emphasizes union and communion of the saints with the Christ. It is used particularly with regard to the eagerness of the bride to be ready for the marriage, and therefore has a strong tone of hope for the future (2 Cor. 11:2; Eph. 5:25–27; Rev. 19:7; 21:2; 22:17). The figure of a wife is also used of the Church, for even though we look forward to a closer relationship with Christ when He comes to earth again, we have a close relationship now (cf. Eph. 5:25–32). The marriage relationship is thus used to illustrate Christ's love and care for the Church as well as the devotion and faithfulness of the Church to Christ.

Other terms and phrases used of the Church include "God's household, which is the Church of the living God, the pillar and foundation of the truth" (1 Tim. 3:15). It is the household, or family, of God (Eph. 2:19), and it supports and upholds the truth. It is God's "field" as well as God's "building," where He not only dwells, but from which He expects fruit (1 Cor. 3:9). It is an "army" equipped with "the full armor of God" so that it can stand against the devil's schemes, using the sword of the Spirit, which is the word of God, and protected by the shield of faith and the helmet of salvation (Eph. 6:10–17). It is a spiritual "fellowship," or partnership, working together with the Lord in the power of the Spirit and in love and care for one another and for the lost (2 Cor. 13:14; Phil. 2:1; 1 John 1:3). We are all "ministers," literally, "servants," doing God's work and building up one another through the gifts and ministries of the Spirit (Rom. 12:6; 1 Cor. 1:7; 12:4–11, 28–31; Eph. 4:11).

Within the Church also is a present manifestation of the "kingdom of God,"[8] the term itself (Gk. *basileia*) referring to the authority, reign, or rule of a king, rather than to territory or subjects.

CHAPTER
10

The Church
and Its
Mission

---

[8]It should be noted that where Mark and Luke have "the kingdom of God," Matthew, writing to the Jews, has in the same contexts "the kingdom of heaven." The terms are synonymous. Jews in New Testament times preferred to avoid the name of God for fear they might take it in vain.

Though human participation in the Kingdom is voluntary, God's kingdom is present, whether or not people recognize and accept it.

There is only one kingdom (rule, authority) of God, variously described in Scripture as the "kingdom of heaven," "kingdom of God," kingdom of "the Son of Man" (Matt. 13:41), "my kingdom" (spoken by Jesus; Luke 22:30), "kingdom of Christ and of God" (Eph. 5:5), and "kingdom of our Lord and of his Christ" (Rev. 11:15).

From the various contexts of the word *kingdom* in the Gospels, the rule of God is seen as (1) a present realm or sphere into which people are entering now and (2) a future apocalyptic order into which the righteous will enter at the end of the age.
. . .

As Pentecostals we recognize the role of the Holy Spirit in the inauguration and ongoing ministry of the Kingdom. . . . The working of the Spirit in the ministry of Jesus proved the presence of the Kingdom.

Jesus described the rule of the Holy Spirit in the kingdom of God. . . . The power of the Kingdom, so manifest in the Cross, the Resurrection, and the Ascension, was passed on to all who would be filled with the Spirit. The age of the Spirit is the age of the Church, the community of the Spirit. Through the Church the Spirit continues the Kingdom ministry of Jesus himself. . . .

The kingdom of God is not the Church. Yet there is an inseparable relationship between the two. . . .

The kingdom of God existed before the beginning of the Church and will continue after the work of the Church is complete. The Church is therefore part of the Kingdom but not all of it. In the present age the kingdom [rule, reign] of God is at work through the Church.[9]

MEMBERSHIP IN THE CHURCH

Through the atoning death of Jesus Christ all human walls of division have been broken down, and in Christ all who are genuine believers are made members of the body of Christ.

---

[9]*Where We Stand* (Springfield, Mo.: Gospel Publishing House, 1990), 185–186, 187, 189, 190.

He [Jesus] came and preached peace to you [Gentiles] who were far away and peace to those who were near [that is, the Jews]. For through him we both have access to the Father by one Spirit. Consequently, you are no longer foreigners and aliens, but fellow citizens with God's people and members of God's household, built on the foundation of the apostles and prophets, with Christ Jesus himself as the chief cornerstone. In him the whole building is joined together and rises to become a holy temple in the Lord. And in him you too are being built together to become a dwelling in which God lives by his Spirit (Eph. 2:17–21).

Clearly, as the Bible tells us, "It is by grace you have been saved, through faith—and this not from yourselves, it is the gift of God—not by works, so that no one can boast" (Eph. 2:8–9). Acts 16:31 expresses the simple truth: "Believe in the Lord Jesus, and you will be saved—you and your household." It is the Lord who adds daily to the Church "those who are being saved" (Acts 2:47).

THE WORK OF THE CHURCH

The Church has a threefold objective. All of the functions of a local body of believers should relate in some significant way to one or more of these three cardinal objectives. If upon examination the local body discovers that its energies are being consumed by activities that do not fit these objectives, it would do well to reassess its priorities. There is a further introductory note which should be interjected here as well: It is God's intention to work through the Church between the first and second advents of Christ. This is the Church Age. An axiom worth pondering is that any activity that does not feed and nourish the Church, no matter how well-intentioned, is simply not God's way of doing things in this age. He has chosen the Church to be His agency for accomplishing His purposes in the world today.

The first objective of the Church is world evangelization. Just as Jesus Christ came to seek and to save the lost, so the extension in this age of His body, the Church, is to share in that central concern (Matt. 18:11). Shortly before His ascension He issued a solemn challenge to the disciples to evangelize the world, making disciples ("learners," "people eager to learn") from all nations, baptizing them "and teaching them to obey everything" He had commanded (Matt. 28:19–20).

A characteristic of the early Jerusalem Church was that it was growing. The Lord added to the Church daily those who were being saved (Acts 2:47). Even under persecution, the Early Church scattered the gospel message, "gossiping the gospel" wherever the members were dispersed (Acts 8:4). The Book of Acts has a theme of growth, both spiritual and numerical, with more and more new centers established as believers in the power of the Spirit continued to spread the good news.[10]

The Early Church was also characterized by emphasis on the spoken Word. Paul recognized that "God was pleased through the foolishness of what was *preached* to save those who believe" (1 Cor. 1:21), and so the work of extending the Great Commission is still to be achieved. The Pentecostal experience has been given to believers with the task of evangelism as its principal objective (Acts 1:8). The power of the Holy Spirit coming upon believers expresses itself not only in tongues as the initial physical, or outward, evidence, but in mighty acts of a supernatural sort, which confirm the verbal testimony of faithful witnesses (Mark 16:15–16; Heb. 2:4). Gifts of the Spirit, such as prophecy, also are means the Holy Spirit uses to convict and convince sinners (1 Cor. 14:24–25).

The second objective of the Church is to minister to God. As a great denominational catechism states, "Man's chief and highest end is to glorify God, and fully to enjoy him forever."[11] An oft-repeated phrase in Ephesians, particularly chapter 1, regarding the purpose of human beings in God's universe is that we should be "to the praise of his [God's] glory." Augustine, bishop of Hippo in North Africa from A.D. 396 to 430, declared that all human beings are restless until they find their rest in God. Human beings

[10]Stanley M. Horton, *The Book of Acts* (Springfield, Mo.: Gospel Publishing House, 1981), 13.

[11]*The Westminster Larger Catechism* (Richmond: Presbyterian Committee of Publication, 1939), 162.

apart from a worshipful relationship to our Creator are disoriented and out of tune. We were created to worship. Now, it is true that worship has many avenues of expression. In a real sense, all of life can be a great hymn of praise to God. The mundane acts of life, including digging weeds, washing the car, and cleaning house, can become an instrument of worship and praise to God.[12] All of life should be of such expression of thanks and praise. However, God has provided the Church, the corporate body of believers, as a special instrument of worship.

One cannot read passages such as 1 Corinthians 11 to 14 without recognizing that the ministry of the Holy Spirit is especially significant in the worship of the Church. Given to the Body of assembled believers are diverse operations of the Spirit, which both edify the worshipers and enrich the worship of God. God and believers are blessed wonderfully in the spiritual worship furnished by the manifest presence of the Holy Spirit. These varied manifestations of the Spirit are generally called gifts of the Spirit; but in the original text of 1 Corinthians 12:1, the word "gift" is not present, but simply the term "spirituals." This word "by itself might include other things directed by the Holy Spirit and expressed through Spirit-filled believers. But in this passage Paul is clearly limiting the word to mean the free gracious gifts or charismata."[13]

All the early Christian writers took the word *spirituals* as spiritual gifts, therefore recognizing them to be supernatural gifts with the Holy Spirit as their immediate source.[15]

---

[15]John Owen, *The Holy Spirit* (Grand Rapids: Sovereign Grace Publishers, 1971), 16.[14]

The implication is that God through the Holy Spirit distributes the various manifestations needful in the worship-

---

[12]Myer Pearlman, beloved teacher and writer, used to say, "If you have to mop the floor, take the mop and say, 'I will not let you go until you bless me.' "

[13]Horton, *What the Bible Says,* 208. The word *charismata* is actually used in 1 Cor. 12:4,9,28,30–31; and 14:1.

[14]Ibid., 208–209.

ing community as He chooses; the "gifts" are given to the Church as a whole. It is true that individuals in the congregation may develop a ministry featuring one or more of the gifts, but none are to be considered one's private property, for the Spirit dispenses His ministrations for the benefit of the Church "just as he determines" (1 Cor. 12:11; 14:12,32).

There are several lists of gifts of the Holy Spirit: 1 Corinthians 12:8–10,28; Ephesians 4:11; Romans 12:6– 8. The first list, 1 Corinthians 12:8–10, is the fullest catalog of spiritual ministries bestowed by the Spirit in the worshiping body. This list is often called the nine gifts of the Spirit. These include three gifts of revelation (the word [or message] of wisdom, the word [or message] of knowledge, and the discerning of [or distinguishing between] spirits), three gifts of power (faith, miracles [miraculous powers], gifts of healings), and three gifts of utterance (tongues, interpretation of tongues, and prophecy).

These supernatural gifts are all concerned with the manifestation of God's character, ways, and eternal purposes. Therefore, every word or message of wisdom that the Spirit gives "will reflect God's plans, purposes, and ways of accomplishing things."[15] It will give divine insight into the need or problem and into God's Word, for the practical resolution of that need.[16]

The word, or message, of knowledge is especially concerned with "the light [enlightening] of the knowledge of the glory of God in the face of Christ" (2 Cor. 4:6) and "the fragrance of the knowledge of him" (2 Cor. 2:14). It reveals applications of the gospel to Christian living and on occasion reveals other facts that only God knows. Donald Gee described it as "flashes of insight into truth" that penetrate beyond the operation of our unaided intellect.[17]

The gift of faith is not ordinary faith, nor is it saving faith. "The vibrant, active Christian is more likely to see this gift

---

[15]David Lim, *Spiritual Gifts: A Fresh Look* (Springfield, Mo.: Gospel Publishing House, 1991), 71.

[16]See Acts 6:1–7; 10:47; 15:13–21; 16:35–40, for example.

[17]Donald Gee, *Spiritual Gifts in the Work of the Ministry Today* (Springfield, Mo.: Gospel Publishing House, 1963), 29.

in action as he claims God's power for present needs. Fervent prayer, extraordinary joy, and unusual boldness accompany the gift of faith. It can include special ability to inspire faith in others, as Paul did on board the ship in the storm (Acts 27:25)."[18]

In the Greek of 1 Corinthians 12:9–10, there are three sets of plurals: *gifts* of healings, *works* of power, and *distinguishings* of spirits. Clearly, no one has *the* gift of healing. The plural may indicate a variety of forms of this gift. It may also indicate that a specific gift is given to the sick person for the particular sickness or disease, the one ministering the gift being the agent through whom the Holy Spirit works.

Works of miraculous power are divine energizings in a broader category than healing. In the Book of Acts, such works encouraged the mission of the Church. Examples may include the judgment on Ananias and Sapphira and on Elymas, the deliverance of Peter from prison, and the preservation of Paul from snakebite.

Prophecy simply means "speaking for God" in a known language. It reveals the progress of the kingdom of God and puts the sinner under conviction by revealing the secrets of his or her heart (1 Cor. 14:24–25). It brings edification and encouragement to the assembled believers (Acts 15:32).

With "distinguishings between spirits" the plurals again indicate a variety of expressions of the gift. We are not to believe every spirit but we must put them to the test (1 John 4:1). In the spiritual battle going on in this world, we need to distinguish who the enemy is. But also the human spirit can be an offender.

The gift of tongues includes kinds, or families, of languages. In the assembly, a message in tongues needs to be interpreted in order to bring edification. Even when the tongue is praise or prayer, there should be interpretation. Interpretation, however, is not necessarily strict translation; rather, it gives the meaning or essential content of what is given in tongues.[19]

CHAPTER 10

The Church and Its Mission

---

[18]Lim, *Spiritual Gifts,* 74–75.
[19]Horton, *What the Bible Says,* 277–279.

The spiritual, worshiping church is a powerful arsenal of supernatural power which God employs in His warfare against the hosts of darkness. In fact, "[w]hatever the need of the Church, the Spirit has some gift to meet it."[20] By combining the four lists given in Romans, Ephesians, and 1 Corinthians "in various ways, it is possible to come up with a total of 18 to 20 gifts."[21] They include "gifts for the establishment of the church and for bringing it to a maturity where all the members can receive their own gifts and contribute to the upbuilding of the local body. . . . Second, gifts of the edification of the local body through individual members. . . . Third, gifts for service and outreach."[22]

The latter group includes the following:

1. Gifts of administration (1 Cor. 12:28), a variety of expressions helping those in leadership.

2. Gifts of helps, or helpful deeds, inspiring us to help others or take someone's part in a difficult situation.

3. Gifts of ministry (service, deaconship), various types of spiritual and practical service, including the distribution of aid or help to the poor, inspiring generosity.

4. Gifts of ruling (directing, caring, giving aid), helping leaders care for souls and make the church concerned about helping others under the leadership God gives.

5. The gift of showing mercy (Rom. 12:8), inspiring gracious and compassionate care for the needy, the sick, the hungry, those with insufficient clothing, and prisoners. It is the last in the list of gifts in Romans 12, but not the least (see Matt. 25:31–46).

All these gifts are needed. The Holy Spirit distributes them according to the need, but we must be willing to respond in faith and obedience. Then the local assembly will be built up both spiritually and in numbers. In fact, as the worshiping body responds in faith, all these spiritual ministries, or gifts, should be in operation in a truly apostolic-patterned church. This is the privilege of believers. It is more than a privilege, really, for increasingly as

---

[20]Ibid., 209.

[21]Ibid., 210.

[22]Ibid., 263–264.

the clouds of darkness roll over the face of the earth, the Church must have all the spiritual resources available to it to withstand the encroachment of secularism, materialism, the occult, New Age philosophies, and other subtle devices of Satan designed to weaken its witness.

Over most of the history of the Church there has been too much dependence on human resources. As long as the funds, equipment, men [and women], materials, and technical skill are available, projects are pushed with every expectation of success. Yet often they fail in spite of everything. On the other hand, some have started out with almost nothing but with a tremendous confidence in God and a dependence on the gifts and help of the Holy Spirit, and the impossible has been done.

It is a great thing to learn to use the human resources available, while depending on the Spirit. The gifts of the Spirit are still God's primary means of building the Church both spiritually and in numbers. Nothing else can do it.[23]

There is a third objective of the New Testament Church: to build a body of saints (dedicated believers), nourishing them so that they become conformed to the image of Christ. Evangelism is the winning of new converts; worship is the Church directed toward God; nurture is the development of new converts into mature saints. God is mightily concerned that newborn babes grow in grace (on the basis of Eph. 4:11–16; cf. 1 Cor. 12:28; 14:12). Paul emphasized repeatedly the yearning God has for evidence of spiritual maturity in the lives of believers (1 Cor. 14:12; Eph. 4:11–13; Col. 1:28–29).

How may one know when one is growing into the image of Christ? How can the Church gauge its success in producing Christian maturity in its membership? Galatians 5:22–26 offers a beautiful set of virtues called the "fruit of the Spirit": love, joy, peace, patience, kindness, goodness, faithfulness, gentleness and self-control.[24] Those who exhibit such traits of character are said to be fulfilling the

---

[23]Ibid., 282.

[24]See "The Acts of the Sinful Nature and the Fruit of the Spirit," in *The Full Life Study Bible* (Grand Rapids Zondervan Bible Publishers, 1990), 395.

law or instruction of Christ. We do need to take an active part in this. Second Peter 1:5–11 tells us:

> Make every effort to add to your faith [or exercise abundantly in your faith] goodness; and to goodness, knowledge; and to knowledge, self-control; and to self-control, perseverance; and to perseverance, godliness; and to godliness, brotherly kindness; and to brotherly kindness, love. For if you possess these qualities in increasing measure, they will keep you from being ineffective and unproductive in your knowledge of our Lord Jesus Christ. But if anyone does not have them, he is nearsighted and blind, and has forgotten that he has been cleansed from his past sins. Therefore, my brothers, be all the more eager to make your calling and election sure. For if you do these things, you will never fall, and you will receive a rich welcome into the eternal kingdom of our Lord and Savior Jesus Christ.

The Church's task is not done until it assists its members in growing spiritually, so that the various gifts of the Spirit are matched by the display of the fruits of the Spirit (cf. 1 Cor. 13).

The Church has a high calling, an upward calling. Paul said, "I press on toward the goal to win the prize for which God has called me heavenward in Christ Jesus" (Phil. 3:14). Hebrews 3:1 reminds us that we "share in the heavenly calling." Ephesians 1:3 says, "Praise be to the God and Father of our Lord Jesus Christ, who has blessed us in the heavenly realms with every spiritual blessing in Christ. For he chose us in him before the creation of the world to be holy and blameless in his sight." The Bible is not referring to predestination of individuals. It is saying that the Church is a chosen body, predestined to be holy. All those who choose to believe become part of the Church and share in its destiny. In the Church "the Christian's position and blessings are spiritual, heavenly, and eternal."[25]

STUDY QUESTIONS

1. How was the word "church" *(ekklēsia)* used in Bible times and how does that use compare with the way it is used today?

---

[25]Ernest Swing Williams, *Systematic Theology,* vol. 3 (Springfield, Mo.: Gospel Publishing House, 1953), 107.

2. What is the evidence that the Church was already in existence before the Day of Pentecost?

3. Both Ephesians and Colossians called Christ the Head and the Church His Body. Is the Head or the Body given most emphasis in Ephesians? in Colossians?

4. What are the three ways the figure of the temple is used with respect to the Church?

5. Some today treat the bride of Christ as a special company of super believers within the Church. What does this kind of teaching lead to and what are the reasons for understanding the Bride to be the whole true Church?

6. What is the relation of the Church to the kingdom of God?

7. What are the conditions for membership in the Church given in the New Testament? How does that compare with conditions for membership in your own local assembly?

8. What priorities does the New Testament give for the work of the Church? What is your own local assembly doing to put these priorities into effect?

9. What is the primary purpose of the Holy Spirit in the ministry of His gifts in the local assembly?

10. When should we expect the Spirit to give His gifts?

11. Which gifts are most often neglected in your own local assembly today?

12. Which gifts are most needed in your own local assembly today?

13. Why is it important that we desire and seek the gifts of the Spirit?

14. How do we grow spiritually and how can we help others to grow spiritually?

11th

th

FUNDAMENTAL
TRUTH

THE MINISTRY

A divinely called and scripturally ordained ministry has been provided by our Lord for the threefold purpose of leading the Church in: (1) Evangelization of the world (Mark 16:15–20), (2) Worship of God (John 4:23–24), and (3) Building a body of saints being perfected in the image of His Son (Eph. 4:11,16).

CHAPTER ELEVEN

The Ministry

CHURCH ORGANIZATION

The Church is more than an organization; it is a living organism. The head of the Church is Jesus Christ (Eph. 1:22–23), who nourishes the Church, giving it spiritual life. However, a living organism must have structure. Nothing is more highly organized in the natural world than the simplest living cell. In the Old Testament the tribes were organized for march as well as for encampment (see Num. 2 to 4). Similarly, the Church is also an orderly, structured arrangement of parts, an arrangement one discovers from examining the pattern of the Apostolic Church. The structure set forth in the New Testament was quite simple, the principle apparently being that only organization necessary for the ongoing life of the Church should be adopted. For example, they did not have deacons until they needed deacons.

A general principle in the development of the Church also seems to be that each local assembly was considered self-governing, without hierarchical connections beyond the local assembly. The exception to this principle is the special authority accorded the apostles, who did, as a matter of fact, exercise an authority over a number of churches. This, however, was because of their special relationship to

Christ, and upon their death this apostolic authority ceased.[1] For example, Paul in his missionary journeys conducted elections for elders and received the respect due one with special authority.[2]

There were two basic types of offices in the Apostolic Church. One was itinerant and charismatic; the other was local and elected. The first involved ministries rather than offices in the modern sense, and was itinerant because those who exercised this function traveled around, generally among a wide range of local assemblies. They were charismatic, given to the whole Church for the exercise of supernatural manifestations that would establish the churches and bring all the believers to the place where they could do the work of ministry (Eph. 4:8,11–14). The other type of office was local. Those who functioned in this category remained in one specific locality. They also were elected, chosen by the local congregation according to prescribed qualifications set forth by the apostles before the churches. (See Acts 6:3; 1 Tim. 3:1–13; Titus 1:6–9.)

Itinerant and charismatic leaders were set apart and given ministry by divine direction. Paul introduces these ministries as Christ's gifts by quoting from Psalm 68:18, "When he ascended on high, he led captives in his train and gave gifts to men" (Eph. 4:8).[3] Ephesians 4:9–10 is a parenthesis that identifies Jesus as the one who ascended on high. Then Paul goes on to show that the gifts given to men are apostles, prophets, evangelists, and pastor-teachers.

---

[1]Matthias was chosen to take the place of Judas because Judas lost his office, but when the apostle James was martyred, no one was chosen to take his place. He will be among the Twelve who will rule the twelve tribes of Israel in the Millennium (Matt. 19:28; Luke 22:30). The Bible gives no indication of any apostles, other than the apostle Paul, who were not commissioned by Jesus before His ascension.

[2]See Acts 14:23, where the word "appointed" is the Gk. *xeirotonē-santes,* which means, literally, "conducting an election by a show of hands."

[3]The picture is taken from the ancient custom of conquerors taking captives, making them slaves, and giving them as gifts to their friends. The ascended Jesus took people captive to himself and gave them as gifts to the Church. Notice how Paul calls himself a servant, literally, a "slave" (Gk. *doulos*), of Jesus Christ (Rom. 1:1; Phil. 1:1).

The primary group of apostles were the Twelve. They had a ministry in the initial establishing of the Church (Acts 1:20,25–26) and when Jesus sits on His glorious throne in the millennial kingdom, they "will also sit on twelve thrones, judging the twelve tribes of Israel" (Matt. 19:28). This marks the twelve apostles as a limited group. However, the New Testament indicates there were other apostles (Gk. *apostoloi,* "ambassadors, sent with a mission") who were also given as gifts to the Church. These included Paul and Barnabas (Acts 14:4,14) as well as Paul's relatives Andronicus and Junias (Rom. 16:7).[4] However, Paul speaks of those who were apostles before he was (Gal. 1:17). He also tells about how Jesus appeared to all the apostles, and "last of all" to him, "as to one abnormally born" (1 Cor. 15:7–8; cf. 9:1). "Thus it appears that the rest of those who are called apostles in the New Testament also belonged to a limited group of which Paul was the last."[5]

The apostolic ministry had three distinct features. First, the apostles were commissioned by the risen Lord Jesus (Acts 1:2) and were first-hand witnesses to the teachings and resurrection of Jesus.[6] Second, the apostles had the unique role of establishing the Church and producing Scripture. This role could not be duplicated after their death, since it was limited to those who had heard Jesus or were able to talk to those who had heard Jesus.[7] The third feature, however, is an apostolic ministry (not office) of signs and wonders applicable to all ages (2 Cor. 12:12). This ministry was involved in the planting of churches. That apostolic function is similar to the task of the pioneer missionary today (2 Cor. 10:16). Paul's journeys supply a vivid and practical pattern for our missionary enterprise.

Prophets were those in the Apostolic Church who had a special ministry of inspired utterance. While the apostles

---

[4]Junias is a feminine name in the Gk.

[5]Stanley M. Horton, *What the Bible Says About the Holy Spirit* (Springfield, Mo.: Gospel Publishing House, 1976), 265.

[6]Notice how Paul defends his apostleship in 1 Cor. 15:8–10; 2 Cor. 12:12; Gal. 1:1,12,16; 2:8.

[7]See the qualifications laid down for the selection of a replacement for Judas (Acts 1:21–22).

and evangelists took the gospel to the unregenerate world, the prophets exercised an edifying ministry to the various churches. For example, "Judas and Silas, who themselves were prophets, said much to encourage and strengthen the brothers" (Acts 15:32). Their messages, however, were not to be taken as infallible, but were to be judged, or evaluated, by the other members of the local church (1 Cor. 14:29–33; 1 John 4:1).

The ministry of evangelist in a very real sense overlapped the ministries of apostles and pastors in the New Testament. The function of the evangelist was to be the first to bring the gospel to those who had not yet heard. In this pioneer sense the function of the evangelist seemed to overlap that of the apostle, who also served in new territory, at the edge of the already evangelized field. The pastor in the New Testament was also exhorted to "do the work of an evangelist" (2 Tim. 4:5). The term was also applied to a layman in the church, the deacon Philip, who exercised the ministry of evangelism and was called "Philip the evangelist" (Acts 21:8). His preaching of the good news was accompanied by miracles, healings, and deliverance from demons. Many in his audiences were saved, baptized in water, and filled with joy (Acts 8:6–8).

"Pastors" could also be translated "shepherds" (Gk. *poimenas*). Jesus called himself the Good Shepherd who gathers the flock, cares for them, knows them, rescues them when they stray, and lays down His life for them (John 10:2–16). He remains the Chief Shepherd (Heb. 13:20; 1 Pet. 5:4). Pastors are undershepherds, having the ministry and responsibility of caring for and protecting God's flock as well as being worthy of their imitation (1 Pet. 5:2–3).

Teachers were given a special ability to explain and interpret the truth of God's revelation (Matt. 28:19–20; Eph. 4:11; 2 John 10). Some were itinerant, going from church to church. However, Ephesians 4:11 seems to connect pastor and teacher as a twofold ministry. The shepherd needed to feed the flock. The very word "shepherd" in the Old Testament (Heb. *ro'eh*) is an active participle meaning, literally, "one who feeds."

First Timothy 3:1–13 gives instruction in the selection of local and elected officers. The first of these officers was the "elder" (Gk. *presbuteros*), a term indicating age and maturity. This term was also used by the Jews to designate the person who was known as the "ruler" of the synagogue (Mark 5:35–38). In the Greek-speaking world of the New Testament, the term "bishop" was used as the equivalent of "elder" (cf. Acts 20:17 and 20:28). "Bishop" (Gk. *episkopos*) literally means "overseer" or "superintendent." Acts 20:28 indicates that they were also expected to have the ministry of shepherd, or pastor. The duties of the office were similar to those of pastors as we think of them today. The elder, or bishop, was in a sense the president of the congregation and was initially elected out of the congregation and given the responsibility of seeing that preaching and teaching were done. The elder did not need to do all the teaching, but, as Paul wrote to Timothy, "The elders who direct the affairs of the church well are worthy of double honor [including financial support], especially those whose work is preaching and teaching" (1 Tim. 5:17).

The use of the plural, "elders," may indicate that each house church had an elder and that the elders in a city met together for the guidance of all the churches. In the history of the Church, the leader of the principal church in a city eventually took the title of bishop and left the title of elder (Gk. *presbuteros*) to his assistants and the pastors of the smaller churches in the city. Later the word "elder" *(presbuteros)* was corrupted into "priest."[8] Since the Bible teaches the priesthood of all believers, we do not believe there should be a priest or shepherd standing between the believer and Christ so that the believer cannot go directly to Him. Jesus is the one and only Mediator between God and humankind. Our pastors serve as teachers, inspirers, and role models for the assembly. Ordination does not make them ministers, it simply recognizes the ministry God has already given them.[9]

The other group of elected officials in the Early Church

---

[8]This is an unbiblical use of the word "priest" and draws attention away from the New Testament word *(hiereus)* used in Rev. 1:6; 5:10; 20:6.

[9]See "The Assemblies of God View of Ordination," in *Where We Stand* (Springfield, Mo.: Gospel Publishing House, 1990), 87–99.

CHAPTER
11
―――
The
Ministry

were the "deacons" (Gk. *diakonos),* originally meaning "a waiter who kept the wine glasses full." It then came to mean a servant who had various duties. Among Christians, deacons were following the pattern of servanthood set by Jesus (Matt. 20:26–28; 23:11; John 12:26). The term was soon used generally for those in the ministry, but then came to be used for an established group of workers elected by the local congregation. These people served as helpers to the elders, principally in the material and mundane matters relating to the assembly, such as the care of money tables for the sake of widows (Acts 6:1–4; Phil. 1:1; 1 Tim. 3:8–13). Church history shows too that they were busy caring for the poor, the sick, and the weak. It should be noted that women seem to have been accorded a role in this ministry, too, for women deacons are mentioned in Romans 16:1 and Philippians 4:3, as well as in 1 Timothy 3:8–11.[10] The deacons, although their ministry was sometimes of a more secular nature, needed to minister spiritually to those they served and were therefore expected to measure up to a high set of spiritual and moral qualifications.[11]

FUNCTIONS OF THE MINISTRY

The various ministers, whether apostles, prophets, evangelists, or pastor-teachers, are considered God's gifts to the Church (Eph. 4:11). The varied tasks of this group of God's servants may be summarized in the following ways.

First, the ministry in the Early Church was expected to lead the Church in world evangelization. The officials, whether itinerant or elected, were not expected to do all the evangelizing. Their task was to equip the believers in the church at large for this and other ministries. Ephesians 4:12 pointedly declares this truth. When persecution struck the Jerusalem church the laypeople were scattered abroad, but they had been so well instructed—and inspired by the

―――――

[10]In 1 Tim. 3:11 "their wives" is simply the Gk. *gunaikas,* "women"; therefore the verse itself is a parenthesis giving additional qualifications for women deacons. (See NASB margin.)

[11]See "Deacons and Trustees," in *Where We Stand,* 77–82.

Holy Spirit—that everywhere they went they fulfilled the ministry of evangelism. There were evangelistic rallies, to be sure, but personal evangelism was the principal means of extending the Early Church. It was expected that converts would be made through the normal concourse of daily encounter, and then they would be brought into the assemblies. The ministers, in other words, were to lead the entire Church in the task of world outreach. Were the ministers alone assigned this task, the world would never be evangelized.

The leadership of the Church also bore a special responsibility in cultivating a climate of worship and leading people into ministry to the Lord (John 4:23–24; Acts 13:1–2). Discipline of the local assembly in matters pertaining to worship, particularly the matter of abuses of the manifestations of the Spirit, occupies 1 Corinthians 11 to 14. In that passage, however, the Bible calls for moderation, not a moderator. The congregation as a whole, as well as the individual members, was to exercise self-discipline.

References to spiritual leadership appear in many places in the New Testament record. Principles that governed worship seem to be edification of the assembly and freedom of expression without quenching the Spirit (1 Thess. 5:19). Of course, the strong assumption throughout the Epistles is that the assemblies were filled with members baptized in the Holy Spirit.

Instruction in spiritual worship includes the beauty of spontaneous expressions of praise and song, suggesting that in the Early Church there was a delightful freedom and sense of expectancy (Eph. 5:18–20). However, lest one imagine that there was a total lack of order, consider such passages as 1 Timothy 4:13, which strongly suggests a regular pattern of Bible reading, the centrality of preaching, and an emphasis on right doctrine (teaching), all within a context of public worship.

A third facet of responsibility charged to the leadership of the New Testament Church was the task of building up believers into mature saints. The stated reason for the various ministries in the Church being classified as "gifts" to the Church is specifically "to prepare God's people for works of service, so that the body of Christ may be built

CHAPTER
11

The
Ministry

up" (Eph. 4:12). The word "prepare" (Gk. *katartismon*) is the word used for "equipping," "completely furnishing," "training with a view of bringing to a level of maturity or full fruition." In the next verse, Ephesians 4:13, the objective is spelled out: "Until we all reach unity in faith and in the knowledge of the Son of God and become mature, attaining to the whole measure of the fullness of Christ." In this verse the word "mature" (Gk. *teleion*) emphasizes the idea of "enabling one to fulfil an intended destiny." The sense of fulfilling God's will for one's life is strongly implied. This is also what being mature implies, for the meaning of that term points to the appropriate use of one's energies, the marshalling of all one's resources, for concentration on ultimate goals without the hindrance of scattered and diverted interests. The expression in this verse that describes the level of maturity the Christian is to achieve, "the whole measure of the fullness of Christ," emphasizes that our model, our pattern, of full obedience to the will of God is the life of Christ himself. Ephesians 4:14–15 gives to us the result of this maturation process, which the Church is expected to produce in the believers through the various ministries entrusted to it.

In summary, one can describe the intended result as stability. The effective result of spiritual ministry in the household of God will be an assembly of saints whose feet are solidly planted, saints whose lives are not easily disturbed by the "waves, and ... wind of teaching" (Eph. 4:14). Into such a solid fellowship it is expected that new converts will be accepted and that those who have suffered the agonies of broken lives will see in this delightful union of believers an attractive quality of life (1 John 1:3–4).

THE CALL TO THE MINISTRY

Paul carefully points out an important truth concerning diversity of ministry (Rom. 12:3–8; 1 Cor. 12:1–30). Within the wonderful unity in the body of Christ, brought about by the work of the Holy Spirit, there is a rich diversity. Not all have the same function, the same gift, the same ministry, or the same office. As the human body needs a wide variety of organs in order to function properly, so the body of Christ requires a diversity of ministries so that the Church may effectively do the bidding of Christ in this world. Out of this great truth of "diversity in unity" shines the concept of God's concern for the individual. Regardless of function, gift, or office, regardless of how glamorous or hidden the task entrusted to one, in the sight of God all are important. Each believer will be rewarded according to individual faithfulness. This great biblical emphasis on the worth and integrity of the individual has tremendous implications for a proper understanding of people and society in the modern world—it militates against totalitarianism and collectivism, such as one finds in communistic societies.

How is it that God brings about the richness of the variety the Church needs? The answer lies in the call of God, sometimes called the doctrine of vocation. <u>The field of toil, the lifework, is not a matter of personal choice for the believer.</u> It is an obedient response to the calling of a sovereign God. God's summons to himself is not only for salvation, but also for service.

In the Gospel record, Jesus is described as calling people with great frequency. His call was to discipleship, that is, to become learners, students. Following Jesus to learn from Him involved leaving the past and surrendering every aspect of one's life to the Master Teacher. It included not only deliverance from sin, but it carried with it a whole new program for living. " 'Come, follow me,' " Jesus said, " 'and I will make you fishers of men' " (Matt. 4:19). Coupled with salvation was the call to service. In a very real sense we are saved to serve. Salvation is more than an escape hatch from hell, it is the gateway to fullness of life and usefulness in the kingdom of God.

In the largest sense all are called to service. All who know Jesus as Savior must continue to be disciples ("learners" who earnestly desire to learn to know and serve Him better). This large view is related to the concept known as the priesthood of all believers (1 Pet. 2:5,9; Rev. 1:5–6). Because Christ made a new and living way into the Most Holy Place (in heaven), all believers have access to the throne of God (Heb. 10:18–22). This is a privilege of the believer's being in the family of God. The powerful

CHAPTER
11

The
Ministry

implication of this great truth is that no human intermediary is needed to plead one's case with God, for Jesus Christ is the Great Mediator—the one and only Mediator—and He has opened the way for the individual to appear before the throne of grace. In this important sense, then, each believer is a priest of God, each believer is a minister of God.

This shatters the medieval idea that salvation was to be dispensed through a special few: the hierarchy of the Church. The sharp division that arose between clergy and laity during this long dark night of church history was broken down by the Protestant Reformation in the sixteenth century, when the New Testament doctrine of the priesthood of all believers was resurrected from the nearly forgotten apostolic past.[12]

However, let us not overlook a very important point here. Although the priesthood of believers gives everyone equal standing before God, not requiring an earthly sacramental system with its round of ritual and pageantry of priestcraft, nonetheless God does call individuals to particular functions in the Church for special service. Though there is no qualitative difference in the worth of the minister as distinct from the layperson, there is a difference in function. And although we should not wish in any way to minimize the calling of the laity—for that also is an important sphere in which a witness for God is made—the Bible does give special attention to the calling of those entrusted with spiritual oversight of the Church. Today, such ministers are usually ordained, which is the Church's recognition that God has given them a ministry and that they are faithfully serving in their calling.[13]

Paul was keenly aware that his apostleship was not of his own choosing. He was aware also that in the providence of God he had been entrusted with awesome responsibility. It was God's doing. God called Paul to be an apostle, making him a "servant" (Gk. *doulos,* literally, "slave") of the Lord and of the Church, separating him to the special ministry

---

[12]The modern "shepherding" movement has fallen into the same trap of setting up another priesthood between the believer and God.

[13]See "Assemblies of God View," in *Where We Stand,* 87–99.

of the Word of God (Rom. 1:1). Again, in writing to the Galatians, Paul underscored the fact that he did not assume this ministry himself, nor was it delegated to him by another person—it was God who put him in the ministry (Gal. 1:1).

Paul's emphasis on servant leadership is in line with the example and commands of Jesus. On one occasion Jesus called a little child and had him stand among the disciples and said, " 'Unless you change and become like little children, you will never enter the kingdom of heaven. Therefore, whoever humbles himself like this child is the greatest in the kingdom of heaven' " (Matt. 18:2–4). Later, Jesus told them, " 'You know that the rulers of the Gentiles lord it over them, and their high officials exercise authority [play the tyrant] over them. Not so with you. Instead, whoever wants to become great among you must be your servant, and whoever wants to be first must be your slave—just as the Son of Man did not come to be served, but to serve, and to give his life as a ransom for many' " (Matt. 20:25–28; see also Luke 22:25–26). Those called to special ministry are not to seek to go to the top, nor are they to seek fame, worldly power, or special privilege. Instead, loving, faithful, humble service, giving themselves for the Lord and for others, will mark all they do. God will take care of their advancement, if it is His will.

That the proclamation of the gospel, its preaching and explanation, requires a special calling from God is evident from this account in the Book of Acts: The leadership in the church at Jerusalem found themselves encountering numerous mundane duties, so that their primary calling, the ministry of the Word and prayer, was being neglected. The appointment of deacons grew out of this awareness. Nothing was to hinder the ministry of the Word. " 'We . . . will give our attention to prayer and the ministry of the word' " (Acts 6:1–4).

A final word should be added here regarding the call to the ministry. Indeed, it is God who sets His call upon individuals in a special manner for the work of the ministry. However, this does not preclude the aspiration of capable earnest young people to such a work. There is a divine-human cooperation evident here. "Here is a trustworthy

CHAPTER

11

The
Ministry

**CHAPTER
11**

The
Ministry

saying: If anyone sets his heart on being an overseer [bishop, pastor], he desires a noble task" (1 Tim. 3:1).

Not all who desire—or even all who prepare for such a work—will be called by God. But it is commendable for keen, capable, energetic, moral, spiritual young people to present themselves before the Lord, making preparation for service and awaiting divine direction. In this age there is likely greater danger of young people shutting their ears to the call of God to the ministry than of finding themselves out of God's will in such full-time service. How important not to mistake the voice of God, not only for one's own personal well-being, not only for the world dying around us, but for the sake of God's glory!

STUDY QUESTIONS

1. Some churches consider themselves free in the sense of not having any formal organization. Why is organization important?

2. Why should the itinerant, charismatic offices be considered primarily as ministries?

3. What were the qualifications of the office of apostle in New Testament times and how does that differ from what might be called apostolic ministry today?

4. What is the primary ministry of prophets in the New Testament Church?

5. How are the ministries of evangelism, pastor, and teacher related?

6. What was the function of the elder-bishop in New Testament times and how does that compare with the function of the pastor in your own local assembly today?

7. What was the function of the deacon in New Testament times and how does that compare with the function of deacons in your own local assembly today?

8. What do you learn about the nature of worship services in the New Testament?

9. How can we help each other become mature, stable saints?

10. What is the essence of a call to full-time ministry?

11. In what sense are all believers to be ministers?

12. Is it wrong to desire a call to full-time ministry? Explain.

12th

th

FUNDAMENTAL
TRUTH

DIVINE HEALING

Divine healing is an integral part of the gospel. Deliverance from sickness is provided for in the atonement, and is the privilege of all believers (Isa. 53:4–5; Matt. 8:16–17; James 5:14–16).

CHAPTER TWELVE

Divine Healing

THE CASE FOR HEALING

Sickness and death came into human experience because of sin. Through the tragedy of the Fall in the Garden of Eden, sin and death passed on to everyone (Rom. 5:12). Part of the curse occasioned by the Fall was the subjection of the human body to the ravages of disease and eventual physical death. Death is considered a curse, a concept clearly taught in Scripture (Gen. 3:19; Prov. 11:19; James 1:15). God promised to deliver His people from the curse of the Egyptians' diseases if they would serve Him (Exod. 15:26; Deut. 28:15–68). Paul likewise taught that "the last enemy to be destroyed is death" (1 Cor. 15:26).

Sickness—and its eventual consequence, death—is surely a penalty for sin (Gen. 2:17), but one must be careful not to make the mistake of assuming that all sickness and every death is the direct consequence of an immediate personal sin. Sickness is in the world because of sin. But Jesus recognized that the curse on humankind is general, afflicting people regardless of personal righteousness or sin (Luke 13:1–4). Sin may be involved as in the case of the man Jesus healed at the pool of Bethesda; Jesus warned him to stop sinning (John 5:14). On the other hand, Jesus made it clear that neither the man born blind nor his parents had sinned. Jesus indicated that in such cases the healing was simply an opportunity to display the work of God in the blind man's life (John 9:1–3; see also Mark 2:12). Until the termination of the present order, it is the lot of humanity to suffer the sicknesses and diseases that are in the world as a penalty of the Fall (Rev. 21:4; 22:2–3). A day will come when there will be no more curse.

The devil himself is the author of sickness and death.[1] God should not be blamed for human tragedy and misery; they are the product of the devil's work (James 1:17). Jesus went about doing good, "and healing all who were under the power of the devil" (Acts 10:38). That Satan, the adversary, is responsible for the physical as well as the spiritual bondage in which people find themselves is strongly supported by the Bible (e.g. Luke 13:11–17; Heb. 2:14–15; and 1 John 3:8).

There is another aspect to the matter of healing. Whether one considers the human being to be made up of three constituent parts (body, soul, and spirit), or two (the material and the immaterial), there is a further truth that needs emphasizing: Human beings would be incomplete as disembodied spirits. We need a body. The Hebrews were so conscious of this that they conceived of each human being as a unity. God himself breathed life into the moist dust He had fashioned to be a man (Gen. 2:7). Going down into the grave was a place of dread, and the Old Testament seers looked ahead with hope to a time of resurrection when the soul and body would be reunited.[2]

In the New Testament, Paul's great emphasis on Resurrection is grounded in the belief that we are incomplete in a disembodied state. (This is implied in 2 Cor. 5:3.) The entire chapter of 1 Corinthians 15 is anchored in the great hope made possible for the believer by the resurrection of Christ as the firstfruits from the dead. What this means

---

[1]See Hugh Jeter, *By His Stripes* (Springfield, Mo.: Gospel Publishing House, 1977), 25.

[2]See Gen. 47:30; Deut. 31:16; 1 Kings 1:21; Job 14:13–15; Dan. 12:2; Heb. 11:19,35.

is that the scriptural view of the human personality assumes a very important role for the physical body.

The ancient Greeks, and other pagans as well, looked on the body as a "prison house" of the soul.[3] Not so the Bible writers. The body is the temple of the Holy Spirit, a habitation for God. And the believer is guaranteed by the resurrection of Christ that his body shall be resurrected, not in its present mortal, frail form, but in a glorified, undying form (1 Cor. 15:42). This great emphasis on physical resurrection in the Scriptures underscores the importance of the body in the sight of God. It is a vehicle for expressing the will of God in this life, and for this reason it is not to be abused. God is interested in the welfare of our bodies.

THE GREAT PHYSICIAN

The next question that comes, then, is whether God is willing to heal our bodies while we live in this world so scarred by the marks of the Fall.

It is God's nature to heal. A great Old Testament title used to describe an aspect of God's nature is found in Exodus: " 'I am the LORD, who heals you' " (15:26). The Hebrew, *'Ani Yahweh roph'eka,* could also be translated "I am the LORD your Physician." *Roph'e* is translated in other Bible passages as "physician" (Jer. 8:22, for example). Its form is an active participle, used to emphasize that it is indeed God's nature to heal. *Ka* is singular and draws attention to an individual, personal relationship. Certainly, if it was His nature to heal then, it is His nature to heal now. He does not change.

Psalm 103:3 speaks of the one "who forgives all your sins and heals all your diseases." However, again, active participles are used, so that literally it reads, "the Forgiver for all your sins [misdeeds, injustice, causing of harm or trouble, falseness], the Physician for all your diseases." There is no disease that He cannot heal. It is His nature to move

---

[3]Plato records Socrates speaking of being "entombed in this which we carry about with us and call the body, in which we are imprisoned like an oyster in its shell" (Phoedrus, 250c). *Plato,* vol. 1, trans. Harold N. Fowler (Cambridge, Mass.: Harvard University Press, 1914), 485.

against all that afflicts and torments those who come to Him believing.

God's healing propensity may be understood in still another way. God is the Giver of Life. Frequently in the Old Testament, episodes of supernatural healing carry the expression "live" to describe the physical recovery. This is appropriate, since God is the Creator, the Source of life itself; and as such, He is the true source of healing. The devil destroys; the Lord God delivers. He makes alive. The Father sent the Son that we might have life, and that more abundantly (John 10:10).

God is love (1 John 4:8). It is His nature to love. God heals because it is an act of love. God's reason for delivering Israel, for loving them as a nation, was not because they were such a great or wonderful people, but because of His love. He had promised to be faithful to the descendants of Abraham, Isaac, and Jacob; and His covenant-keeping character was therefore displayed (Deut. 7:7–8). Deeply woven into this relationship God had with His people was His love, so much so that a good rendering of the term for "faithfulness" in the Old Testament is "steadfast love."

God, the great Physician, is our Healer because He is Lord of the universe. He is sovereign over His creation. He has power to wound and to heal (Deut. 32:39). God can employ sickness for His own ends, although one must always bear in mind that He is not the author of sickness. Miriam was made sick, then well, as an object lesson in judgment to the people (Num. 12:10–15). King Jehoram was permitted by God to suffer a fatal illness as a matter of judgment on sin (2 Chron. 21:18–19). Job was permitted to undergo a severe physical testing, but it is clear from the biblical record that the disease and trouble that plagued Job were brought upon him by Satan. God, the Sovereign of heaven and earth, merely permitted this satanic activity within prescribed bounds for a higher purpose and actually used it to win a victory over Satan (see Job 1:20–22; 19:25). Important to bear in mind is that God stood above and beyond the works of the adversary, ultimately displaying His delivering power.

HEALING IN THE ATONEMENT

Sin brought with it sickness and death. God by nature is against sin, sickness, and death. His love and grace made a way for deliverance from the penalties of sin. Through the atonement wrought by Christ at Calvary not only was the curse of sin broken, but our deliverance from sickness was also cared for. Healing was in the plan of God from before the dawn of time.

Since God is the Great Physician, *Yahweh roph'eka,* it is not strange that under the Law provision was made for forgiveness and for both spiritual and physical restoration. The Law gives special attention to the priests, whose ministry points to our great High Priest, who is touched with the feeling of our infirmities (and thus sympathizes with our weaknesses; Heb. 4:14–15).

The priests, through the sprinkling of the blood of the sacrifices, made atonement for the sins of the people. An examination of the atonement in the Hebrew Bible shows that in most cases it refers to a ransom price paid for redemption and restoration. This points to the redemption through Christ, His shedding His blood in our behalf and in our stead. "God presented him as a sacrifice of atonement, through faith in His blood" (Rom. 3:25). He would be the One who would protect us from God's wrath by taking away our sin.

The phrase "sacrifice of atonement"[4] translates the Greek *hilastērion,* "a means of expiation or making atonement in order to remove the guilt of sin." The same Greek word is used also of the place of propitiation or making atonement. It is used in this sense in Hebrews 9:5 and in the Septuagint (Greek) versions of Exodus 25:17 of the "atonement cover" ("mercy seat," KJV; that is, the place from which mercy was extended). This was the solid gold lid placed on the top of the ark of the covenant.

The reference to the Atonement and atonement cover ("mercy seat") has its background in Leviticus 16, which deals with the annual Day of Atonement provided in the Law. On that day the high priest went to sprinkle the blood

---

[4]"Propitiation," KJV.

of a sin offering on that solid gold cover of the ark of the covenant. Inside the ark were the two stone tablets inscribed with the Ten Commandments, the heart of God's covenant with Israel. These commandments the people had broken; the broken Law called for judgment and death. But when the blood of a spotless lamb[5] was sprinkled, representing the sinless life of Christ, God saw the sinless life instead of the broken Law and could give mercy, blessing, restoration, and healing.

The primary purpose of the atonement was cleansing from sin (Lev. 16:30).[6] It is also clear, however, that atonement brought release from the penalty and consequences of sin in order to bring restoration of God's blessing and favor.

When the people complained after the judgment that followed the rebellion of Korah, Dathan, and Abiram, God sent a plague on the Israelites. Moses then sent Aaron out into the congregation to make atonement for them, and the plague was stopped (Num. 16:46–48). We read also that when the men of Israel were numbered, they were to give one-half shekel atonement money for their redemption and prevention of a plague upon themselves (Exod. 30:12,15). Atonement, then, provided for the consequences of sin, including sickness. The Bible makes it clear that there is no way an individual can pay a sufficient price for personal redemption, so God, out of His love and for the glory of His own name, provided the atonement (Rom. 3:25–26; cf. Pss. 65:3; 78:38; 79:9; Rom. 3:21–28).

That this atonement provided not only for the sin but also for its consequences is pictured by Hosea buying back his wife at a great cost to himself when she had deserted him, gone after false gods, and was to be sold in the slave market (Hos. 3:1–5; 13:4,14; 14:4). This atonement is further illustrated by the bronze serpent hung up on a pole in the desert when God's judgment caused poisonous snakes to bite the Israelites. All the people had to do to live was

---

[5]The Heb. uses the word "lamb" for a young goat as well as a young sheep. The sin offering here called for a goat.

[6]Cf. Rom. 5:11, where "atonement" (KJV) is the same word translated "reconciliation" in Rom. 11:15 and 2 Cor. 5:18–19.

look at the bronze serpent (see Num. 21:9). All this found its fulfillment and was accomplished through Christ at Calvary (John 3:14–16). There He made a full Atonement for the whole person. The New Testament speaks of this as redemption, which has essentially the same meaning as atonement. Through Christ we have received redemption and the forgiveness of sins (Rom. 3:24; Eph. 1:7; Col. 1:14; Heb. 9:15). Again, atonement provides for the consequences of sin. Even where sickness is not the direct result of sin, it is still in the world because of sin. Therefore it is among the works of the devil Jesus came to destroy (1 John 3:8) and is thus included in the provisions of the atonement.

The Bible indicates, however, that until Jesus comes we—along with the rest of creation (affected by the results of Adam's sin)—groan because we have not yet received the redemption of our bodies (Rom. 8:22–23). Only when the dead in Christ rise and we are changed do we receive the new bodies, which are like His glorious body (1 Cor. 15:42–44,51–54).

In the parallel between redemption and atonement, we see that the provision for our bodies is the redemption spoken of in Romans 8:23. We receive the forgiveness of sins now in connection with the redemption of our souls. We shall receive the redemption of our bodies when we are caught up to meet the Lord and are changed into His likeness (1 Cor. 15:51–54; 2 Cor. 5:1–4; 1 John 3:2). Divine healing is a foretaste of this and, like all the blessings of the gospel, flows from the atonement.[7]

The Book of Isaiah, called by some "the Old Testament Gospel," clearly predicted that the benefits of the atonement would extend to physical healing. In the great fifty-third chapter of this wonderful Old Testament book, Christ is presented as the Suffering Servant, who in His own person becomes the penalty offering for sin, making atonement even for those who despise and reject Him. Verse 5 gives us this wonderful prophetic announcement: "By his wounds we are healed." The context of this verse demands

---

[7]The previous material was adapted from *Where We Stand* (Springfield, Mo.: Gospel Publishing House, 1990), 47–50.

that it not be spiritualized to cover "soul-sickness" only, for the preceding verses speak vividly of physical suffering.[8]

Matthew gives a more literal rendering of verse 4: " 'He took up our infirmities and carried our diseases' " (Matt. 8:17), "infirmities" including all kinds of sickness. For Isaiah, the coming Messiah who would make atonement for His people would cure diseases not only of the soul, but of the body as well. The passage in Matthew is a definite link between the Old Testament prophecy and the ministry of our Lord Jesus. Matthew records that during Jesus' Galilean ministry, He "healed all the sick," which "was to fulfill what was spoken through the prophet Isaiah" (v. 17). Clearly the Holy Spirit inspired the Gospel w. ter to declare that the ministry of Jesus was an anticipation of the benefits of the Cross and was the realization of the promise given about seven hundred years before.

The apostle Paul saw in the death of Christ a remarkable fact. Christ was made a curse for us so that we might be set free from the law's curse on sin (Gal. 3:10–14). The implications of this truth are staggering! Those who by faith reach out to appropriate the full dimensions of their salvation in Christ can receive in their own bodies deliverance from the curse. Death itself is the last enemy to b· destroyed, and death will be the common lot of believers until the time of the resurrection and Rapture, when we shall all be changed and our new bodies become immortal and imperishable, no longer subject to death, sickness, disease, or decay (1 Cor. 15:53–54). But deliverance from the ills that plague the body presently is an aspect of the curse that God has put into subjection to the faith of the believers.

— Divine healing is an integral part of the gospel. It flows from the Atonement. When Jesus said, " 'It is finished' " (John 19:30), the work necessary for the redemption of the whole person—spirit, soul, and body—was complete.
⁓ The ministry of Christ was a healing ministry, for He bound up broken souls and bodies. Divine healing was "not some-

---

[8]Infirmities ("griefs," KJV) is the same word used of physical sickness and disease in 2 Chron. 16:12; 21:15,18–19; Isa. 38:9. "Sorrows" is the same word used of physical pain in Job 33:19.

thing peripheral" in His ministry, but was an important witness to His identity (see John 10:37–38).[9] He went about preaching, teaching, and healing. Provision for all to enter into this ministry and its benefits was made possible by Calvary (Matt. 10:7–8; Mark 16:15–20; Luke 4:18–19; 10:9).

HEALING AVAILABLE TODAY

It is God's will for believers to enjoy the benefits of divine healing today. During Jesus' earthly ministry, He and His disciples healed all who came to them (Matt. 8:16; Acts 5:12,16). Jesus carefully selected a group of followers to whom He entrusted the task of carrying on His ministry, for He fully intended that greater works (in the sense of more numerous works) than He had done should mark the lives and ministries of His disciples (John 14:12–13). Just before He ascended to heaven, Jesus gave this ringing promise to His faithful apostles and disciples: "These signs will accompany those who believe: in my name . . . they will place their hands on sick people, and they will get well" (Mark 16:17–18).

The Apostolic Church practiced divine healing, as Jesus clearly intended. (The authority of Matt. 10:1 was never rescinded.) It was expected that supernatural deliverance from physical disorders should characterize the normal assembly in the first century. The Book of Acts shows it did. Not for two centuries or more did the practice of divine healing disappear from the Church. It was one of the last vestiges of supernatural power that the decaying church lost as the years wore on.[10] Eventually the medieval church distorted the practice laid down in James 5:14 by making the biblical provision for healing into a sacrament of last rites, which they named "Extreme Unction." Instead of encouraging faith for healing, all it was supposed to do was help a dying person through the pains of death.[11]

---

[9]*Where We Stand,* 45.

[10]Jeter, *Stripes,* 57–59. See also Joseph Pohle *The Sacraments,* vol. 4, ed. Arthur Preuss (St. Louis: B. Herder Book Co., 1945), 1–2, 44–45.

[11]Vatican II has since changed the name "Extreme Unction" to "Anointing of the Sick."

**CHAPTER
12**

Divine
Healing

James sets down the principles believers in all ages should observe for receiving divine healing (James 5:14). It is useful to notice that healing was to occur within the local assembly—it was not necessary to travel to a great shrine or a great healer. The "prayer of faith" speaks of the conditions necessary for receiving healing. It is by grace through faith that all God's gifts and blessings are received. Prayer is the avenue of communication between heaven and earth, the key that unlocks the resources of God for needy people. The sick are to exercise the initiative, calling for the elders of the church to pray with and for them.

A further condition for healing is supplied in this very important passage. Though the Bible does not say that every sickness is caused by sin, some are. Therefore, the provision is made that if candidates for healing have sinned, they are to confess their sins. This indicates that the way must be clear, cleared if need be by confessing sin, for receiving blessing from the hand of God. Our relationship to the Lord is not mechanical, it is personal. Anything that hinders personal fellowship with a holy God stands in the way, jeopardizing the reception of the fruits of Christ's atonement in our lives.

It is important to notice also that no one in the New Testament demanded healing. People came to Jesus asking Him for it. They did not look on healing as their right, but as a gracious privilege extended to them. It is clear also that as the privilege of believers, the promise of healing did not rule out suffering for Christ's sake and the gospel's. And whenever such suffering becomes necessary, we are expected to be prepared to follow His example (Heb. 5:8; 1 Pet. 2:19,21; 4:12–14,19). Nor are we to look at divine healing as a substitute for observing practices of good physical and mental health. Jesus recognized the need of the disciples to get away from the crowds and rest awhile (Mark 6:31). Jethro saw that if Moses did not delegate some of his responsibilities to others, he would wear out (Exod. 18:18).

INNER RENEWAL

Divine healing is not a means of avoiding the aging process. Although it is true that Moses retained his natural strength and a clear eye until the day of his death (Deut. 34:7), this privilege was not granted to David or Elisha (1 Kings 1:1–4; 2 Kings 13:14). The gradual breakdown of old age, pictured so poignantly in Ecclesiastes 12:1–7, is the common experience of believers as well as unbelievers. And although healing is still available to the aged, the part that is healed usually continues to age like the rest of the body; an eighty-year-old who is healed is still eighty years old. We do not yet have redemption of the body. However, the Bible does not tell us this to discourage us; it tells us this to make us realize that we must encourage and cultivate our life in the Spirit, for the Spirit gives life to our mortal bodies, ultimately through resurrection, and resurrection is our real hope (Rom. 8:11). In fact, even though "outwardly we are wasting away [gradually dying], yet inwardly we are being renewed day by day" (2 Cor. 4:16). Actually, it is this inner renewal that makes us best able to have the faith to claim the privilege of divine healing. To the woman healed of the issue of blood, Jesus said, " 'Your faith has healed you. Go in peace and be freed from your suffering' " (Mark 5:34). Great faith then receives healing through the simple word of the Lord.

CHAPTER
12
———

Divine
Healing

FAITH HELPED

But Jesus did not turn away from those who had little faith or weak faith. Those who are sick often find it not easy to express faith, and Jesus did a variety of things to help them. Sometimes He laid His hands on them or touched them (see Mark 5:23; 6:5; 8:22–23; 10:13; Luke 4:40; 13:13). Once, He put clay on the eyes of a blind man and gave him the opportunity to express obedient faith by washing in the pool of Siloam (John 9:6–15). At other times people expressed their faith by touching Him or His clothing (Matt. 9:21; 14:36; Mark 3:10; 5:28; 6:56; Luke 6:19). In the Book of Acts, Peter took hold of the right hand of the cripple at the Beautiful Gate of the temple to help him up, "and instantly the man's feet and ankles became strong. He jumped to his feet and began to walk" (Acts 3:7–8). Later, there was a time when people were healed when Peter's shadow fell on them (Acts 5:15–16). At Ephesus, "God did extraordinary miracles through Paul, so that even hand-kerchiefs [sweat cloths] and [work] aprons that had touched him were taken to the sick, and their illnesses were cured and evil spirits left them" (Acts 19:11–12).

There was no magic or virtue in the means used to encourage faith, however. Their faith had to be in the Lord, not in the clay, the shadow, the work aprons, or the prac-tice of the laying on of hands. This seems to be the reason for the great variety of means used, lest people get their eyes on some particular means rather than on God himself.

SICKNESS AND DEMONS

Problems have arisen when some have taught that all sickness and disease is caused by demons. The New Tes-tament recognizes that demons do cause sickness and dis-ease and can cruelly torment people.[12] But Jesus did not treat all sickness and disease as the result of demon pos-session or demon activity. The demon-possessed are dis-tinguished as a separate class, distinct from those "who were ill with various diseases, those suffering severe pain . . . those having seizures, and the paralyzed" (Matt. 4:24). It is obvious also that when Jesus touched the leper and said "Be clean!" that no demon was involved in the leprosy (Luke 5:12–13). The paralyzed man brought to Jesus by His friends did need to have his sins forgiven. Even so, the forgiveness did not automatically bring healing. It was when Jesus spoke the word that the man was healed (Luke 5:24–25). For all that, there is no indication of any demon power involved in his paralysis. "[M]any passages make a clear distinction between sicknesses and diseases not caused by demons and those caused by demons (Matt. 4:24; 8:16; 9:32–33; 10:1; Mark 1:32; 3:15; Luke 6:17–18; 9:1, etc). In none of these examples is there any indication that any of these sicknesses caused by demons were of people in right relation to God. We must remember also that all of these examples took place before Pentecost."[13]

___

[12]See Matt. 9:32–33; 12:22; 17:14–16; Mark 9:20–22; Luke 13:11,16. Demons can take possession of the bodies of unbelievers and even use their voices to talk (Mark 5:15; Luke 4:41; 8:27–28; Acts 16:18).

[13]*Where We Stand,* 19–20.

It should be noted also that though demons can tempt and harass Christians, they cannot read our minds nor can they possess, inhabit, or "demonize" any true believer, one indwelt by the Holy Spirit. Our bodies are temples of the Holy Spirit (2 Cor. 6:15).[14] When demons do attack us, we are not told to cast them out. Rather, we are to put our armor on, take our stand, and the shield of faith will extinguish all the flaming arrows of the evil one, all of which come from outside us (Eph. 6:10–16). We have the power to resist the devil, who will then flee from us (James 4:7; 1 Pet. 5:8–9). We have been armed with divine power to demolish strongholds (2 Cor. 10:4). Jesus defeated Satan with the Word (Matt. 4:4,7,10). We too can win victories with the Word, the sword of the Spirit (Eph. 6:17). Finally we note that "Christ's enemies accused Him of having a demon. It is a subtle trick of the devil that makes sincere people accuse Christians today of having a demon. Clearly, there are deliverances, but calling them deliverances from demon possession is unscriptural."[15]

HEALING AND THE MEDICAL PROFESSION

Others have tried to set divine healing in opposition to or in competition with the medical profession. This need not be so. Physicians through their skills have brought help to many. It is true that the Lord is the great Physician. It is also true that the Bible condemns King Asa because "even in his illness he did not seek help from the Lord, but only from the physicians" (2 Chron. 16:12). But Asa had already sought help from Syria in an act of unbelief and disobedience, refusing to rely on the Lord (v. 7). In other words, the emphasis is not that he consulted physicians (which in this case may have been heathen physicians), but that

---

[14]For a biblical discussion of the whole matter of demon activity and demon possession see Opal L. Reddin, ed. *Power Encounter: A Pentecostal Perspective* (Springfield, Mo.: Central Bible College Press, 1989); "Can Born-Again Believers Be Demon Possessed?" in *Where We Stand,* 15–23; and "Power Over Satan and Demons" in *The Full Life Study Bible,* Donald C. Stamps, ed. (Grand Rapids: Zondervan Bible Publishers, 1992), 80.

[15]*Where We Stand,* 23.

he refused to seek help from the Lord. It is evident that physicians had an honorable place in Israel (Jer. 8:22). Jesus also presented the medicinal use of oil and wine by the Good Samaritan in a favorable light (Luke 10:34). Luke the doctor was a dear friend of the apostle Paul (Col. 4:14). When the woman with the issue of blood was healed, we are told she "had suffered a great deal under the care of many doctors and had spent all she had, yet instead of getting better she grew worse" (Mark 5:26). If it were wrong for her to go to physicians, this would have been the perfect place for Jesus to have said so. But He did not. Instead, He accepted the faith she then expressed and commended her for it. Even today God has performed many miracles for people given up by doctors.[16]

Jesus also sent the ten lepers back to show themselves to the priests (Luke 17:14). Under the Law the priests were in charge of diagnosis, quarantine, and health (Lev. 14:2ff.; Matt. 8:4). In effect, Jesus recognized that human diagnosticians have their place. The priests, however, were agents of the Lord, and in this sense it is possible to take all healing as divine, whether instantaneous or gradual (cf. Luke 5:14; 17:14). On the other hand, those healed in the Bible did not testify to divine healing until the healing was actually accomplished by divine power.

We recognize that there have been abuses of the doctrine and practice of divine healing today. But we must not let that cause us to retreat from a positive proclamation of the truth of the Scriptures. The apostles were able to say to the lame man, "What I have I give you" (Acts 3:6).[17]

It is instructive to observe that as part of the provision God arranged for in the Church was the ministry of "healings," listed as one of the manifestations of the Holy Spirit (1 Cor. 12:28). Each local church is expected to have the manifestation of the power of God present. It is God's gift to the Church.

---

[16]See Gordon Wright, *In Quest of Healing* (Springfield, Mo.: Gospel Publishing House, 1984), 88–98.

[17]Much of the preceding material was adapted from *Where We Stand,* 50–54.

THE PURPOSE OF HEALING

Actually, there are two major purposes for divine healing to be exercised in the Church today, just as there were in the Early Church. First, divine healing attests the power of God. Jesus healed on many occasions to arrest attention, to authenticate His message. In fact, in that day it was expected that divine healing would be the credentials of the Messiah (Luke 5:23–24). The Apostolic Church also established its credentials by the demonstration of the power of God (repeatedly), which frequently was displayed through physical deliverances (1 Cor. 2:4). Signs and wonders (which included healings) were attendant marks with which God blessed the preaching of the gospel in the first century, confirming the Word (Heb. 2:3–4).

Second, divine healing attests the love of God. Christ healed, to be sure, to authenticate His message, but He also healed because of His great compassion on suffering humanity (Matt. 9:36; Mark 1:41). It is God's nature to love. Healing is a breakthrough of that love in a world bound by the curse of sin. On the one hand, Jesus won a victory over death through His resurrection. On the other hand, its effect will not bring an end to death for believers until the time of our resurrection or (if we are still alive at that time) our being caught away for the meeting with the Lord in the air. In this way the victory over death has been assured and the chains of sickness can now be broken. God's love is exhibited in His provision within the church for divine deliverance from physical suffering.

WHY ARE NOT ALL HEALED?

As has been observed, it is important to develop doctrine (teaching) from Scripture and not from human experience. Some who shrugged their shoulders in the opening years of the twentieth century, saying that Pentecostal manifestations were not being experienced, argued that they were obviously not for the present day. Thank God there were hardy souls, filled with faith and with a profound belief in the Word of God, who dared to believe that the practice of the Church should not be the determining factor in developing doctrine or deciding what was truth. Just so, simply because many are not healed should not be the determining factor in one's doctrine or teaching today.[18] There are mysteries that transcend our understanding in this realm. Some answers we must leave with God. But we do know that it is God's nature to heal; we know that healing has been provided for in the atonement of Christ. We know that Christ committed to the church not only the ministry of reconciliation but of healing.

Faith is the key that unlocks the door to divine blessing. When we have done our part, we must leave the rest to God. As someone has wisely said, "Where there is a greater atmosphere of faith, there will be more healings." Even the Lord Jesus did not perform many miracles in an atmosphere of unbelief (Matt. 13:58). The provision is available. Positive preaching and teaching encourage faith. The Church must be alive in faith to experience the supernatural today.

We humbly admit that we do not have all the answers to why some people are not healed. But we know and have experienced the biblical truth that God does heal today.[19]

STUDY QUESTIONS

1. What is the relation between sickness and sin?

2. For what is Satan responsible in terms of sickness?

3. What is the meaning of the name *Yahweh roph'eka* and why is it significant for us today?

4. Does God ever use sickness as punishment? Explain.

5. What is the significance of the atonement cover ("mercy seat") with relation to divine healing?

6. What is included in the atonement that Jesus accomplished on Calvary?

7. What part did healing have in the ministry of Jesus on earth? in the ministry of the disciples?

8. What is the significance of the oil in James 5:14?

9. What is wrong with "demanding" healing from the Lord?

---

[18]For additional discussion on this topic see Wright, *In Quest,* 115–136.

[19]See "Hindrances to Healing," and "Earnestly Contend for the Faith," in Jeter, *By His Stripes,* 92–99, 189–195; and "Divine Healing," in *Study Bible,* 20–21; Wright, *In Quest,* 137–159.

10. When will we receive the redemption of the body and what will that redemption include?

11. What is the value of such things as anointed hand-kerchiefs and prayer cloths?

12. What are the two major purposes of divine healing? How should they affect our prayers for healing?

13*th*

FUNDAMENTAL
TRUTH

THE BLESSED HOPE

The resurrection of those who have fallen asleep in Christ and their translation together with those who are alive and remain unto the coming of the Lord is the imminent and blessed hope of the Church (Rom. 8:23; 1 Cor. 15:51–52; 1 Thess. 4:16–17; Titus 2:13).

CHAPTER THIRTEEN

The Blessed Hope

THE RESURRECTION OF BELIEVERS

Until the victory of Jesus on the cross, the whole human race was held in slavery by the fear of death (Heb. 2:14–15). But Jesus, by His death, defeated the devil and removed God's wrath that was against us because of our sins. Then He was raised to life for our justification (Rom. 4:25). Death therefore holds no terror for the believer. Because we are justified, we live in fellowship with Christ. We can say with the apostle Paul, "To me, to live is Christ and to die is gain" (Phil. 1:21). That is, to die is gain in Christ, to die is more of Christ, for we will be "at home with the Lord" (2 Cor. 5:8). Yet Paul's real hope was in the resurrection of the believers at the coming of the Lord. Notice how he commended the Thessalonians because they had "turned to God from idols to serve the living and true God, and to wait for his Son from heaven, whom he raised from the dead—Jesus, who rescues us from the coming wrath" (1 Thess. 1:9–10).

A central theme of the preaching in the Early Church was the resurrection of Jesus and how His resurrection also becomes the guarantee of ours. His resurrection is the ground for our faith and hope. One of the great affirmations of the New Testament is found in the words of Jesus: " 'Because I live, you also will live' " (John 14:19). Paul calls it a mystery, something not revealed in Old Testament times but now made clear. "We will not all sleep, but we will all be changed—in a flash, in the twinkling of an eye, at the last trumpet. For the trumpet will sound, the dead will be raised imperishable, and we will be changed. For the perishable must clothe itself with the imperishable, and the mortal with immortality. When the perishable has been clothed with the imperishable, and the mortal with immortality, then the saying that is written will come true: 'Death has been swallowed up in victory' " (1 Cor. 15:51–54). "We" simply means all true believers, all who are "in Christ." Paul previously compared the present body to a bare grain, which must be buried if it is to be changed into a whole wheat plant (1 Cor. 15:37). Here he qualifies this by saying we shall not all die. He is not saying that he himself would be alive when Jesus comes. Rather, he is emphasizing that all believers, both living and dead, will be changed at the time of the Resurrection.

Like the body of Jesus, the resurrection body of which the risen Jesus is the animating life will be neither this mortal body of ours today nor yet bodiless spirit. It will be neither mortal body nor pure spirit, but a 'spirit body.' A real body, but a 'spirit body.' Reality is not solidarity. Inability to pass through closed doors does not constitute reality. Is air less real than lead, or sound less real than sod, or light less real than stone? There is the flesh of a baby, so soft that you can hardly feel it, and the flesh of a rhinoceros, which you cannot pierce with a rifle bullet. So is the resurrection body—real, with a glorious reality such as we have never known on earth, a 'spirit body' of human life immortalized by the risen life of Jesus.[1]

The Bible states that we shall be like Jesus when we see Him as He is (1 John 3:2). Our bodies will be touchable like His after the Resurrection (Luke 24:39). They will be glorious (endowed with splendor and beauty), powerful, and heavenly (like Jesus' body, ready to ascend into heaven

---

[1]Nathan R. Wood, from a lecture given at Gordon Divinity School, Boston, Mass., 1944.

without a space suit and ready to live in heaven without discomfort). That change will be supernatural and sudden. The trumpet call, unlike the trumpets of the Book of Revelation, which are trumpets of judgment, will be a call to assemble to meet the Lord in the air. Then "we will be with the Lord forever" (1 Thess. 4:17). Some today are saying that there is no hope, fearing that if the nuclear bombs do not destroy the earth, pollution will. But God is not going to let circumstances go that far. Jesus will come again and bring an end to human corruption as He brings in His glorious kingdom.

CHAPTER
13

The Blessed
Hope

JESUS IS COMING AGAIN

More than three hundred times—an average of one verse in every twenty-six—the New Testament refers to the truth of the second coming of Jesus Christ. Therefore, in spite of the fact that some have exercised more zeal than wisdom in making spectacular predictions about events surrounding the Second Coming, let us not mistake the truth that the Scriptures place great emphasis on this strategic teaching.

The Early Church lived in the midst of the expectation that their beloved Lord would return. Not until the third century was this hope dimmed in the Church. Thereafter, centuries of neglect settled in on the teaching of the Second Coming. Then, during the nineteenth century, it was restored, becoming a matter of considerable interest to a revived Church.

Today, in much of the evangelical wing of the Church, there is common agreement on the fact that Jesus Christ is indeed coming again. Even in the larger world of modern theology it is interesting to observe that (after talk of the death of God passed off the scene, the theology of hope, which deals with the doctrine of the last things, became more prominent.) However, regardless of theological fads, it is enough for us to settle our convictions on the truth as it is revealed in God's Holy Word. And He has stated categorically, over and over, "I am coming again."

Why is this doctrine, this teaching, so strategic? For one thing, it is a key to history. We are moving inexorably to

CHAPTER
13

The Blessed Hope

a consummation of all things. Most non-Christian religions and philosophies have a cyclical view of history. The Hindus look at history as a wheel of life, endlessly going around and around, no beginning and no end. But the Bible teaches a linear view of history. There was a beginning, a central event—the cross[2] (and the resurrection)—and there will be a final consummation, in which God will bring His plan to its glorious fulfillment. World events will not continue in an endless, unyielding procession. There is coming a moment when the present order, or dispensation, will come to an end. The sorrows of a world blighted by sin, marred by war, crushed by enmity, will be terminated by the advent of the Prince of Peace. When the nations have fulfilled their allotted course in God's panorama of history, He will announce, "It is enough," and Jesus will once again physically invade the world order. All things are pointing to His coming. Jesus Christ is the focal point of all history. Apart from Him there is no meaning to our existence (Col. 1:16–17).

This teaching, so frequently mentioned in the Bible, is important also because it is the hope of the Church. Death is not our hope, nor is the prospect of converting the world. (See Matt. 13:18–30; 36–43). Our hope as the Church is for the appearance of the Bridegroom. This concept of the sure hope of resurrection is inseparably linked with the picture of the Church as the Bride of Christ (Acts 23:6; Rom. 8:20–25; 1 Cor. 15:19; Titus 2:13; 1 Pet. 1:3; 2 Pet. 3:9–13).

There is further significance to the doctrine of the Second Coming: It is an incentive to holy living. The awareness that our Lord may come without warning stirs believers from their lethargy, to rekindle the fire of first love. Self-purification is the responsibility of alert believers, for to us has been given the spiritual resources to live in a manner

---

[2]When Jesus said, "It is finished" (John 19:30) He meant His sufferings and death paid the full price for our redemption. But we do not yet have the fullness of our salvation and inheritance. That is yet to come, when Jesus returns (Rom. 13:11; 8:23; Heb. 9:28). The victory of the cross has aspects that are already available. But other aspects of the victory are "not yet" ours.

pleasing to our Lord (Matt. 25:6–7; 2 Pet. 3:11; 1 John 3:3). Watchfulness is the proper attitude of believers; we are to be keen, alert, looking continually for the coming of Christ (Matt. 24:44; Mark 13:35–36; 1 Thess. 5:8; 1 John 2:28).

The teaching of the Second Coming has also the value of stimulating Christian service. Believers who ardently look for the return of Christ will constantly be reevaluating the priorities that govern their manner of living. They will put in highest place a vital relationship to the Lord, and very near the top will be the rendering of service in the name of the Lord—for this alone has eternal value. They will be witnesses, warning their unsaved neighbors and colleagues to flee from the wrath to come, and to be preparing for the coming of the Lord (Matt. 24:45–46; Luke 19:13; 2 Cor. 5:10–11).

But how is Jesus going to come again? He will return personally (John 14:3; 21:20–23; Acts 1:11). He will return unexpectedly (Matt. 24:32–51; Mark 13:33–37). He will return in glory (Matt. 16:27; 19:28; Luke 19:11–27). He will come in a physical mode; the angel announced to the crowd on the Mount of Ascension that " 'this same Jesus, who has been taken from you into heaven, will come back in the same way you have seen him go into heaven' " (Acts 1:11). This real, physical, literal return of the Lord Jesus Christ to this earth precludes any spiritualized interpretation, for example, conceiving of His coming as occurring somehow in the Spirit on the Day of Pentecost or at the time of one's conversion or possibly, as some teach, at one's death.

Why is Jesus coming again? He is coming to receive His own unto himself (John 14:3). We are to receive a new body, and as a complete person, be united forever with the Lord (1 Cor. 15:35–54; 2 Cor. 5:1–5; 1 Thess. 4:17). Those dead already at the time of His coming shall be raised, and those still alive at that time shall be changed, both becoming glorified beings in an instant, "in a flash, in the twinkling of an eye" (1 Cor. 15:52; 1 Thess. 4:17). He is coming again to judge and to reward. Christ will come to judge believers, apportioning rewards commensurate with deeds done in this life, especially with regard to motives (Matt. 25:14–30; Luke 19:11–27; 1 Cor. 13:3; 2 Pet.

1:11). The use of opportunity, talent, and time will be appropriately recognized. This is the believers' judgment (sometimes called the judgment seat of Christ, or the *Bēma* judgment).[3] It is not a judgment with regard to sins, for believers have already been judged in the person of Christ at Calvary (Isa. 53:5–6; John 5:24; 2 Cor. 5:21).

The second coming of Christ will also remove that which restrains. What is it that restrains the total onslaught of evil in this world? Some think 2 Thessalonians 2:6–8 refers to the Holy Spirit; some, to the power of law and order itself; others, to the Church. Perhaps the best solution is that the removal of the Church, the agency through which the Holy Spirit chiefly works in this age, is the restraining influence to which this passage alludes. The Holy Spirit certainly will continue on earth much as He did prior to the Church Age.[4] Without His life-giving presence this world would go out of existence.

THE RAPTURE

The definition of the term "Second Coming" is broad, used in at least two different ways. Sometimes this term is used of the total end-time drama, encompassing both the rapture of the Church and the revelation of Christ in triumphant glory (2 Thess. 1:7), when He will stand on the Mount of Olives (Zech. 14:4). Sometimes the term is used specifically of the revelation of Christ, in distinction to the Rapture, which precedes it. The first phase of the Second Coming, then, used in this broader sense, refers to the rapture of the Church. Abruptly and without warning, Jesus will catch away those who are prepared for His coming, but He will not descend to earth itself at that time (1 Thess. 4:16–18; 2 Thess. 2:1). Those "in Christ," both those resurrected and those still alive, will together be "caught up"

---

[3]*Bēma*, the Gk. word found in 2 Cor. 5:10, is often used by theologians to distinguish it from the Great White Throne of Revelation 20:11.

[4]For further discussion see Donald C. Stamps, ed., *The Full Life Study Bible* (Grand Rapids: Zondervan Bible Publishers, 1990), 448.

(Gk. *harpagēsometha*), "snatched away powerfully"[5] in the clouds (possibly clouds of glory) for a meeting with Him in the air—above the earth.

Because Matthew 24:30–31 mentions the angels gathering the elect after it mentions all nations mourning when they see the Son of Man coming on the clouds of the sky with power and great glory, some take this to mean that the Church will not be caught away until after Jesus comes to destroy the armies of the Antichrist at the end of the Tribulation. But Matthew 24 does not give events in the order of their occurrence. Jesus had no intention of revealing the day or the hour (Matt. 24:36). The words "At that time" ("then," KJV) in Matthew 24:30 translate a very general Greek word *(tote),* meaning that these events will all occur in the same general period of time, but not necessarily in the order given.

Jesus further emphasizes that when the Rapture takes place, everything in the world will still be going on as usual. In New Testament times, the economy was agricultural and men went daily into the fields. Since there were no tight containers to keep insects out of flour, a daily task of women was to clean the grain and grind fresh flour in the small stone hand mills for their daily bread. So when Jesus says, " 'Two men will be in the field; one will be taken [taken along to be with Jesus] and the other left [abandoned, left behind to suffer the judgments about to come on the earth], two women will be grinding with a hand mill, one will be taken and the other left' " (Matt. 24:40–41), He means people will be going about their daily tasks when He comes again. Everything will seem to be "business as usual." Then, without any special warning, one shall be snatched away to meet the Lord in the air, while the person

---

[5]The Gk. is a future passive tense of *harpazō,* a word used to describe robbers snatching up their plunder, eagles snatching up their prey, and, in the New Testament, Paul being caught up with great power into the third heaven (2 Cor. 12:2). The Latin translated this word *raptus,* which is the root of our English word *rapture.* Thus, "be caught away" could be translated "be raptured," and our word "rapture" becomes a legitimate term for designating this event the Bible has prophesied. See Stanley M. Horton, *It's Getting Late* (Springfield, Mo.: Gospel Publishing House, 1975), 49.

by his or her side will be left to suffer the wrath of God that is about to be poured out on the earth.[6] There is no indication whatever of the world being dominated by the Antichrist at this time or of the armies of the Antichrist being gathered for the battle of Armageddon. It seems obvious, therefore, that the Church will be caught away prior to the great judgments of the Tribulation period, so vividly pictured in the Book of Revelation.[7]

Paul is very emphatic here that the dead in Christ will be united with the living who remain and both groups will be caught up together in one body to meet the Lord and to be with Him forever. Some today teach multiple raptures. They use the parables of Jesus to split the Church into various groups, such as the bride, the friends of the bridegroom, the virgins, the guests, and the servants. But this is pressing the analogy too far. We must be careful that we do not become like Nicodemus when he pressed the analogy of birth too far by asking how we could go back into our mothers' wombs and be born again (John 3:4).

If we examine the parables of the wedding, we see that all of them center around Christ. When the bride is mentioned, other groups are not, and vice versa. We see also that both Jews and Gentiles are referred to as guests. The twelve apostles are referred to as friends, or guests, of the bridegroom ("children of the bridechamber," KJV, Matt. 9:15). Jesus was actually using different aspects of the wedding feast to express different aspects of our relation to Him. The "Bride" is one of those aspects and represents the whole of the true Church in a close relation to Jesus that will find its complete fulfillment at the Marriage Supper of the Lamb (Rev. 19:7–8).

Another common teaching is that the Rapture will be limited to a special group of "overcomers," and that the main body of the Church will be left behind to go through the Tribulation or to go up in later raptures. If we examine

---

[6]See Stanley M. Horton, "One Is Taken; One Is Left," *Pentecostal Evangel,* 15 September 1973, 6.

[7]See Stanley M. Horton, "I Believe in the Pre-Tribulation Rapture," *Pentecostal Evangel,* 2 July 1989, 8–9; Stanley M. Horton, "Counted Worthy to Escape," *Pentecostal Evangel,* 15 August 1976, 6–7.

what the Bible has to say about overcomers, however, we see that only those who overcome will eat from the tree of life, they will not be hurt by the second death or the lake of fire, and will not have their names blotted out of the Book of Life (Rev. 2:7,11; 3:5). To overcome means to conquer, to win. If we do not win, we lose. These verses in the Book of Revelation indicate that those who do not overcome lose out forever. Who then are the overcomers? First John 5:4 tells us, "This is the victory that has overcome the world, even our faith." All the born-again believer has to do to overcome is to believe (be an obedient believer and keep on believing) that Jesus is the Son of God. Then God gives us the victory through our Lord Jesus Christ (1 Cor. 15:57). He makes us winners.[8]

THE GREAT TRIBULATION

Following the Rapture will be a time of terrible tribulation, predicted by the sages of old, even from Old Testament days. Daniel speaks of a time of trouble, such as never existed before (12:1). Matthew 24:21–29 describes this as a period of "great tribulation" (KJV). Revelation 3:10 refers to it as "the hour of trial that is going to come upon the whole world to test those who live on the earth." Jeremiah foretells the impending and ominous darkness to come as "a time of trouble for Jacob" (Jer. 30:4–7). Isaiah and Zechariah speak of a time of God's indignation with the inhabitants of this earth (Isa. 24:17–21; Zech. 14:1–3).

When shall this terrible time of suffering come? Matthew 24:30 pictures the Great Tribulation as ending with the return of Christ in glory, the time of His revelation. It is quite apparent, therefore, that the time of trouble, which many passages of Scripture point to as coming at the end of the age, is between the Rapture and the revelation of Christ. We have further assurance that the Rapture will take place before the Tribulation in 1 Thessalonians 5:9–11: "God did not appoint us to suffer wrath but to receive salvation through our Lord Jesus Christ. He died for us so

---

[8]Much of the above material is adapted from Horton, *Getting Late*, 50–54.

CHAPTER
13

The Blessed
Hope

that, whether we are awake or asleep, we may live together with him. Therefore encourage one another and build each other up, just as in fact you are doing." Jesus is our Preserver, Deliverer, Rescuer, from the wrath to come. His blood avails to save us from wrath (Rom. 5:9). During the Tribulation God will pour out His wrath on the world. "Whether we are awake or asleep" refers to the Thessalonians' concern over what would happen to the dead in Christ. They will rise first and we shall all be caught up for the meeting with the Lord in the air. "And so we will be with the Lord forever" (1 Thess. 4:17). In other words, we will be kept from the wrath to come by being caught up in the Rapture to live forever with Jesus (1 Thess. 1:9–10; 5:9).[9]

This is strong evidence that no part of the true Church will be left on earth while the judgments of God fall during the Tribulation. These judgments will be wrath (Rev. 6:16–17; 11:18; 14:10,19; 15:1,7; 16:1,19; 19:15). And as John points out, "The rest of mankind that were not killed by these plagues still did not repent" (Rev. 9:20). This precludes the presence of believers on earth at that time.[10] In Revelation 16, the judgments are such that no one could hide anywhere on earth and escape all of them. "Many other passages also speak of the day of wrath which will reveal the righteous judgment of God on impenitent, disobedient hearts (Rom. 2:5; Eph. 5:6; Col. 3:6). But we as believers are not destined for this wrath."[11]

Quite often those who argue that the Church will go through the Tribulation, being on earth during the time of the Antichrist and these judgments, emphasize one thing: They say God has not promised that the Church will escape tribulation and suffering. The point they miss is that the Bible uses the word "tribulation" (Gk. *thlipsis*) in two different ways. Sometimes the word refers to the distress, persecution, trouble, pressure, and anguish of heart brought on us by a godless world. The same Greek word translated

---

[9]The context of 1 Thess. 5:9 shows the wrath is that which comes after the Rapture, i.e., during the Tribulation.

[10]Horton, "Pre-Tribulation Rapture," 8–9.

[11]Horton, *Getting Late,* 69.

"tribulation" is translated "troubles" ("affliction," KJV) when Paul speaks of our light (slight) troubles (which in comparison to eternity are but for a moment, and which "are achieving for us an eternal glory that far outweighs them all" [2 Cor. 4:17]). But the tribulation judgments of the Book of Revelation are not in the same class; they represent God's wrath. We are not looking for wrath; whether we live or die we are looking for the Rapture, after which we will be together with Jesus forever (1 Thess. 5:10). With this in mind, Paul again tells the Thessalonians to encourage one another, build each other up. Then, to indicate his confidence in them, he adds, "just as in fact you are doing." This is parallel to the exhortation to encourage one another in 1 Thessalonians 4:18. Clearly, Paul still had the Rapture in mind.[12]

How long will the Great Tribulation last? The Scripture does not clearly say. However, there are several references that may be helpful to look at; they seem to be indicators that point to a period of seven years. A key here is the unraveling of the mystery of Daniel's 70 weeks (Dan. 9:24–27). The first 69 weeks, however they are to be interpreted, are said to end with the crucifixion of the Messiah (Dan. 9:26). Many believe that an interlude occurs between the 69th and 70th weeks, in effect postponing the 70th week indefinitely. The interlude is the age of grace, or the Church Age. When the restraining influence, the Holy Spirit's working in and through the Church, is removed at the time of the Rapture, apparently this is the signal for the unleashing of the events which fall into that fateful, terrible 70th week. The "week" seems to have the significance of 7 years. Supporting this view are the references in Daniel 7:25; 12:7 and Revelation 12:14—in which the latter half of this period is called "time, times, and half a time," or 3 ½ years, or 42 months (Rev. 11:2; 13:5), or 1,260 days (Rev. 11:3; 12:6).

ANTICHRIST

The earthly leader of the Great Tribulation, Christ's archenemy, is called Antichrist. "Anti" has the basic mean-

---

[12]Ibid., 69–70.

ing in the Greek "instead of " or "in place of," not "against." He will not call himself the Antichrist—He will claim to be the real Christ. Although there are biblical allusions and characterizations of Antichrist throughout the Old and New Testaments, the clearest representation of this foe of God is given in 2 Thessalonians 2:3–9. He is pictured as the embodiment of lawlessness (cf. Dan. 7:24–25; 2 Thess. 2:3,8–9). He claims to be deity (2 Thess. 2:9–10). It is probable that the Beast referred to in Revelation 13 is another name for Antichrist, for this monster is pictured as having authority ascribed only to Antichrist.[13] Antichrist will unmask his apparent beneficence toward the state of Israel by perpetrating an act of sacrilege, showing himself to be a great deceiver and an enemy of God. This sacrilege that he will perform is called in Daniel "the abomination that causes desolation" (cf. Dan. 11:31; 12:11; Matt. 24:15; Mark 13:14). The desecration of the temple by Antiochus IV, Epiphanes, a Syrian ruler in 168 B.C., is probably the immediate fulfillment of Daniel's prophecy, but that it has a longer-range eschatological significance is borne out by the New Testament references to this term "abomination of desolation"—which Jesus saw as still future.

The destiny of Antichrist is swift, certain judgment at the time of the intervention of Christ the King at His revelation (Rev. 19:11–16). The Battle of Armageddon, the last great conflict of the nations, which will be instigated by Antichrist, will culminate in the triumph of our Lord and the consignment of the Antichrist and his allies to the lake of fire.

THE TIME OF CHRIST'S COMING

The Lord pointed out with care that dates should not be set for His second coming: " 'No one knows about that day or hour, not even the angels in heaven, nor the Son, but only the Father. Be on guard! Be alert! You do not know when that time will come' " (Mark 13:32–33). He indicated to the disciples just moments before He ascended

---

[13]Stanley M. Horton, *The Ultimate Victory* (Springfield, Mo.: Gospel Publishing House, 1991), 184–186.

to heaven that it wasn't for them " 'to know the times or dates the Father has set by his own authority' " (Acts 1:7). The date of Christ's return is none of our business. (Jesus told us what our business is in the next verse.) Yet there are some guidelines that should be noted in a general way, since we are to be alert, on guard, lest we be unprepared.

It is in view of this need to stay alert that we speak of the blessed hope as imminent. We do not mean that Jesus could have returned immediately after His ascension. Not long before Jesus made His triumphal entry into Jerusalem, He told a parable because "the people thought that the kingdom of God was going to appear at once." The parable depicted "a man of noble birth" who "went to a distant country to have himself appointed king and then to return. So he called ten of his servants and gave them ten minas. 'Put this money to work,' he said, 'until I come back . . .' " (Luke 19:11–27). The man's going to a distant country indicates a considerable period of time. The money given implies that the servants were expected to be faithful in the responsibilities given them. There would be time to work. On the other hand, since they did not know the exact time of the nobleman's return, they could not put off doing their master's business.

The Christians in the first century hoped Jesus would return in their lifetime. But, like the apostle Paul, they were not disappointed when they realized this would not be so, for they knew a crown was waiting (2 Tim. 4:8). We too must keep in mind the Great Commission (Matt. 28:19–20; Acts 1:8), and the fact that "this gospel of the kingdom will be preached in the whole world as a testimony to all nations, and then the end will come" (Matt. 24:14). In any case, it is good for us always to think of Jesus as "coming soon." Jesus emphasized this when He said:

"You also must be ready, because the Son of Man will come in an hour when you do not expect him. Who then is the faithful and wise servant, whom the master has put in charge of the servants in his household to give them their food at the proper time? It will be good for that servant whose master finds him doing so when he returns. . . . But suppose that servant is wicked and says to himself, 'My master is staying away a long time,' and he then begins to beat his fellow servants and to eat and drink with the drunkards. The master of that servant will come on a day when he does not expect him and at an hour he is not aware of. He will cut him to pieces and assign him a place with the hypocrites, where there will be weeping and gnashing of teeth" (Matt. 24:44–51).

John further emphasizes the importance of keeping the hope of the Lord's coming before us by saying, "Everyone who has this hope in him purifies himself, just as he is pure" (1 John 3:3). Thus, Jesus and the entire New Testament show that it is good for us to live in the tension between the hope that He is coming soon and the recognition that the gospel must be preached to all nations before the end comes (Matt. 24:14). It is also true that there is a sense in which the kingdom (rule) of God is already present but has not yet arrived in the fullness that Jesus will bring when He returns in glory.

Peter warned against false teachers and then went on to draw special attention to scoffers who will say, " 'Where is this "coming" he promised?' " (2 Pet. 3:4). To them he pointed out: "With the Lord a day is like a thousand years, and a thousand years are like a day. The Lord is not slow in keeping the promise, as some understand slowness. He is patient with you, not wanting anyone to perish, but everyone to come to repentance" (2 Pet. 3:8–9). That is, God does not look at time the way we do, nor is He limited by time the way we are.[14] We look at things from the standpoint of our short lives. He looks at things from the standpoint of eternity. He is also concerned about the fulfillment of the Great Commission and is giving us time for that. But we can be sure that in His time God will say, "It is enough," for "the day of the Lord will come" (2 Pet. 3:10).[15]

---

[14]See Stanley M. Horton, *Ready Always* (Springfield, Mo.: Gospel Publishing House, 1974), 111–113.

[15]Because Peter is concerned about the judgment on the false teachers, he jumps over the time of the Rapture and the Millennium and goes to the time of the final judgment, all of which is on the "day of the Lord," which in itself is the whole period rather than a twenty-four-hour day.

Paul also warned against false teachers who were disturbing the Thessalonians after Paul had encouraged them with the hope of the Rapture. By such things as a purported prophecy or a report or letter, which they falsely claimed to have come from Paul, they said, "The day of the Lord has already come" (2 Thess. 2:1–2). Paul denies the claim of these false teachers as emphatically as possible: "Don't let anyone deceive you in any way, for that day will not come until the rebellion occurs and the man of lawlessness is revealed" (2 Thess. 2:3). That is, the first things on the Day of the Lord[16] will be this rebellion (possibly the events of Ezekiel 38 and 39) and then the revelation of the Antichrist. Paul means that since these things had not yet occurred, then neither had the day of the Lord; we can therefore still look forward to being caught away in the Rapture.[17]

Christ's coming is also imminent with respect to signs. The "wars and rumors of wars" and the other things Jesus mentioned in Matthew 24 are not signs of the end (v. 6), but are simply things that will characterize this age. What Jesus meant was that we cannot wait for perfect conditions to spread the gospel but must do so in the midst of the world the way it is. Other "signs" mentioned in other passages refer to the Second Coming in the specific sense of the revelation when Jesus will return in glory to judge the earth and set up His millennial kingdom. Jesus also said, "When these things begin to take place, stand up and lift up your heads, because your redemption is drawing near" (Luke 21:28). This seems to mean that we should focus our attention on the Lord, not on the signs.

From this it is evident there are no signs in particular that will allow us to date the Rapture. So despite some modern speculations and attempts at date setting, His coming for us will remain unannounced (Matt. 24:36; 25:13; Mark 13:32; 1 Thess. 4:16–17; Titus 2:13). Even though God the Father is working out His plan, from our point of

---

[16]Not "before" the Day of the Lord. The word "first," KJV, means first on the day, not first prior to the day. See Horton, *Getting Late,* 100–101.

[17]Ibid., 94–101. See also *Study Bible,* 445–446.

view the rapture of the Church could occur at any time. God wants us to live in a state of readiness.

Important to this view that the Rapture will take place before the Tribulation is the assurance that God characteristically delivers His people from tribulation (Luke 21:34–36; 1 Thess. 5:9–10; 2 Thess. 1:4–10; Rev. 3:10).[18] We have indeed a blessed hope!

STUDY QUESTIONS

1. Why was the resurrection of Jesus a central theme in the preaching of the Early Church?

2. What will our new resurrection bodies be like?

3. Why is the coming resurrection of believers and the second coming of Christ a "blessed" hope for us today?

4. Why should we look at the end of the present age as a consummation rather than simply an end?

5. How should the hope of the Second Coming affect our daily living?

6. What are the reasons for expecting a literal, personal return of Jesus to earth?

7. The word "rapture" is from the Latin *rapere,* "to seize," in its participial form *raptus,* "seizing." How does that fit with the translation "caught up" and with the suddenness of the Rapture?

8. Will the Rapture and the meeting with Jesus in the air be for all true believers, or for just a certain group? Explain.

9. Who are the overcomers?

10. What is the evidence that the Rapture will take place before the Great Tribulation?

11. What will the Antichrist be like?

12. What is the danger of trying to set dates for the Lord's return?

____

[18]See "The Rapture of the Church," in *Where We Stand* (Springfield, Mo.: Gospel Publishing House, 1990), 125–130.

14th

FUNDAMENTAL TRUTH

THE MILLENNIAL REIGN OF CHRIST

The second coming of Christ includes the rapture of the saints, which is our blessed hope, followed by the visible return of Christ with His saints to reign on the earth for one thousand years (Zech. 14:5; Matt. 24:27,30; Rev. 1:7; 19:11–14; 20:1–6). This millennial reign will bring the salvation of national Israel (Ezek. 37:21–22; Zeph. 3:19–20; Rom. 11:26–27) and the establishment of universal peace (Ps. 72:3–8; Isa. 11:6–9; Mic. 4:3–4).

CHAPTER FOURTEEN

The Millennial Reign of Christ

The Rapture was discussed in the previous chapter, but it would be well for us to consider again Titus 2:11–14: "The grace of God that brings salvation has appeared to all men. It teaches us to say 'No' to ungodliness and worldly passions, and to live self-controlled, upright and godly lives in this present age, while we wait for the blessed hope— the glorious appearing of our great God and Savior, Jesus Christ, who gave himself for us to redeem us from all wickedness and to purify for himself a people that are his very own, eager to do what is good."[1]

THE REVELATION OF CHRIST

The revelation of Christ is the second phase of the Second Coming; it will occur sometime following the Rapture, the first phase. On that wonderful occasion, Jesus "will stand on the Mount of Olives, east of Jerusalem, and the Mount of Olives will be split in two from east to west, forming a great valley, with half of the mountain moving

---

[1]See Stanley M. Horton, "I Believe in the Pre-Tribulation Rapture," *Pentecostal Evangel,* 2 July 1989, 8–9; Stanley M. Horton, "Counted Worthy to Escape," *Pentecostal Evangel,* 15 August 1976, 6–7.

**CHAPTER
14**

The
Millennial
Reign of
Christ

north and half moving south. . . . Then the Lord my God will come, and all the holy ones with him" (Zech. 14:4–5). This promise of a literal, physical descent to earth is corroborated by the angelic messengers who announced to the stunned crowd at the Ascension that Christ would return " 'in the same way you have seen him go into heaven' " (Acts 1:11). Since He left visibly from the Mount of Olives, one may gather that He will return visibly to that location.

Revelation 1:7 points to this open, public coming of Christ: " 'Look, he is coming with the clouds, and every eye will see him, even those who pierced him; and all the peoples of the earth will mourn because of him.' " When He returns in power and glory in the revelation phase of the Second Coming, He will bring His saints with Him (Joel 3:11; 1 Thess. 3:13; Jude 14).

The purposes of the revelation are various. Jesus will come to reveal himself and to display His saints. The Rapture occurs suddenly and is apparently hidden from the gaze of the undiscerning people of the world. The revelation, however, is public. People who refused to recognize Him during the Church Age and who refused to take note of the disappearance of thousands at the time of the Rapture will be forced to acknowledge the King of kings at the revelation of Christ (Joel 3:11–12; Zech. 14:5; Matt. 16:27; 24:29–31; Col. 3:4; 1 Thess. 3:13; 1 John 3:2).

He is coming in power and glory to judge His enemies. The Beast, the False Prophet, and the armies who supported these adversaries of God will come under the wrath of the Judge. These terrible forces, which participated in the time of unprecedented tribulation, will be overthrown and destroyed (2 Thess. 2:8–9).

The evil spirits coming from the Beast, the False Prophet, and the Dragon (Satan) go forth to conquer Jerusalem at the end of the time of Great Tribulation (Zech. 12:1–9; 13:8–9; 14:12; Rev. 16:12–16). Just as victory seems in their grasp, the Lord Jesus descends from heaven with His valiant armies, probably including both the saints and the angels (Rev. 19:11–16). Christ the King triumphs wonderfully at this critical moment, and the leaders of the wicked hosts are cast into the lake of fire (Ps. 2:3–9; 2 Thess.

2:8; Rev. 19:19–20). The way is thus prepared for an earthly rule of Christ, the inauguration of a new regime known as the Millennium.[2]

The revelation of Christ at His second coming not only crushes the manifestation of Satan's power, that is, the False Prophet and the Beast, but also binds Satan himself (Rom. 16:20; Rev. 20:1–2). For a thousand years he remains bound before his eventual release and final consignment to the lake of fire with the rest of his emissaries.

THE MILLENNIUM

The return of Jesus in power and glory is vividly described in Revelation 19:11–16:

I saw heaven standing open and there before me was a white horse, whose rider is called Faithful and True. With justice he judges and makes war. His eyes are like blazing fire, and on his head are many crowns. . . . He is dressed in a robe dipped in blood, and his name is the Word of God. The armies of heaven were following him, riding on white horses and dressed in fine linen, white and clean. Out of his mouth comes a sharp sword with which to strike down the nations. "He will rule them with an iron scepter." He treads the winepress of the fury of the wrath of God Almighty. On his robe and on his thigh he has this name written: KING OF KINGS AND LORD OF LORDS.

The white horse means He comes as a mighty conqueror. "Faithful and true" means He is genuine and real: He is the real Jesus, the same Jesus (the Living Word) who was born in a manger. His robe dipped in blood shows He is the same Jesus who died on the cross. "Rule . . . with an iron scepter" is literally "acting the part of a shepherd with an iron rod." This, along with making war, wielding a sharp sword, is in fulfillment of Daniel 2:34–35,44–45, where the "stone" destroys the kingdoms of this world and then becomes a kingdom that fills the earth. The "fine linen" of the armies who follow Him identify them as the Church

---

[2]Millennium is from the Latin *mille* "thousand" and *annus* "year."

(Rev. 17:14; 19:8), who from the time of the Rapture are "with the Lord forever" (1 Thess. 4:17).[3]

THE VIEWS OF MILLENNIALISM

The Early Church looked forward to Christ's return to establish His kingdom and reign in Jerusalem as the true and final Heir of David's throne. They accepted as literal Jesus' promise that the twelve apostles would sit on twelve thrones judging and ruling the twelve tribes of a restored Israel (Matt. 19:28).

Paul commends the Thessalonians because they "turned to God from idols to serve the living and true God, and to wait for his Son from heaven" (1 Thess. 1:9–10). They could identify with singing the new song of Revelation 5:9–10, which celebrates not only redemption by the blood of the Lamb, but also the fact that Christ had made them kings and priests who would reign on the earth.

As time went on, the hope of some believers grew cold. But there continued to be those in the early centuries who emphasized Christ's millennial reign on earth. They were sometimes called "Chiliasts," from the Greek word *chilia*, "one thousand." Then, after Christianity was made the official religion of the Roman Empire, a change began to take place. The pastors of the assemblies no longer took the role of servant leaders. Instead, they followed the pattern of the government of the Roman Empire and built up a hierarchy of power.

When the capital of the empire was moved from Rome to Constantinople, this left a political vacuum in Rome; so the Bishop of Rome stepped into the gap to take political leadership, making his seat a throne. The other bishops began to look at their churches as a power base, their attention diverted from the blessed hope of the Church by earthly power and authority. As a result, postmillennialism[4]

---

[3]See Stanley M. Horton, *The Ultimate Victory: An Exposition of the Book of Revelation* (Springfield, Mo.: Gospel Publishing House, 1991), 281–284.

[4]"Post" means "after." That is, they believe Christ's return will be after the "present" millennium.

arose, teaching that the millennial kingdom started with Christ's resurrection and will end with His second coming, and therefore there will be no future kingdom of God on earth.[5] The only kingdom advocates of such teaching were concerned about was the one they could build for themselves using the people as their servants.

Later, amillennialism arose, teaching that there will be no millennium on earth (the "a" in amillennialism means "no"). These views were carried over into the Protestant churches of the Reformation. Because they denied a future millennium on earth, they had no room in their theological systems for any restoration of an earthly Israel. Therefore, they spiritualized the kingdom prophecies of the Old Testament about Israel and applied them to the Church. They declared that Israel by rejecting Jesus as the Christ had forfeited all of the promises God had given to them. They also spiritualized the Book of Revelation and claimed that Satan was bound at the Cross, so that the gospel could be spread in a marvelous way without his hindrance. They taught further that when Christ returns there will be a general judgment of both the righteous and the wicked at the same time. Then Christ will immediately set up His eternal kingdom, with no millennium in between. Later amillennialists taught that whatever millennium there might be is going on now (either spiritually on earth or else in heaven).[6]

Admittedly the Book of Revelation uses figures of speech. But those figures represent realities. The Antichrist is pictured as a beast, but he will be a real person, as 2 Thessalonians 2 shows. There are also some very plain and literal statements in Revelation, especially in its opening and closing chapters. The thousand years are mentioned six times in Revelation 20. That kind of repetition in the Bible indicates emphasis, which gives us every rea-

---

[5]Augustine, bishop of Hippo in North Africa, A.D. 396–430, was probably one of the chief promoters of this type of postmillennialism, though he is also claimed by amillennialists.

[6]It is sometimes difficult to distinguish between postmillennialists and amillennialists. They share much in their teachings, and both spiritualize the Scripture heavily.

son to take the thousand years of the Millennium literally. And though the kind of chain that will bind Satan is not specified, the fact that he will be bound is clear.

It is also clear from the Bible that Satan was not bound at the cross. Christ did indeed rise victorious. The Cross and the Resurrection are the guarantee of Satan's final defeat. Yet the Bible makes it clear that the believer's "enemy the devil prowls around like a roaring lion looking for someone to devour" and we must "resist him, standing firm in the faith" (1 Pet. 5:8–9). We must still put on spiritual armor, for we are still in a spiritual battle and need to use the shield of faith to "extinguish all the flaming arrows of the evil one" (see Eph. 6:10–18). Revelation 20:2–3 says, however, that Satan *will* be bound, thrown into the Abyss, which will be locked and sealed over him, "to keep him from deceiving the nations anymore until the thousand years" are ended. Therefore it is not until after Christ comes in glory that the binding of Satan takes place.

In more recent times another form of postmillennialism arose. Its advocates made the Millennium an extension of the Church Age and taught that in time there will be a great spread of Christianity over the world. Then when the Church converts the world as a whole, Jesus will return for a general judgment of both the righteous and the wicked at the same time. Those who hold this view usually say that unless you believe that the world is going to be converted before Jesus comes, you do not believe in the power of the gospel.

Another recent resurgence of postmillennialism has captured the imagination of many.[7] Some go so far as to say that we must become (or recognize ourselves as) little gods and take over the kingdoms of this world, that when this is done, Jesus will come and we can turn it all over to Him. They, like the earlier postmillennialists and amillennialists, spiritualize the plain prophecies of the Bible and twist them to fit the system they have conceived.

The idea that the world must be converted and the king-

---

[7]These include such doctrines as "Kingdom Now," "Restorationism," and "Dominion Theology." See L. Thomas Holdcroft, "Is the Kingdom Now?" *The Pentecostal Minister* (Fall 1988), 15–19.

doms of this world be taken over by the Church before Jesus comes is the product, not of Scripture, but of human thinking. Anything can be made to seem logical if you leave out some of the facts. But when we search the Scriptures we see that Jesus had to warn His disciples that some of the gospel seed would fall by the wayside, some on stony ground, some among weeds. There would be good ground, but there would also be much opposition (Matt. 13:1–23). In Matthew 24:11,24, Jesus warned that false teachers and false prophets would arise. He also indicated that toward the end they would become worse. The Book of Acts shows how the Church grew in numbers. It also shows how opposition grew and continued. There is no formal conclusion to the Book of Acts, so we can expect the same activities to continue throughout the Church Age. Both Paul and Peter indicate that as we approach the end of the age there will be "terrible times," times difficult for Christians to live in (2 Tim. 3:1–5; 1 Pet. 4:12–19; 2 Pet. 3:3).

All this emphasizes strongly that the kingdom must be brought in through judgment. The great image Nebuchadnezzar saw in Daniel 2 is an inclusive representation of the world system, including its sequence of empires followed by feet of iron and clay: a mix of nationalistic states, some strong, some brittle (repeatedly breaking up). Though Babylon gave way to Medo-Persia, Medo-Persia to Greece, Greece to Rome, and Rome to the variety of states that have followed, the image still stands. And we still have with us Babylonian astrology, Medo-Persian ethics, Greek philosophy, and Roman ideas (e.g., that might makes right); there never has been a really new world order. Then the stone, representing Christ and His kingdom, comes. It does not penetrate the image and convert or transform it. It hits the image, the present world system, in the feet and the entire image is reduced to powder and blown away. Not until then does the stone become a great mountain, representing the millennial kingdom that fills the earth. Even what we might term good things in the present world system must be destroyed to make way for the better things of the millennial kingdom. This fits in with Psalm 2:8–9; 2 Thessalonians 1:7–8; Revelation 12:5; 19:11–21. Revelation 2:26–29 also indicates that all faithful believers—

CHAPTER
14

The Millennial Reign of Christ

who are consequently overcomers, winners—will be with Christ and share in His triumph, taking part in acting as a shepherd with a rod of iron and dashing the nations "to pieces like pottery." Therefore, the rod of iron and the dashing to pieces apply to the judgment that must precede the establishment of the millennial kingdom, not to the Millennium itself.

The premillennial view is the only one that takes the Bible as literally as it is intended to be.[8] It sees that God has fulfillments for both the Church and national Israel. It looks for Jesus to return and fulfill the promise that He will sit on the throne of David and will establish His kingdom on the earth.

GOD'S PROMISES TO NATIONAL ISRAEL

God promised Abraham personal blessings, blessings for his numerous seed (Israel), and blessing for all the families of the earth (Gen. 12:3; 17:5,7; 22:17–18). To put it another way, the promise to Abraham included the seed, the land, and the nations. The seed included the numerous seed, Israel, and the unique Seed, Christ, through whom the future blessings of redemption and the Holy Spirit would come.

The land was also an integral part of the promise to Abraham and to Israel.[9] Ezekiel saw a future restoration of the land, especially in chapters 36 and 37. In this connection Ezekiel emphasizes the importance of the Name of the Lord. The Name represents His nature and character. He will live up to His Name; He will be the kind of faithful God He says He is. God is going to restore Israel both materially and spiritually even though they have profaned His holy Name. He will do it to honor His holy Name, that is, to demonstrate His holy nature and character. This is God's positive holiness whereby He has dedicated himself to carrying out His will and plan. Consequently, there is

---

[8]Premillennialists believe Jesus will return before the Millennium.

[9]God promised the land between the River Euphrates and the River of Egypt (Gen. 15:18–19).

no way that Ezekiel's prophecy can be spiritualized and applied to the Church.

Ezekiel 36:24–27 shows God will bring Israel out of all countries and will bring them back to their own land. Then He will cleanse them, restore them spiritually, and put His Spirit within them. That is, they will come back to their land first in unbelief. Chapter 37 brings out the same thing by means of a symbolic vision in which by the power of the prophetic word, dry bones come together (flesh, muscles, skin, come on them) but have no breath in them. Then Ezekiel was told to prophesy again. Thus, by a further action of the prophetic Word, life comes into these corpses. The dry bones, God explains, pictures Israel scattered among all nations, their hope completely dry. That never happened during the seventy years in Babylonian exile, for they had Jeremiah's prophecy of the return after seventy years before them. But after the twelve tribes were again scattered in A.D. 70 and 135, they went for centuries with no hope of ever going back to the Promised Land. Therefore, Ezekiel looks forward to a future restoration. But God did not reveal to him how long it would be after they returned in unbelief before He would grant the spiritual restoration. From this passage, however, it is clear that the land is still an important part of God's promise. The Law of Moses was added to the promise (Gal. 3:19)—but without doing away with it (or any part of it). When the Law's work was finished the promise was still there and is still an important part of God's Word. God's faithfulness thus guarantees Israel's restoration to the Land.

Isaiah 65:17 speaks of God creating a new heavens and a new earth in the future. Then 65:18 begins with a strong adversative (Heb. *ki- 'im)*, which is best translated "nevertheless."[10] That is, though there will be a new heavens and a new earth, the present Jerusalem will also have its fulfillment. The rest of chapter 65 fits millennial conditions in the coming kingdom age. They do not fit the description of the new heavens and earth given in the Book of Reve-

---

[10]See William L. Holladay, *A Concise Hebrew and Aramaic Lexicon of the Old Testament* (Grand Rapids: Wm. B. Eerdmans Pub. Co., 1971), 156.

lation. Rather, they are parallel to the descriptions of Christ's coming kingdom given in Isaiah 11:4–10.

The apostle Paul had a great love for the people of Israel who were rejecting the gospel. He would have been willing to give up his own eternal salvation if that would have guaranteed theirs (Rom. 9:1–5). He knew that was impossible, but that was how much he loved them. He also asked the question in Romans 11:1, "Did God reject his people?" Paul's literal response is "Let it not be!" (Gk. *mē genoito,* which the KJV paraphrases "God forbid!" the NIV, "By no means!"). God is not going to let it happen. Surely this makes it clear that God has not thrown aside His people! The context shows the Bible is talking about literal, national Israel and shows that God has not changed His mind about His promises.

Remember too that the twelve apostles will judge, or rule, the twelve tribes of Israel (Matt. 19:28; Luke 22:30). This clearly calls for a literal restoration of Israel. There is no way the Church can be divided into twelve tribes.

Again, the premillennial view is the only one that has a place for the restoration of national Israel and for the literal fulfillment of the prophecies of peace and blessing that Isaiah and other prophets foresaw:

1. There will be universal peace. "They will beat their swords into plowshares and their spears into pruning hooks. Nation will not take up sword against nation, nor will they train for war anymore" (Isa. 2:4).

2. The glory of the Lord will rest on a rebuilt temple. Ezekiel saw the glory departing (Ezek. 9:3; 10:4,18; 11:23). Later he saw it returning: "I saw the glory of the God of Israel coming from the east. . . . the glory of the LORD filled the temple" (Ezek. 43:2,5).

3. Jesus will reestablish David's throne. " 'I will raise up to David a righteous Branch, a King who will reign wisely and do what is just and right in the land' " (Jer. 23:5).

4. There will be joy. "The ransomed of the Lord will return. They will enter Zion with singing; everlasting joy will crown their heads. Gladness and joy will overtake them, and sorrow and sighing will flee away" (Isa. 35:10; see Isa. 51:11; 55:12; 61:10; Jer. 31:12).

5. The earth will be blessed. "I will send down showers in season; there will be showers of blessing. The trees of the field will yield their fruit and the ground will yield its crops" (Ezek. 34:26–27).[11]

The Millennium is going to be a wonderful, glorious time. The world will be cleansed of its present pollution and renewed to a state superior to that of Eden before the Fall.[12]

Our hope is not solely fixed on the future, however. We have encouragement for the present in Acts 3:19, where Peter spoke of times of refreshing. The Greek indicates that whenever people repent (change their hearts, minds, and attitudes), seasons of refreshing follow—right up until the time of Jesus' return. Thus, the blessed hope should stir us to seeking revival now.

STUDY QUESTIONS

1. What are the purposes of the revelation phase of Christ's second coming?

2. What are some of the passages that show that the Early Church took the Second Coming literally?

3. What brought about the rise of postmillennialism and amillennialism?

4. What reasons do premillennialists have for not spiritualizing the Book of Revelation to the extent that amillennialists and postmillennialists do?

5. When will Satan be bound?

6. What are the dangers of some of the newer forms of postmillennialism?

---

[11]The preceding was adapted from Ernest Swing Williams, *Systematic Theology*, vol. 3 (Springfield, Mo.: Gospel Publishing House, 1953), 235–236.

[12]Horton, *Ultimate Victory*, 293–298. See also Pss. 2:8; 24:7–8; Isa. 9:7; 11:6–19; 35:1–2; 61:3; Ezek. 40 to 48; Dan. 2:44; Hos. 1:10; 3:5; Amos 9:11–15; Mic. 4:1–8; Zech. 8:1–9; Matt. 8:11; 19:28; Acts 15:16–18; Rev. 2:25–28; 11:15.

CHAPTER
14
___

The
Millennial
Reign of
Christ

7. What is going to happen to the present world system when Jesus returns in glory?

8. Who is most concerned that national Israel be re-established in the Promised Land with a new heart, a new spirit, and the Holy Spirit within them? Explain.

9. What will conditions be like during the Millennium?

10. How can we have times of refreshing now?

15th

FUNDAMENTAL
TRUTH

THE FINAL JUDGMENT

There will be a final judgment in which the wicked dead will be raised and judged according to their works. Whosoever is not found written in the Book of Life, together with the devil and his angels, the beast and the false prophet, will be consigned to everlasting punishment in the lake which burneth with fire and brimstone, which is the second death (Matt. 25:46; Mark 9:43–48; Rev. 19:20; 20:11–15; 21:8)

CHAPTER FIFTEEN

The Final Judgment

THE DESTINY OF THE HUMAN RACE

At the end of this life, what happens to us? This is one of the most important questions a thinking person can ask. How wonderful that the Book of books supplies the necessary information to relieve the anxiety about our existence beyond time! Although the details are not given, sufficient light has been provided by the inspired writers of Holy Scripture so that believers need not dread the unknown.

What happens at death? Death is the separation of the spirit and the body (John 11:11,13; 2 Cor. 5:1–9). Death is the wages of sin, and everyone dies because everyone has sinned (Rom. 6:23; 5:12). Death is also the ultimate manifestation of sin from which we will finally be delivered (1 Cor. 15:26). Christ has vanquished death, annulling its consequences through His mighty triumph on the cross (2 Tim. 1:10). However, until the final disposition of things, everyone—believer and unbeliever—is subject to death. The triumph is that death is not final for the believer. For unbelievers (although there is a resurrection of the "wicked dead" for purposes of judgment), their ultimate state is

CHAPTER
15

The Final
Judgment

eternal separation from God, which is the second death (Rev. 20:14).

Every human being will have immortality, which means a future in which existence is not subject to annihilation (Rom. 2:7; 1 Cor. 15:53–54). Even if immortality is a future condition beyond the grave, eternal life, Christ's life in us, is a present possession of believers. Through the Holy Spirit we have the first installment of our inheritance and we are already sealed, accepted by God as His children, because of the living Christ who lives within (Gal 2:20; Eph. 1:13–14).

Between the time of death and the resurrection of the body is the intermediate state. Some have taught psychopannychy, soul sleep: the whole person dies and the soul and spirit go out of existence until called back into existence at the resurrection. But the Bible teaches a conscious existence. When Moses and Elijah appeared with Jesus on the Mount of Transfiguration, they were still Moses and Elijah (they had not been reincarnated into someone else) and they knew what was going on (see Luke 9:28–31). The account of the rich man and Lazarus points in the direction of consciousness for the departed (see Luke 16:19–31). And from the cross Jesus promised the dying thief, "Today you will be with me in paradise" (Luke 23:43). The apostle Paul, reflecting on death, indicated that to die would mean being ushered at once into the presence of the Lord (Phil. 1:21–24).

The location of the godly dead is pictured in the Old Testament in several ways. David wrote, "I will dwell in the house of the LORD forever" (Ps. 23:6). Proverbs 15:24 reads literally, "The path of life is to the place above for the wise in order to avoid (keep away from) Sheol beneath." The sons of Korah wrote of those who trust in themselves, "Like sheep they are destined for the grave. ... But God will redeem my life from the grave; he will surely take me to himself" (Ps. 49:14–15). The psalmist Asaph added, "You guide me with your counsel, and afterward you will take me into glory. Whom have I in heaven but you? And earth has nothing I desire besides you" (Ps. 73:24–25). These verses have structure that shows the guidance is on earth and the glory is in heaven. Asaph goes on in the next verse to say, "My flesh and my heart may fail, but God is the strength of my heart and my portion forever." Though the Old Testament does not give details, it seems clear from these passages that the righteous had a hope to be with the Lord in heaven.

The meaning of the Hebrew term *She'ol* is debated: Some take it to mean the grave; others interpret it as the place of the intermediate state between death and resurrection; still others take it to have a broader meaning, including both the grave and the place of the intermediate state. In most contexts Sheol is something to be avoided. It is often, as in Psalm 9:17 and Proverbs 15:24, the destiny of the wicked in contrast to the destiny of the righteous. Because Jacob spoke of going to Sheol to his son Joseph (Gen. 37:35), some later rabbis decided there must be two compartments in Sheol, separated by a handbreadth or perhaps even a fingerbreadth.[1] But Luke 16:26 declares there is a great unbridgeable, "yawning" space between the fires of Hades and the place where Abraham and Lazarus were.

In the New Testament the Greek word *Hadēs* is substituted for the Hebrew *She'ol,* and Hades in the New Testament is always a place of punishment. It is also a place of conscious existence "in torment" (Luke 16:23). Some make the Greek *Gehenna*[2] (Matt. 5:22; 23:33, for example) the equivalent of *Hadēs,* but it is rather a term describing the lake of fire, which is the second (i.e., eternal) death.

The New Testament does make it clear, however, that there is a hell. Hades to the Greeks was a shadowy place. But Jesus refers to its fire that causes torment (Luke

---

[1]That is, they supposed there must be a place for the righteous in Sheol since Jacob spoke of going there and assumed his son was there already. However, since Jacob "refused to be comforted" (Gen. 37:35) and there is no record of his seeking God again until after he received the news that Joseph was alive, it may be just as probable that he thought Sheol was God's judgment on them both.

[2]Gehenna is the Aramaic name of the Valley of Hinnom, on the south of Jerusalem. King Ahaz made it a place of idolatrous worship (2 Chron. 28:3; see 2 Chron. 33:6; Jer. 7:31; 32:35). Therefore, King Josiah, under his reforms, had it polluted, making it a garbage and trash dump, a place of abomination. Jesus spoke of it as a type of place of eternal punishment (Matt. 25:46; Mark 9:47–48; cf. Rev. 14:11).

16:24,28). This is a subject from which we naturally turn away, for it is grim indeed. Yet it is part of the biblical record. God could not be the holy God He is without providing an appropriate place for those who have chosen to rebel against Him.

Just as hell is real, so is heaven. It is the abode of those who are children of God (joint heirs with Jesus Christ, those sharing in eternal life), a place in the very presence of God himself.[3] We live here in the world not by sight but by faith. In heaven we will find the reality of everything we took by faith on earth.

The intermediate state is followed by resurrections and judgments, issuing ultimately in the final destination of the righteous and the wicked.

THE JUDGMENTS

Hebrews 9:27 speaks pointedly of the coming time of accountability, when all will stand before the righteous Judge to give account of what they have done during their lives on earth. "Man is destined to die once, and after that to face judgment." There is clearly no second chance, no reincarnation, after death. The Scriptures do not teach, however, that there will be a single, general judgment of everyone. Some passages do speak of the judgments in a general way, without showing time in between them. But, just as the Old Testament can speak of the first coming of Christ in one verse and His second coming in the next (compare Zech. 9:9–10), so the Bible does not always give the time in between the resurrections or between the judgments. But there is a progressive revelation that makes it quite apparent that there are at least four specific episodes of judgment during the final stages of time's great dramatic climax.

There is the judgment seat of Christ. This judgment is for believers only. It is not a judgment on sin, for the

---

[3]Paul identifies the third heaven (where God's throne is) with paradise. See chap. 16. "Paradise" (Gk. *paradeisos*), from the Persian for "an enclosed park," is used in the New Testament only of the place of blessedness in heaven.

believer by accepting Christ as Savior has had his sins judged at the Cross already. This judgment is a matter of appropriate rewards for stewardship of opportunity and energy during one's life on earth. A system of rewards is part of Christ's teaching about the hereafter, given elaborate treatment in the Gospels, especially in the parables. The same principle is clearly stated by Paul in Romans 14:10 and 2 Corinthians 5:10. In 1 Corinthians 3:11–15 Paul points out that all believers are building an edifice, some of permanent material: gold, silver, and precious stones; some of impermanent material: wood, hay, and stubble. Our deeds will be examined by the fire of God's judgment. Motives especially will be judged (1 Cor. 13:3).

Before whom do believers appear for this judgment? Revelation 1:13–17 pictures the glory of the triumphant Christ, before whose eyes nothing can be hidden. In view of the responsibility entrusted to believers as stewards of precious opportunity, it is necessary that we first subject our own lives to judgment so that we will not come under later judgment (1 Cor. 11:31). If we are responsive to the gentle urging of the Holy Spirit and seek daily to allow Christ to live through us, "we may be confident and unashamed before him at his coming" (1 John 2:28).

There will be a judgment of Israel. Who can read Old Testament prophecy, such as Isaiah 43:5–10, and New Testament comments, such as Romans 9 to 11, without being keenly aware that the entrance of the modern state of Israel onto the stage of world affairs is surely a miracle of God? But before their millennial restoration there must first come a time of suffering, the time of "Jacob's trouble," the Great Tribulation which will take place between the Rapture and the revelation of Christ (see chapter 14). Out of this time of deep difficulty Israel will call upon the Lord (Zech. 12:9 to 13:1).

There will be a judgment of angels. This is mentioned in 1 Corinthians 6:3, but no details are given except that believers will be with Christ, sharing in that judgment. He will be there, for the Father has given all judgment to the Son (John 5:22).

Some interpret the parable of Matthew 25:31–46 as a separate judgment of the nations just after the Battle of

Armageddon: upon the revelation of Jesus Christ and just at the close of the Great Tribulation period. There are two common interpretations of this parable. One says that there will be some saved during the Great Tribulation. They will be living among the lost who have survived the Tribulation. The judgment will make a separation based on works of love and kindness to those belonging to Christ, perhaps especially converted Jews (cf. Gen. 12:1–3; Isa. 10:12; 47:5–6).

Another common view notes, however, that (1) the acts of kindness are acts of individuals toward individuals; (2) Jesus counted His disciples as His family (Matt. 12:48–50); (3) His disciples are the "little flock" who are to receive the Kingdom (Luke 12:32); therefore, they are "the least of these" (Matt. 25:40,45); and (4) the issue of this judgment is not simply a matter of entering into the Millennium. For those on the left hand it is eternal punishment in fire prepared for the devil and his angels; for those on the right hand it is entrance into an eternal inheritance prepared since the creation of the world. This view also notes that at the judgment seat of Christ and also at the final Great White Throne Judgment, works, or deeds, are judged. They suggest therefore that in this parable Jesus put both the judgment seat of Christ and the Great White Throne in the same picture for the sake of the lesson.[4] Consequently, He did not show that the thousand years of the Millennium come between the two judgments. In fact, that period was not yet revealed. Not until Revelation 20 is the time in between judgments made known. Revelation 20 shows also that prior to the Great White Throne Judgment, Satan leads a final rebellion.

SATAN'S FINAL REBELLION

After Christ's millennial reign, Satan will be released for a short time. God probably allows this as another evidence that His justice is righteous. It is a terrible thing to throw

---

[4]See James Oliver Buswell, *A Systematic Theology of the Christian Religion,* vol. 2 (Grand Rapids: Zondervan Publishing House, 1962), 417–423.

people into the lake of fire which was prepared for the devil and his angels (Matt. 25:41) and was never intended for the human beings God created. It would seem reasonable that if people could only know how wonderful the reign of Christ will be, they would all believe in Him and follow Him. But the release of Satan shows that even after the world has seen peace and blessing for a thousand years under Christ's rule, some will still follow Satan when they get the opportunity to do so. Clearly they are self-willed rebels, saying to God, "Leave us alone!" Therefore, there is nothing a holy God can do but separate them from His presence forever.

Satan's rebellion after his release ends with his followers being consumed by fire from heaven. Then Satan himself is cast into the lake of fire forever. After that the Great White Throne appears.

THE GREAT WHITE THRONE

Though the throne is God the Father's judgment throne, Jesus declared, "The Father judges no one, but has entrusted all judgment to the Son" (John 5:22): The one Mediator between God and humankind becomes the Mediator in judgment. Therefore, Jesus will be the One actually sitting on the throne. And so great will His majesty in judgment appear that the present earth and heaven will "flee away" (KJV), there being "no more place in God's plan" for them.[5] Thus, the way is made for the creation of a new heavens and a new earth (discussed further in chapter 16).

Those who appear before the Great White Throne are "the dead, great and small" (Rev. 20:12). Since the righteous who take part in the first resurrection already have their new bodies, which are immortal and incorruptible, they are the living, not the dead. Therefore, the dead who stand before that throne to be judged must be "the rest of the dead" (Rev. 20:5) who did not have part in the first

[5]Stanley M. Horton, *The Ultimate Victory: An Exposition of the Book of Revelation* (Springfield, Mo.: Gospel Publishing House, 1991), 301.

CHAPTER
15
———

The Final
Judgment

resurrection to life at the time of the Rapture.[6] They are the "wicked dead," including those who were killed after the Millennium when they chose to follow Satan.

Some suppose that those who were not killed during the Tribulation and were brought into the Millennium plus those who are born during the Millennium will have an opportunity to be saved and follow Christ and then come before the Great White Throne to receive rewards. But the Bible does not tell us this. Only the "dead" appear in this second resurrection, which is the resurrection to judgment (John 5:29). Those saved during the Millennium will probably receive new bodies before the thousand years are over—possibly after a period of probation.

For the judgment, books are opened. The wicked will then be judged according to what they have done. Then the Book of Life is opened. Though the wicked are judged by their deeds, salvation is not by works. Their works, their deeds, are simply the evidence of their unbelief. In other words, the Book of Life is opened as a witness to the fact that they were not among those who had placed their faith in Jesus and followed Him with trust and obedience.

The Great White Throne Judgment makes a final disposition of the unsaved. The epoch between eternity past and eternity future, this brief interlude called time, is a period of probation. There is opportunity for choice in this fleeting season, but once a settled character has been achieved in this world, and one passes out into the world beyond, there is no more opportunity for change. The decisions in this life are irreversible; they are utterly crucial, since the destiny of the individual is for eternity. No, the Scriptures do not teach the annihilation of the wicked, nor a mindless state of Nirvana, as the Buddhists teach, nor the opportunity for a second chance after death. This is why it is urgent that our lives be geared to the strategic, utterly important task of evangelism, of being ambassadors for Christ, seeking to win men and women to Him. Witnessing is the chief task of the Christian. Those we meet day by day are never-dying souls who have an eternal des-

———
[6]Ibid., 303.

tiny at stake. And apart from the salvation provided in Jesus
Christ, there is no hope for the unregenerate.

THE LAKE OF FIRE

After the witness from the Book of Life that their names
are not included, the wicked are thrown into the lake of
fire, the lake of burning sulfur,[7] which is the second death.
In the Bible, death often means separation: The second
death is a final separation from God and from the inheritance of the saints. The wicked will miss the glories of the
new heavens and the new earth as well as the new Jerusalem.

Jesus refers to the final punishment of the wicked as
"outer darkness" (Matt. 22:13, KJV), which implies final
separation from God, for "God is light; in him there is no
darkness at all" (1 John 1:5). Revelation 22:15 also indicates that the wicked dead will be "outside," not only
outside the New Jerusalem, but outside the whole new
creation of the new heavens and the new earth.[8]

Death and Hades will also be thrown into the lake of
fire. That is, death and Hades will have no part in the new
creation but will be merged with the second death, the
lake of fire in outer darkness, and be forever separated from
the light of Christ. In this way "the last enemy," death, will
be destroyed (1 Cor. 15:26), for in the new heavens and
the new earth there will be no more tears, no more dying.
Only in the outer darkness of the lake of fire will such
lamentation be heard (Matt. 8:12; 13:49–50; Luke 13:28).
It will be full of remorse, bitterness, frustration, and raging
lusts that cannot be fulfilled. Death and judgment will not
change a sinner's nature. Only the blood of Jesus can do
that.

Those thrown into the lake of fire "will be tormented
day and night for ever and ever" (Rev. 20:10). Jude 7 also
speaks of the punishment of eternal fire. Some today claim
that the word "eternal" means only "age-lasting." This is a
case where a little knowledge of Greek is a bad thing. The

---

[7]"Brimstone," KJV, is an old word for sulfur.
[8]Horton, *Ultimate Victory,* 336.

252 Bible Doctrines: A Pentecostal Perspective

CHAPTER
15
The Final
Judgment

Greek word *aiōnios,* translated "eternal" or "everlasting," is used of eternal life, eternal death, and the eternal God. We are all in trouble if God is only "age-lasting." Moreover, the Bible describes the fires of divine judgment in ways that have nothing to do with time. By its very nature the fire is unquenchable (Matt. 3:12; Luke 3:17) and therefore endless.

It should also be noted that God's promise of life to the obedient believer means more than the gift of bare existence. Everyone already has that. The gift of eternal life brings blessings and eternal fellowship with God and Christ, as well as a sharing in the glory to come. So the second death as a penalty does not mean mere loss of existence. It means everlasting punishment and everlasting separation from God and from the faith (including trust), hope (including continuing blessings), and love that remain for the believer (see 1 Cor. 13:13).

It is not God's will that any should perish. He wants everyone to come to repentance (2 Pet. 3:9). God has put many things in the path of humankind to turn them from sin and to the salvation He has provided in Christ. But the choice is up to the individual.

STUDY QUESTIONS

1. Why do believers not have to fear death?
2. What is the evidence for conscious existence after death, in the intermediate state?
3. What hope did the Old Testament saints have?
4. What happens to the wicked and unbelieving at death?
5. How do we know that heaven and paradise are real?
6. Who comes before the judgment seat of Christ and what can they expect there?
7. Why is Satan allowed to lead a final rebellion after the Millennium?
8. Who comes before the Great White Throne and what judgment can they expect?
9. What is the second death and what will it be like?
10. What is God's purpose in revealing in the Bible the coming judgments to the world?

16th

th

FUNDAMENTAL
TRUTH

THE NEW HEAVENS AND THE NEW EARTH
"We, according to his promise, look for new heavens and a new earth wherein dwelleth righteousness" (2 Pet 3:13 [KJV]; Rev. 21–22).

CHAPTER SIXTEEN

The New Heavens and the New Earth

The apostle Paul relates an experience of being caught away into the "third heaven" (which he also identified as "paradise" [2 Cor. 12:2,4]).[1] His idea of three heavens included (1) the atmospheric heavens surrounding the earth (Dan. 7:13; Hos. 2:18); (2) the starry heavens (Gen. 1:14–18); and (3) the third heaven, where the throne of God is and which is the present home of all believers who have died and gone to heaven (2 Cor. 5:8; Phil. 1:23). Just where it is in relation to the rest of God's creation the Bible does not reveal.

THE NEW REPLACES THE OLD

Both the Old and New Testaments, however, speak of a new heavens and a new earth (see Isa. 65:17; 66:22; Rev. 21:1). Some believe a good case can be made for the renovation of the present heavens and earth rather than a new creation. For example, the Bible does speak of "everlasting hills" (Gen. 49:26; Hab. 3:6, KJV) and of the earth being

---

[1]Paul in vv. 2 and 5 speaks of "a man," to soften the "boasting" (v. 1). Then v. 7 makes it clear that "the man" was indeed Paul himself.

"established forever" (Pss. 78:69; 104:5; 125:1–2) and remaining "forever" (Eccles. 1:4).

However, let us examine what Peter says: "The heavens will disappear with a roar; the elements will be destroyed by fire, and the earth and everything in it will be laid bare. ... That day will bring about the destruction of the heavens by fire, and the elements will melt in the heat" (2 Pet. 3:10,12).

The word in 2 Peter 3:10 translated "disappear" ("pass away," KJV; Gk. *pareleusontai*) sometimes means "pass by," "pass on," or "pass through." But it also does mean "pass away," "come to an end," "disappear." This seems to be its clear meaning in Matthew 5:18; 24:35; Mark 13:31; Luke 16:17; 21:33.

The word translated "destroyed" ("melt," KJV; Gk. *luthēsetai*) sometimes means "to unloose," "untie," "break" (break bonds or seals). But it is also used of a ship breaking up and being destroyed (Acts 27:41), tearing down a building, destroying the works of the devil (1 John 3:8), and of abolishing laws. Other uses include "repeal," "bring to an end," "do away with." Then, another Greek word, *tēketai,* in 2 Peter 3:12 means "melt away" and confirms that the earth, the stars, and the planets will be destroyed.

The word "new" used of the new earth is also used of our new nature as a new creation (2 Cor. 5:17; Gal. 6:15; Eph. 4:24). Yet we still retain our identity as the same person. However, it is more commonly used of something brand new, such as new wineskins (Matt. 9:17; Mark 2:22), a new piece of cloth (Mark 2:21). It is also used of things previously unknown, not previously present, unheard of— such as a new name (Rev. 2:17) and a new covenant, which covenant is entirely different from the old one given at Mt. Sinai (Jer. 31:31; Luke 22:20; Heb. 8:8). It is also used of the New Jerusalem, which already exists in heaven (Gal. 4:26) and comes down to the new earth from heaven. It is, therefore, clearly not the present Jerusalem renovated, but a marvelous new one coming to a marvelous new earth.

"Passed away" in Revelation 21:1 (Gk. *apēlthan*) is also used of going away, passing from one condition to another. But it also used of leprosy leaving (Mark 1:42), of a woe being over with, past, and others about to take its place (Rev. 9:12).

Then, since fire is often used in the Bible of cleansing or purifying, it may be taken that the heavens and earth are simply renovated, renewed, and restored to a better state by going through the fire. Yet it is also used of burning something up.

Habakkuk 3:6 speaks of everlasting, or "age old," hills scattered, which seems to mean they were not as ever-lasting as people thought they were. Ecclesiastes 1:4, "Generations come and generations go, but the earth remains forever," simply makes a contrast between generations of people that come and go while the earth is still here. "Forever" (Heb. *le'olam*) is often used of the distant past or future when the speaker is not able to see an end, even though there might eventually be one. In Ecclesiastes 1:10 the same expression is translated "long ago." Some also take Ecclesiastes 1:4 to mean that there will always be an earth, even though the present earth is replaced by a brand new one.

The Psalmist makes a similar contrast between the permanence of God and the impermanence of the present creation. "Perish," used of the heavens and earth in Psalm 102:26, is used of Jonah's gourd vine (Jon. 4:10) and of things being destroyed, vanishing, or being blotted out.

Remember that at the appearance of the Great White Throne the present earth and heaven flee away from the One on the throne, and "there was no place for them" (Rev. 20:11). Actually, the simplest meaning is that they are not anywhere; they go out of existence—annihilated! Isaiah 51:6 prophesies that "the heavens will vanish like smoke, the earth will wear out like a garment." Psalm 102:25–26 says, "In the beginning you [God] laid the foundations of the earth, and the heavens are the work of your hands. They will perish, but you remain; they will all wear out like a garment. Like clothing you will change them and they will be discarded." The picture of changing clothes implies putting on a brand new set, which in turn indicates the creation of a brand new heavens and earth.

CHAPTER

16

The New
Heavens
and the
New Earth

CHAPTER
16

The New
Heavens
and the
New Earth

Peter prophesied that this judgment[2] would be by fire that will make the very elements of the universe (the stars and planets) disappear in fervent heat (2 Pet. 3:7–13[3]). In other words, the same thing will happen to them that happens when matter and antimatter (such as an electron and a positron) come together. There is a flash of energy, going off as heat, and then nothing. However God does it, the disappearance of the present earth and heaven will make way for the creation of a brand new heavens and earth where there will be no more sun or moon. Some wonder how this will affect people. The believers will already have their new bodies, immortal and incorruptible, so the destruction of the present universe will not affect them. The dead, who come before the Great White Throne, will also be given some kind of body, for they are resurrected for this judgment (John 5:29). Therefore, neither will they be affected by what happens to the present heaven and earth.

John, in his vision on the island of Patmos, gives details about the new earth that show it will indeed be different from the present earth. There will be no more sea (Rev. 21:1). Sometimes a symbol of restlessness, instability, and danger (Isa. 57:20; James 1:6), the absence of seas may be a way of emphasizing the perfection and peace in the new earth. But seas are not always spoken of in a negative sense (Isa. 11:9; 48:18; Hab. 2:14). Oceans cover the major part of the present earth, and microorganisms (primarily diatoms) in the sea are necessary to replace oxygen and keep the balance in our present atmosphere. Consequently, without seas, the whole environment of the new earth will be different. It seems evident, however, that our new bodies, like Christ's glorified body, will be perfectly suited for both earth and heaven, no longer being dependent on oxygen or a pressurized atmosphere.

---

[2]"Peter, however, does not go into all the details that will accompany and follow Christ's return. They are all part of the Day of the Lord that will lead to final judgment. So Peter jumps ahead in order to draw a lesson from that judgment." Stanley M. Horton, *Ready Always* (Springfield, Mo.: Gospel Publishing House, 1974), 115.

[3]Some take 2 Pet. 3:10 to mean simply a rearrangement of the elements; however, v. 11 speaks of everything being destroyed, and this is emphasized in v. 12.

THE NEW JERUSALEM

More important, the new earth will become the site of the New Jerusalem, which will come down from God out of heaven. Its dimensions (Rev. 21:16)—about 1,380 miles to its height, width, and depth (using the ancient furlong, the Greek *stade* of about 607 feet or 192 meters)—describe a cube, like the holiest place in the tabernacle and the temple, and probably indicate that the new earth will be larger than the present earth.

The initial mention of the Holy City, the New Jerusalem, in Revelation 21:2–3 lets us know that God's dwelling will be with the redeemed of humanity, for He will live with them and they will be His people and He will be their God. In this way, God's purpose for both Israel and the Church will finally be completely fulfilled. (See Gen. 17:7; Exod. 19:5–6; Lev. 11:45; 2 Sam. 7:14; 2 Cor. 6:16,18; Gal. 3:29; 1 Pet. 2:5,9–10). The effects of sin will never be felt again. Believers will experience the full inheritance and final consummation of all that was purchased for them on Calvary by the death of Jesus and the shedding of His blood. There will, therefore, be no more tears and no more death, for death is the wages of sin (Rom. 6:23), and we have the promise that God "will swallow up death forever" (Isa. 25:8) and death will be "swallowed up in victory" (1 Cor. 15:54). Then there will be no more of the kind of separation death brings, nor will there be anything to cause sorrow, pain, grief, or guilt. Nothing will ever mar the fellowship we shall share with the Lord and with each other.

What a glorious vision of the New Jerusalem John saw! Though the angel promised to show John the Bride (Rev. 21:9), this simply means that his concern was for the inhabitants of the city rather than the city itself. The Bible often identifies a city with its inhabitants. (Cf. Matt. 23:37, where Jesus wept over Jerusalem but with its inhabitants in mind.) Therefore, it was a real city John saw in this vision, the home of the saved.

John saw the city filled and radiant with the glory of God, a far greater glory than Moses saw on Mount Sinai (Exod. 33:18–22) or than was manifest in the Holy of

CHAPTER
16
———

The New
Heavens
and the
New Earth

Holies in the tabernacle and temple (Exod. 40:34; 2 Chron. 7:1). Its wall draws attention to the security it provides. The wall also draws attention to the fact that the city is real, having physical dimensions. Its gates are inscribed with the names of the twelve tribes of Israel, but they are open and everyone may go in and out freely. There is no wall between Israel and the Church, however, and the twelve foundations with the names of the twelve apostles on them indicate that the city is the final home and headquarters for both Israel and the Church as one great body of God's redeemed people.

Inside the walls the city is pure gold, transparent like glass. Here John seems to find human language inadequate for describing what he saw. We do not have any gold transparent like glass today. We can pound out gold until it is only a few molecules thick and place it on a window as gold leaf, but it is not transparent like the glass of the window. The Bible seems to be telling us that the new creation will include new substances more beautiful than anything we now know or can imagine.

Most important, there is no temple in the city, for the whole city is filled with the glory and presence of God. By this we see that the New Jerusalem will be the headquarters for the Father, the Son, and the Holy Spirit. No longer will God make His chief manifestation in heaven. The Father and the Son will be personally present in a special way in the New Jerusalem, and the throne of God will be there. Spiritually, all believers will also be indwelt by the Spirit and will continue to be together "a holy temple in the Lord . . . a dwelling in which God lives by his Spirit" (Eph. 2:21–22).

Christ will personally be the "lamp," the source and transmitter of light and energy, so there will be no need of the sun or moon. That is, God will mediate to us divine light and energy directly through Christ. We, however, will still be finite, dependent beings, without a source of energy within ourselves. This is further indicated by the tree of life with its leaves for the "healing" (health, well-being) of the "nations," that is, all believers from all backgrounds, as they walk in the light of the Lord (Rev. 22:2). Not only will there be no sickness or pain, but we shall know in supreme measure what it means to have the Lord as our Shepherd, so we shall lack nothing that we need. He will provide a fullness of life, strength, and joy (cf. Ps. 16:11).

What a wonderful hope! The curse will be gone. Our worship of the Lord will be unhindered, inspiring, and beautiful. We have a foretaste of that now through the Holy Spirit, but what we experience then will be beyond our present imagination. We shall see the Lord and His name will be in our foreheads (Rev. 22:4), forever identifying us as belonging to Him.

God in His love reminds us of the necessity of the destruction of the present material universe (along with everything an unregenerate world values), so that it all can be replaced by the new heavens and the new earth. God's purpose is not merely to satisfy our curiosity about our bright, eternal future. He wants us to share in some new things now. He invites us to enjoy springs of living water (John 4:14; 7:37–39). He wants us to stay close to Jesus. Those who do not, those who turn away because of fear, unbelief, lust, or selfish pride, will lose everything. Those who follow false cults and false religions will also end in the lake of fire.

God has made us as believers joint-heirs with Christ (Rom. 8:16–17): the heir of all things (Ps. 2:8; Heb. 1:2). Consequently, those who believe in Jesus and obey Him will also inherit all things. We can be sure this includes wonderful things and wonderful, ever-new opportunities that our eternal God and His Christ have prepared for us. In fact, the graphic, concrete language of the New Testament may be at best a pale reflection of the riches and glory to which they point.

To sum it up, we know that the New Jerusalem will be a place of surpassing beauty and light (Rev. 21:23; 22:5). There will be fullness of knowledge there (1 Cor. 13:12). It will be a place of interesting activity, but it will, above all, be a place of rest from frustrating toil and tumult (Rev. 14:13; 21:4). It will not be sheer inactivity, however, for there will be meaningful service there (Rev. 7:15; 22:3). It will be filled with joy (Rev. 21:4). There will be wonderful fellowship (John 14:3; 2 Cor. 5:8; Phil. 1:23; 1 Thess. 4:13–18; Heb. 12:22–23). There will be no more heart-

CHAPTER
16

The New
Heavens
and the
New Earth

ache, no more loneliness, no more suffering. And it will be permanent, never in jeopardy of being disrupted, for sin— once for all, and forever—will have been broken by the Mighty Conqueror![4]

STUDY QUESTIONS

1. What is meant by the "third heaven"?

2. What are the chief arguments for considering the new earth merely renovated?

3. What are the chief arguments for considering the new earth a brand new creation?

4. What effect will the judgment of the present earth have upon people?

5. Why does the Bible tell us about what is going to happen to the present heavens and earth?

6. What does the Bible tell us about the new earth?

7. What are the reasons for taking the New Jerusalem as a real city?

8. Who will inhabit the New Jerusalem?

9. Why is there no temple in the New Jerusalem?

10. What will be our relation to Christ in the New Jerusalem?

11. What is God's purpose in telling us about the New Jerusalem?

___

[4]Some of the material in this chap. was adapted from Horton, *Ready Always,* 117–125; *Ultimate Victory,* 307–340.

A STATEMENT OF FUNDAMENTAL TRUTHS APPROVED BY THE GENERAL COUNCIL OF THE ASSEMBLIES OF GOD, OCTOBER 2-7, 1916.

This Statement of Fundamental Truths is not intended as a creed for the Church, nor as a basis of fellowship among Christians, but only as a basis of unity for the ministry alone (i. e., that we all speak the same thing, 1 Cor. 1:10; Acts 2:42). The human phraseology employed in such statement is not inspired nor contended for, but the truth set forth in such phraseology is held to be essential to a full Gospel ministry. No claim is made that it contains all truth in the Bible, only that it covers our present needs as to these fundamental matters.

1. THE SCRIPTURES INSPIRED.

The Bible is the inspired Word of God, a revelation from God to man, the infallible rule of faith and conduct, and is superior to conscience and reason, but not contrary to reason. 2 Tim. 3:15, 16; 1 Pet. 2:2.

2. THE ONE TRUE GOD.

The one true God has revealed Himself as the eternally self-existent, self-revealed "I AM;" and has further revealed Himself as embodying the principles of relationship and association, i. e., as Father, Son and Holy Ghost. Deut. 6:4; Mark 12:29; Isa. 43:10, 11; Matth. 28:19.

3. MAN, HIS FALL AND REDEMPTION.

Man was created good and upright; for God said, "Let us make man in our image and in our likeness." But man, by voluntary transgression, fell, and his only hope of redemption is in Jesus Christ the Son of God. Gen. 1:26-31; 3: 1-7; Rom. 5:12-21.

4. THE SALVATION OF MAN.

(a) Conditions to Salvation.

The grace of God that brings salvation to all men has appeared through the preaching of repentance toward God and faith toward the Lord Jesus Christ; whereupon man is saved by the washing of regeneration and renewing of the Holy Ghost which is shed upon him richly through Jesus Christ our Saviour; and, having been justified by grace through faith, he becomes an heir of God according to the hope of eternal life. Tit. 2:11; Rom. 10: 13-15; Luke 24:47; Titus 3:5-7.

(b) The Evidences of Salvation.

The inward evidence to the believer of his salvation, is the direct witness of the Spirit. Rom. 8:16. The outward evidence to all men is a life of righteousness and true holiness, Luke 1:73-75; Titus 2:12-14; the fruit of the Spirit, Gal. 5:22, and brotherly love, Jno. 13:35; Heb. 13:1; 1 Jno. 3:14.

5. THE PROMISE OF THE FATHER.

All believers are entitled to, and should ardently expect, and earnestly seek the promise of the Father, the baptism in the Holy Ghost and fire, according to the command of our Lord Jesus Christ. This was the normal experience of all in the early Christian Church. With it comes the enduement of power for life and service, the bestowment of the gifts and their uses in the work of the ministry. Luke 24:49; Acts 1:4; 1:8; 1 Cor. 12:1-31.

6. THE FULL CONSUMMATION OF THE BAPTISM IN THE HOLY GHOST.

The full consummation of the baptism of believers in the Holy Ghost and fire, is indicated by the initial sign of speaking in tongues, as the Spirit of God gives utterance. Acts 2:4. This wonderful experience is distinct from and subsequent to the experience of the new birth. Acts 10:44-46; 11:14-16; 15:8, 9.

7. ENTIRE SANCTIFICATION, THE GOAL FOR ALL BELIEVERS.

The Scriptures teach a life of holiness without which no man shall see the Lord. By the power of the Holy Ghost we are able to obey the command, "be ye holy for I am holy." Entire sanctification is the will of God for all believers, and should be earnestly pursued by walking in obedience to God's Word. Heb. 12:14; 1 Pet. 1:15. 16; 1 Thess. 5:23, 24; 1 Jno. 2:6.

8. THE CHURCH A LIVING ORGANISM.

The Church is a living organism; a living body; yea the body of Christ; a habitation of God through the Spirit, with divine appointments for the fulfillment of her great commission. Every local assembly is an integral part of the General Assembly and Church of the First-born, written in heaven. Eph. 1:22, 23; 2:22; Heb. 12:23.

9. THE MINISTRY AND EVANGELISM.

A divinely called and a Scripturally ordained ministry for the evangelization of the world, is the command of the Lord, and the chief concern of the Church. Mk. 16:15-20; Eph. 4:11-13.

10. THE LORD'S SUPPER.

The Lord's Supper, consisting of the elements, bread and the fruit of the vine, is the symbol expressing our sharing the divine nature of our Lord Jesus Christ, 2 Pet. 1:4; a memorial of his suffering and death, 1 Cor. 11:26; and a prophecy of His second coming, 1 Cor. 11:26; and is enjoined on all believers "until He comes."

11. BAPTISM IN WATER.

The Ordinance of Baptism by a burial with Christ should be observed as commanded in the Scriptures, by all who have really repented and in their hearts have truly believed on Christ as Saviour and Lord. In so doing, they have the body washed in pure water as an outward symbol of cleansing while their heart has already been sprinkled with the blood of Christ as an inner cleansing. Thus they declare to the world that they have died with Jesus and that they have also been raised with Him to walk in newness of life. Math. 28:19; Acts 10:47-48; Rom. 6:4; Acts 20:21; Heb. 10:22.

12. DIVINE HEALING.

Deliverance from sickness is provided for in the atonement, and is the privilege of all believers. Isa. 53:4, 5; Matth. 8:16, 17.

13. THE ESSENTIALS AS TO THE GODHEAD.

(a) Terms Explained.

The terms "Trinity" and "Persons," as related to the Godhead, while not found in the Scriptures, yet are words in harmony with Scripture, whereby we may convey to others our immediate understanding of the doctrine of Christ respecting the Being of God, as distinguished from "gods many and lords many." We, therefore, may speak with propriety of the Lord our God who is One Lord, as a Trinity or as one Being of three Persons, and still be absolutely Scriptural. (Examples: Matth. 2:6; 8:16, 17; Acts 15:15-18.)

(b) Distinction and Relationship in the Godhead.

Christ taught a distinction of Persons in the Godhead which he expressed in specific terms of relationship, as Father, Son, and Holy Ghost; and that this distinction and relationship, as to its existence, is an eternal fact, but as to its mode it is inscrutible and incomprehensible, because unexplained. (That is, it is not explained as to how there can be three persons in the Godhead.) (Luke 1:35; 1 Cor. 1:24; Matth. 11:25-27; 28:19; 2 Cor. 13:14; 1 Jno. 1:3, 4.)

(c) Unity of the One Being of Father, Son and Holy Ghost.

Accordingly, therefore, there is that in the Father which constitutes Him the Father and not the Son; there is that in the Son which constitutes Him the Son and not the Father; and there is that in the Holy Ghost which constitutes him the Holy Ghost and not either the Father or the Son. Wherefore, the Father is the Begetter; the Son is the Begotten; and the Holy Ghost is the one proceeding from the Father and the Son. Therefore, because these three eternally distinct and related persons in the Godhead are in a state of unity, there is but one Lord God Almighty and His name one. Jno. 1:18; 15:26; 17:11, 21; Zech. 14:9.

(d) Identity and Co-operation in the Godhead.

The Father, the Son and the Holy Ghost are never identical as to Person; nor confused as to relation; nor divided in respect of the Godhead; nor opposed as to co-operation. The Son is in the Father and the Father is in the Son as to relationship. The Son is with the Father and the Father is with the Son as to fellowship. The Father is not from the Son, but the Son is from the Father, as to authority. The Holy Ghost is from the Father and the Son proceeding, as to nature, relationship, co-operation and authority. Hence, neither Person in the Godhead either exists or works separately or independently of the others. Jno. 5:17-30.

(e) The Title, Lord Jesus Christ.

The appellation "Lord Jesus Christ" is a proper name. It is never applied, in the New Testament, either to the Father or to the Holy Ghost. It therefore belongs exclusively to the Son of God. Rom. 1:1-3, 7; 2 Jno. 3.

(f) The Lord Jesus Christ, God with us.

The Lord Jesus Christ, as to His divine and eternal nature, is the proper and only Begotten of the Father; but, as to His human nature, He is the proper Son of Man. He is, therefore, acknowledged to be both God and man; who, because He is God and man, is "Immanuel," God with us. Matth. 1:23; 1 Jno. 4:2, 10, 14; Rev. 1:13, 14-17.

(g) The Title, Son of God.

Since the name "Immanuel" embraces both God and man in the one Person, our Lord Jesus Christ, it follows that the title, Son of God, describes His proper Deity, and the title, Son of Man, His proper humanity. Therefore, the title, Son of God, belongs to the order of eternity, and the title, Son of man, to the order of time. Matth. 1:23, 21; 2 Jno. 3; 1 Jno. 3:3; Heb. 7:3; 1:1-13.

(h) Transgression of the Doctrine of Christ.

Wherefore, it is a transgression of the Doctrine of Christ to say that Jesus Christ derived the title, Son of God, either from the fact of the incarnation, or because of His relation to the economy of redemption. Therefore, to deny that the Father is a real and eternal Father, and that the Son is a real and eternal Son, is a denial of the distinction and relationship in the Being of God; a denial of the Father and the Son; and a displacement of the truth that Jesus Christ is come in flesh. 2 Jno. 9; Jno. 1:1, 2, 14, 18, 29, 49; 8:57, 58; 1 Jno. 2:22, 23; 4:1-5; Heb. 12:3, 4.

(i)   **Exaltation of Jesus Christ as Lord.**

The Son of God, our Lord Jesus Christ, having by himself purged our sins, sat down on the right hand of the Majesty on high; angels and principalities and powers having been made subject unto Him, And, having been made both Lord and Christ, He sent the Holy Ghost that we, in the name of Jesus, might bow our knees and confess that Jesus Christ is Lord to the glory of God the Father until the end, when the Son shall become subject to the Father that God may be all in all. Heb. 1:3; 1 Pet. 3:22; Acts 2:32-36; Rom. 14:11; 1 Cor. 15:24-28.

(j)   **Equal honor to the Father and the Son.**

Wherefore, since the Father has delivered all judgment unto the Son, it is not only the express duty of all things in heaven and in earth to bow the knee, but it is an unspeakable joy in the Holy Ghost to ascribe unto the Son all the attributes of Deity, and to give him all the honor and the glory contained in all the names and titles of the Godhead, (except those which express relationship. See paragraphs b, c and d) and thus honor the Son even as we honor the Father. Jno. 5:22, 23; 1 Pet. 1:8; Rev. 5:6-14; Phil. 2:9, 8; Rev. 7:9, 10; 4:8-11.

14. THE BLESSED HOPE.

The Resurrection of those who have fallen asleep in Christ, the rapture of believers which are alive and remain, and the translation of the true church, this is the blessed hope set before all believers. 1 Thess. 4:16, 17; Rom. 8:23; Tit. 2:13.

15. THE IMMINENT COMING AND MILLENIAL REIGN OF JESUS.

The premillenial and imminent coming of the Lord to gather His people unto Himself, and to judge the world in righteousness while reigning on the earth for a thousand years is the expectation of the true Church of Christ.

16. THE LAKE OF FIRE.

The devil and his angels, the Beast and false prophet, and whosoever is not found written in the Book of Life, the fearful and unbelieving, and abominable, and murderers and whoremongers, and sorcerers, and idolators and all liars shall be consigned to everlasting punishment in the lake which burneth with fire and brimstone, which is the second death.

17. THE NEW HEAVENS AND NEW EARTH.

We look for new heavens and a new earth wherein dwelleth righteousness. 2 Pet. 3:13; Rev. 21 and 22.

Bible Doctrines: A Pentecostal Perspective

Adoption. At salvation the new believer is made part of the family of God and receives divine favor as His child (Gal. 4:5; Eph. 1:5; 2:19). Adoption also includes a future aspect: when believers receive their new bodies at the resurrection and Rapture and share the privileges of Christ's throne.

Amillennialism. The view that there will be no future reign of Christ on earth. Some spiritualize the Millennium and make it represent Christ's present reign in heaven during the entire Church Age.

Anglican. Belonging to the Church of England (Episcopal).

Annihilationism. The teaching that the wicked cease to exist at death or after a period in the Lake of Fire.

Anointed. In the Old Testament refers to an act of dedication to God's service by pouring oil on the person's head. In the New Testament it refers to an empowering, or energizing, by the Holy Spirit.

Antichrist. A false Christ who will appear at the end of this age, become a world dictator, and demand worship.

Antisupernatural. Denies the existence and reality of the supernatural. Tries to explain everything in terms of natural law.

Apocrypha. Books written during the period between the Book of Malachi and the birth of Jesus. The Jews did not include them in the Hebrew Bible and all the Protestant reformers rejected them as not being inspired.

Apostasy. A deliberate and total turning away from Christ and His teachings.

Apostle. A "sent one," or ambassador. Specifically, those chosen personally by Jesus to be with Him and to be primary witnesses to His resurrection and His teachings (Matt. 10:2–42; Acts 1:21–22; 1 Cor. 9:1).

Apostolic Age. The period between Christ's ascension and the death of the apostle John near the end of the first century A.D.

Ark of the covenant. In the Old Testament a gold-plated box that was the receptacle for the stone tablets inscribed with the Ten Commandments received on Mt. Sinai by Moses.

Armageddon. "The mountain of Megiddo," the site of the final battle between Christ and the Antichrist (Rev. 16:16).

Arminians. Followers of James Arminius (1560–1609) who taught that God chose to save all who will believe in Christ, that it is possible to resist the grace of God, and that it is possible for true believers to fall away and lose their salvation.

Ascension. Christ's bodily return to heaven forty days after His resurrection (Acts 1:3,9; Eph. 1:20–21).

Atonement. The covering of human sin by the payment of the price of Christ's death and the shedding of His blood. It blots out sin and guilt and makes possible reconciliation with God.

Attributes of God. The special traits, characteristics, or qualities of God that constitute His nature and being.

Autographs. The original handwritten manuscripts produced by the human authors of Scripture. These were probably circulated and copied so many times that they wore out. None of them are now known to exist. However, copies from close to the time they were written do exist.

Backsliding. A lessening of Christian commitment to do God's will.

Barbarian. In New Testament times this was a term used

of anyone who could not speak Greek. KJV uses the term often; NIV uses it once (Col. 3:11), resorting more often to "foreigner," "non-Greek," etc.

Bishop. (Old English *bisceop* from the Greek *episcopos,* "overseer," "superintendent.") In the New Testament a synonym for the "elder" (Gk. *presbuteros*) who was the president of the congregation. In later history it became the title of the chief pastor of a church.

Book of Life. A book containing the names of those who are born-again believers (Luke 10:20; Phil. 4:3; Heb. 12:23; Rev. 21:27), and therefore "fellow citizens with God's people" (Eph. 2:19).

Born again. Also means "born from above," a spiritual birth to a new life of obedience to Christ Jesus when a person puts faith in Him (John 3:3). It is evidenced by a sincere desire to please Him, show His love, and avoid sin and evil.

Bridegroom, The. Jesus Christ, who anticipates His future union with His bride, the Church, when He comes again at the end of the age.

Calvary. The Latin translation of the Greek *kranion* and the Aramaic *Golgotha,* "a skull." One ancient tradition says it was so called because Adam's skull was supposed to be there.

Calvin, John. A reformer (1509–1564) who taught God's absolute sovereignty demanded absolute predestination of those who should be saved and who should be lost. He failed to see that God is sovereign over himself and therefore able to give human beings true free will.

Camp meeting. On the American frontier thousands of people would pitch their tents around a clearing and have an open-air revival meeting. Later, large tents or plain auditoriums would accommodate the people as they worshiped.

Canon. The list of books accepted by the Church as Scripture inspired by the Holy Spirit.

Canonical. Accepted as part of the canon of the Bible.

Charismatic. Related to or possessing powerful spiritual gifts. The charismatic movement came into being through the emphasis and practice of charismatic gifts of the Holy Spirit.

Christ. Greek *Christos,* "Anointed One." Used as a title of Jesus as God's anointed Prophet, Priest, and King. A translation of the Hebrew *Mashiach,* "Messiah," also meaning "anointed one."

Church council. A meeting of representatives from individual churches to discuss matters of doctrine and practice.

Church Age. The period between Christ's resurrection and His second coming.

Circumcision. The cutting off of the foreskin of the penis. It was a sign of God's covenant with Abraham (Gen. 17:9–14) and became a sign of being a Jew.

Clergy. Those ordained by the Church to perform pastoral and teaching functions.

Collectivism. The theory advocating collective control over production and distribution of goods and services.

Communions. Groups of Christians who share common beliefs and are in communion with Christ and with each other.

Consecration. The setting apart of a person or thing for the Lord's use, or service. Also used of the seeking of a richer, deeper Christian life, wholly committed to God.

Conversion. The turning of a life from sin to serving Christ. It involves repentance that confesses and forsakes sin and that places faith and trust in Christ.

Conviction. The Holy Spirit's work in convincing a person of being a sinner and needing Jesus as Savior.

Covenant. A solemn, binding agreement. God's covenants are agreements by which He pledges to bless those who accept the covenant.

Day of Atonement. The tenth day of the seventh month (our Sept.-Oct.) of the Old Testament year. On that day the high priest offered sacrifices to make atonement for the sins of all the people of Israel (Lev. 16).

Deacon. A word meaning "servant," "helper." An office in the local church. Both men and women served as deacons (Rom. 16:1; 1 Tim. 3:8–13).

Deity. Being God, having the nature of God.

Demons. Spirit beings, sometimes called evil or unclean spirits, who work under Satan. Some believe they are fallen angels.

Denomination. A group of churches with a particular name who are organized and work together on the basis of a set of beliefs and practices they accept.

Depravity. Moral and spiritual corruption or pollution.

Desecration. Treating something that is holy with irreverence and contempt, usually in an outrageous way.

Devil. "Slanderer" (Gk. *diabolos*). The chief of the evil spirits, also known as Satan.

'**Discipleship and submission movement.** Teaches that a person should choose someone to be a "shepherd" (always a man) and submit to him. Also called the shepherding movement.

Doctrine. Teaching, especially teaching concerning biblical truths.

Dominion. Authority, sovereignty.

Easy believism. The idea that a person can express a mental belief in the gospel and in Jesus as Savior without any genuine repentance and without any responsibility to follow and obey Him.

Edification. The building up and strengthening of the believers.

Efficacious. Achieves what God intends.

Empirical data. Data received through the physical (five) senses.

Enduement. From the Greek, *enduō,* meaning "to be clothed upon." Used of the reception of the Holy Spirit's power.

Eternal kingdom. The final state of the saved in the new heavens and the new earth, with the New Jerusalem as their home and headquarters.

Eternal punishment. The final, endless punishment of the wicked in the lake of fire.

Evangelicalism. Affirms the inspiration and authority of the Bible and the truth of its teachings, with emphasis on the need for personal conversion and regeneration by the Holy Spirit.

Faculty. Ability, power, capability to act or do; natural aptitude.

Faith. Belief in God and Christ expressed in wholehearted, trustful obedience. Biblical faith is always more than believing something is true. It always has God and Christ as its object.

Fall of man. Adam and Eve's initial act of disobedience by which they lost their close relationship with God.

Fellowship. The sense of unity and partnership with God and Christ and with one another as Christians pray and work together in a spirit of mutual encouragement.

Firstfruits. In the Old Testament each year the first part of the crop was given to God. This came to include the meaning of "the best."

Folklore. Customs, stories, and sayings passed down from previous generations by word of mouth.

Fundamentalist. Conservative evangelical who emphasizes the inerrancy and literal interpretation of the Bible and takes a stand against antisupernatural liberalism.

Gnostics. Those who, beginning in the second century A.D., taught that salvation comes through special superior knowledge. Some taught physical matter is evil, and most denied the humanity of Christ.

Godhead. Originally, "Godhood." The nature of God, existing as one God in three divine Persons.

Grace. God's Riches At Christ's Expense; His generosity to humanity.

Great Commission. Jesus' command to spread the gospel to the whole world.

Great Tribulation. The period of the outpouring of God's wrath as judgment on the ungodly world system at the end of the age.

Great White Throne Judgment. The final pronouncement of judgment on the wicked (Rev. 20:11–14).

Heathen. Pagan; worshipers of false gods.

Heresy. An opinion or way of thinking that contradicts the teachings of the Bible.

Hierarchical. Referring to a system of church government that has several levels, the flow of authority coming from the top down.

Hieroglyphics. Picture writing used in ancient Egypt.

Holiness. Separation from sin and dedication to the worship and service of the Lord.

Holiness movement. A movement originating in the

mid-nineteenth century that emphasizes John Wesley's teaching on total sanctification and Christian perfection.

Holy. God is supremely holy and separate from all sin and evil in an awesome way. He is also dedicated in a positive sense to carrying out His will and plan. People are holy to the extent they are like Him.

Holy Ghost. Another term for the Holy Spirit, the third person of the one Godhead. "Ghost" is an old English word for "spirit."

Humanistic. Asserts human self-sufficiency while rejecting the supernatural. Secular humanism makes human reason its god.

Idolatry. The worship of anything other than the true God.

Immersion. Baptism that submerges the individual in the water.

Imminent. About to happen, or having the potential of happening at any time.

Immortal. Not subject to death and decay; living forever.

Impenitent. Refusing to repent or change one's attitude toward sin and toward the gospel.

Imputed righteousness. Christ's righteousness credited to the believers in Christ who accept His gift of salvation. God then treats the believer just as if he or she had never sinned.

Incarnation. The act by which the eternal Son of God became a human being without giving up His deity.

Intercession. Prayer on behalf of another person or persons.

Intuitively. Perceived or known directly without being reasoned out.

Irrationality. A way of thinking that distrusts human reason or that lacks clarity and coherence.

Itinerant. Traveling from place to place.

Judaism. The religion and culture that developed from Phariseeism among the Jews after the temple was destroyed in A.D. 70.

Justification. God's act of declaring and accepting a person as righteous in His sight. God pardons sinners who

274 **Bible Doctrines: A Pentecostal Perspective**

accept Christ and treats them as not guilty—just as if they had never sinned.

Kingdom of God. The reign, rule and royal power of God—in the believer's hearts, in the Church, in the world, and eventually in the millennial kingdom to be ruled on earth by Christ.

Laity. Originally the people of God as a whole. Later used as a term for Christians not ordained by the church as ministers.

Lake of fire. The place of final eternal punishment for Satan, his demons, and the wicked.

Layman. A member of the laity (not ordained to the ministry).

Liberalism. A movement that denies the supernatural and redefines Christian teachings and practices in terms of current human philosophies.

Lord. "Master," "owner." A term used of God and representing the personal name of God (Yahweh) in the Old Testament and used of both God and Jesus in the New Testament.

Luther, Martin (1483–1546). Leader of the German Reformation. He emphasized justification by faith alone rather than by works.

Manicheans. Followers of Mani (ca. A.D. 216–ca. 276), a Persian who taught there would be an ongoing struggle between the kingdom of light and the kingdom of darkness for 1468 years. It emphasized denial of bodily desires as a means of salvation.

Manuscript. A handwritten book. Before A.D. 100 these were scrolls or rolls. After that they were bound books.

Marriage Supper of the Lamb. A great celebration of the union of Christ and the Church. It takes place just before Jesus comes in triumph to destroy the armies of the Antichrist and establishes the millennial kingdom.

Materialism. Teaches that matter and its laws are the ultimate, or only, reality. The term is also used of putting the highest value on material well-being and the acquiring of material goods.

Mediator. One who goes between two parties in order to reconcile them. Jesus is the only Mediator between God and human beings (1 Tim. 2:5).

Messiah. "Anointed One." See "Christ."

Millennial Reign. The thousand-year reign of Christ on earth.

Ministry. Service rendered to God or to others. God has a ministry for every believer.

Miracle. An act of divine intervention where God's power is greater than and supersedes any natural forces that are present.

Missionary. One who ministers to other cultures and communicates the gospel across cultural lines.

Modernism. Protestant theological liberalism with its critical approach to the Bible and a willingness to accept current scientific theories even when they appear to contradict the Bible.

Monarchians. A second- and third-century movement that stressed the unity and oneness of God. Some made Jesus just a man. Others taught that God appears sometimes as the Father, sometimes as the Son, sometimes as the Holy Spirit.

Mount of Olives. The hill (2,723 feet elevation) east of Jerusalem's temple area.

New covenant. The covenant promised in Jeremiah 31:31 and put into effect by the death of Jesus (Heb. 8:6; 9:15–17).

New-age philosophies. A loosely-tied group of teachings based on oriental philosophies with an emphasis on nature worship, often including a smattering of Christian terminology

Normative. Having scriptural authority concerning what Christians are to believe and do.

Occult. The secret knowledge of supposed supernatural forces or agencies, especially in spiritism, fortune-telling, witchcraft, and astrology. These are dangerous ventures into Satan's territory.

Omnipresent. God is everywhere present and nothing is hidden from Him.

Ontological. Related to being, or existence.

Ordained. Publicly recognized by the Church as having a God-given ministry.

Ordinance. A practice commanded by Jesus and continued as a memorial in obedience to Him. The two specific ordinances are water baptism and the Lord's Supper.

Ordination. The public recognition by the Church of a God-given ministry.

Orthodox. From the Greek *orthōs,* "upright," "straight," "correct," "true," and *dokeō,* "think," "believe." Refers to correct teachings and practices as established by the Church. Used by Evangelicals of correct biblical teachings. The eastern churches took the name "orthodox" when the western (Roman Catholic) church split off from them.

Overcomers. "Winners," "victors:" all believers who maintain their faith in Christ (Rom. 8:37; 1 John 5:4).

Pantheism. The belief that God and nature or the universe are identical: "God is all, all is God."

Passover. The annual memorial ceremony by which the Jews remember deliverance from the death of the firstborn, the tenth plague God brought on Egypt in order to deliver them from Pharaoh (Exod. 12:1–32).

Pentecost. "Fiftieth," a name for the harvest feast which occurred fifty days after Passover. On the first Pentecost after the resurrection of Jesus the Holy Spirit was poured out on 120 believers to empower them.

Pentecostal. The movement that began in 1901 and emphasizes the restoration of the baptism in the Holy Spirit with the evidence of speaking in other tongues and the restoration of the gifts of the Holy Spirit.

Personal devotions. Private, personal worship and Bible study.

Postmillennial. Refers to the teaching that the millennium is the Church Age or an extension of the Church Age, with Christ ruling but not personally present.

Predestination. The teaching that God chooses something in advance. He predestined that Jesus would be the Head of the Church and that the Church is a chosen Body that He will glorify when Jesus returns. Calvinists believe God predestines individuals to be saved. This comes from Calvin's philosophy, not from the Bible.

Premillennialism. Teaches that Jesus will personally return at the end of the Church Age and will establish His kingdom on earth for a thousand years. Emphasizes the literal interpretation of the Bible.

Probation. The teaching that our present life is preparation for the future life.

Prophet. A speaker for God. In the Old Testament, God used prophets to give His message to His people and to the world. They were "forthtellers" rather than foretellers. New Testament prophets are gifted by the Holy Spirit to give messages of encouragement (Acts 15:32; 1 Cor. 14:3).

Providential. Involving God's care and guidance.

Puritans. A sixteenth-century movement in England that attempted to purify the English Church by introducing more Calvinistic reforms, along with a simplicity of worship.

Rapture. The snatching away of true believers for a meeting with Jesus in the air.

Reconciliation. The bringing of people to God in a restored fellowship.

Redeem. Refers to Christ's paying the penalty for our sins by His death on the cross and the shedding of His blood.

Redeemer. Jesus Christ, who alone was able to free us from sin.

Redemption. See "Redeem."

Reformation. The sixteenth-century movement led by Martin Luther that attempted to reform the Roman Catholic Church.

Regeneration. The Holy Spirit's work of giving new life to the sinner who repents and believes in Jesus.

Relativism. Teaches that any concept, meaning, or truth changes when the situation changes, or changes from one group of people to another. Often denies that there is any absolute truth.

Repentance. Greek, *metanoia*, "a change of mind." That is, a change of basic attitudes toward God and Christ that involves a turning away from sin and a seeking of God's rule and righteousness.

Revelation of Christ. The return of Christ in power and glory to destroy the forces of the Antichrist and establish the millennial kingdom.

Revival. The work of the Holy Spirit in renewing the spiritual vitality of individuals and churches. True revival makes evangelism easier.

Righteousness. Right relationship with God within His covenant, the believer lining up with the standards of justice and truth God has provided in the Bible.

Ritualistic. Dependent on prescribed forms of words and ceremonies.

Sabellians. Followers of Sabellius (third century A.D.), who taught that God is one Person who revealed himself in three forms, modes, or manifestations, in succession.

Sacramental. Refers to the belief that grace is dispensed through religious rites called sacraments.

Saint. Translates the Greek *hagios,* "a holy person." In the New Testament all believers are saints, not because they have reached perfection but because they have turned their backs on the world to follow Jesus. They are headed in the right direction.

Salvation. Includes all that God has done and will do for the believer in delivering from the power of sin and death and restoring to fellowship as well as assuring future resurrection and the full inheritance He has promised.

Sanctification. The work of the Holy Spirit that separates believers from sin and evil and dedicates them to the worship and service of the Lord. There is an initial act of sanctification at conversion and a continuing process of sanctification as we cooperate with the Holy Spirit in putting to death wrong desires.

Sanctify. "Separate to God," "make holy."

Sanctuary. "Holy place."

Satan. The Hebrew name of the devil, meaning "accuser," "adversary." He opposes God and all believers.

Scythian. Warlike Indo-Aryan tribes who moved from Central Asia and made several invasions of the Middle East beginning in the eighth century B.C. By 100 B.C. they had settled in the Crimea, near the Black Sea.

Seal. A mark or impression stamped on something by a signet ring or a small cylinder with an engraved end. It was used to authenticate or identify a document or object. Spiritually it identifies a person as belonging to Christ.

Second death. Eternal punishment in the lake of fire.

Secularism. Life and thought that ignore God and religion.

Seminary. An institution of higher education for the training of ministers and missionaries.

Septuagint. The translation of the Old Testament from Hebrew to Greek made during the two hundred years before Christ. A later tradition said it was done by seventy (or seventy-two) men. As a consequence, it is often referred to by the Roman numerals for seventy, LXX.

Shekel. Originally a weight of about ten grams. Later a coin of that weight.

Sovereign. Having supreme authority and rule. God's sovereignty includes his right to choose according to His own nature and will.

Speaking in other tongues. Speaking in a language given by the Holy Spirit.

Spiritualized. Given a spiritual meaning not in the literal or actual sense of the word or teaching.

Supernatural. Beyond the human or natural realm or activities. Used by Bible believers to describe God's activities that go beyond the ordinary events of nature.

Supernatural manifestations. Gifts distributed by the Holy Spirit and exercised by those receiving the gifts.

Tabernacle. The tent made by Israel in the wilderness as a place for God to manifest His presence in the midst of His people.

Teleological. The argument from design or purpose for the existence of God.

Testament. "Covenant" or "will." Used also to designate the two major portions of the Bible.

Theology of hope. Theodore Moltmann's construction of theology in terms of the future hope.

Totalitarianism. The theory that the centralized authority of the state should have total control over the individual citizen.

Transcendental meditation. A Hindu religious practice of meditation with the intent of securing happiness.

Transfiguration. The experience of Jesus on top of one of the mountains in Galilee during which His inner glory shown out like lightning flashes.

Transgression. Translates the Hebrew *pesha'*, "rebellion," and the Greek *parabasis*, "overstepping," "violation," describing sin that refuses to conform to the limits or standards set by God.

Translation of persons. The taking of persons into heaven without dying.

Tribulation. Greek, *thlipsis,* "pressure," "oppression," "affliction," "distress caused by circumstances." Also used of the Great Tribulation at the end of the age just preceding Christ's return in glory.

Typology. The study of Old Testament persons or events that foreshadow or anticipate New Testament truth, especially as relating to Jesus Christ.

Unregenerate. Not born again; without spiritual life.

Version. A translation of the Bible.

Vicarious. Totally for the benefit of another, or as a substitute for another.

Virgin Birth. The birth of Jesus Christ brought about by God's creative act through the Holy Spirit so that Mary became His mother without His having a human father.

Virtue. In the KJV this is another translation of the Greek *dunamis,* "power" (Mark 5:30; Luke 6:19; 8:46), and the Greek, *aretē,* "moral excellence" (2 Pet. 1:3).

Vision. Sometimes another word for a dream. Sometimes used of a supernatural appearance that brings divine revelation.

Vocation. The call of God to a life of faith and obedience and to particular ministries.

Witnesses. Those who testify concerning their experiences and knowledge of the truth of the gospel, especially with the intent of turning others to Jesus.

Zoroastrians. Followers of the Persian Zarathustra (sixth century B.C.) who taught that there are two gods, one good and one evil, that keep the world in a constant struggle between light and darkness. The good god, Ahura Mazda, demands good works.

BIBLIOGRAPHY

Bible Doctrines: A Pentecostal Perspective

Anderson, Christopher. *The Annals of the English Bible.* Abridged and Continued by S. I. Prime. New York: Robert Carter & Brothers, 1849.

Archer, Gleason L. Jr. *A Survey of Old Testament Introduction.* Revised Edition. Chicago: Moody Press, 1981.

Bauer, Walter, William F. Arndt, F. Wilbur Gingrich, eds., *A Greek Lexicon of the New Testament.* Translated by Frederick W. Danker. Chicago: The University of Chicago Press, 1971.

Bicket, Zenas. "The Holy Spirit—Our Sanctifier." *Paraclete* 2, No. 3 (Summer 1968), 3–6.

Boyd, Frank M. *The Spirit Works Today.* Springfield, Mo.: Gospel Publishing House, 1970.

Broughton, Hugh. *A Censure of the Late Translation for Our Churches.* ca. 1612. S.T.C. 3847.

Brumback, Carl. *Like a River: The Early Years of the Assemblies of God.* Springfield, Mo.: Gospel Publishing House, 1977.

——————————. *Suddenly From Heaven.* Springfield, Mo.: Gospel Publishing House, 1961.

Buswell, James Oliver. *A Systematic Theology of the Christian Religion.* 2 Vols. Grand Rapids: Zondervan Publishing House, 1962.

Cairns, Earle E. *Christianity Through the Centuries.* Grand Rapids: Zondervan Publishing House, 1981.

Dalton, Robert C. *Tongues Like as of Fire.* Springfield, Mo.: Gospel Publishing House, 1945.

Erickson, Millard J., ed. *Christian Theology.* Grand Rapids: Baker Book House, 1986.

Finegan, Jack. *Light From the Ancient Past.* 2d Ed. Princeton, N.J.: Princeton University Press, 1959.

Fjordbak, Everitt M. *Sanctification.* Dallas: Wisdom House Publishers, n.d.

Frodsham, Stanley H. *With Signs Following.* Rev. Ed. Springfield, Mo.: Gospel Publishing House, 1946.

Gee, Donald. *Spiritual Gifts in the Work of the Ministry Today.* Springfield, Mo.: Gospel Publishing House, 1963.

Geisler, Norman L. *Inerrancy.* Grand Rapids: Zondervan Publishing House, 1980.

General Council of the Assemblies of God. General Council Minutes. Oct. 1–7, 1916.

The General Council of the Assemblies of God Statement of Fundamental Truths. Revised. Springfield, Mo.: Gospel Publishing House, 1983.

Gish, Duane T. *Evolution: The Fossils Say No!* 2d Ed. San Diego: ICR Publishing Co., 1973.

Haley, John W. *Alleged Discrepancies of the Bible.* Grand Rapids: Baker Book House, 1977.

Harris, Ralph W. *Our Faith and Fellowship.* Springfield, Mo.: Gospel Publishing House, 1963.

Harrison, Everett F. *Introduction to the New Testament.* Grand Rapids: Wm. B. Eerdmans Pub. Co. 1982.

Harrison, R. K., Bruce K. Waltke, Donald Guthrie, Gordon D. Fee. *Biblical Criticism: Historical, Literary and Textual.* Grand Rapids: Zondervan Publishing House, 1980.

Harrison, Thomas F. *Christology.* 2d Ed. Rev. Springfield, Mo.: Published by the author, 1985.

——————. *Soteriology.* 2d Ed. Rev. Springfield, Mo.: Published by the author, 1986.

Holdcroft, L. Thomas, "Is the Kingdom Now?" *Pentecostal Minister* (Fall 1988), 15–17.

Horton, Stanley M. *The Book of Acts.* Springfield, Mo.: Gospel Publishing House, 1981.

——————————. "Counted Worthy to Escape." *Pentecostal Evangel,* 15 August 1976, 6–7.

——————————. "I Believe in the Pre-Tribulation Rapture." *Pentecostal Evangel,* 2 July 1989, 8–9.

——————————. *It's Getting Late.* Springfield, Mo.: Gospel Publishing House, 1975.

——————————. "One is taken; one is left." *Pentecostal Evangel,* 16 September 1973, 6.

——————————. "Paraclete." *Paraclete* 1, No. 1 (Winter 1967), 5–8.

——————————. "The Pentecostal Perspective," in *Five Views on Sanctification.* Melvin E. Dieter. Grand Rapids: Zondervan Publishing House, 1987.

——————————. "Perspective On Those New Translations." *Pentecostal Evangel,* 11 July 1971, 6–8.

——————————. *Ready Always.* Springfield, Mo.: Gospel Publishing House, 1974.

——————————. *The Ultimate Victory: An Exposition of the Book of Revelation.* Springfield, Mo.: Gospel Publishing House, 1991.

——————————. *What the Bible Says About the Holy Spirit.* Springfield, Mo.: Gospel Publishing House, 1976.

——————————. "Why the Bible is Reliable." *Pentecostal Evangel,* 14 January 1973, 8–11.

Hoy, Albert L. "Sanctification." *Paraclete* 15, No. 4 (Fall 1981).

In the Last Days: An Early History of the Assemblies of God. Springfield, Mo.: Assemblies of God, 1962.

Jeter, Hugh. *By His Stripes.* Springfield, Mo.: Gospel Publishing House, 1977.

Kendrick, Klaude. *The Promise Fulfilled.* Springfield, Mo.: Gospel Publishing House, 1961.

Kenyon, Sir Frederic. *Our Bible and the Ancient Manuscripts.* 5th Ed. Rev. London: Eyre & Spottiswoode, 1958.

——————————. *The Story of the Bible.* 2d Ed. Grand Rapids: Wm. B. Eerdmans Pub. Co., 1964.

Lewis, Jack P. *The English Bible From KJV to NIV: A History and Evaluation.* Grand Rapids: Baker Book House, 1981.

Lim, David. *Spiritual Gifts: A Fresh Look.* Springfield, Mo.: Gospel Publishing House, 1991.

McFarlane, K. B. *John Wycliffe*. London: The English Universities Press, 1952.

McGee, Gary B. "A Brief History of the Modern Pentecostal Outpouring." *Paraclete* 18, No. 2 (Spring 1984), 18–23.

Menzies, William W. *Anointed to Serve: The Story of the Assemblies of God*. Springfield, Mo.: Gospel Publishing House, 1971.

Morrison, Frank. *Who Moved the Stone?* London: Faber & Faber, 1930.

Nelson, P. C. *Bible Doctrines*. Springfield, Mo.: Gospel Publishing House, 1948.

The New Testament Greek-English Dictionary. Springfield, Mo.: The Complete Biblical Library, 1990.

Niebuhr, Reinhold. *Moral Man and Immoral Society*. New York: Charles Scribner's Sons, 1932.

Palma, Anthony D., "Baptism *by* the Spirit." *Advance* (June 1980), 214–216.

_____. *The Spirit*. Springfield, Mo.: Gospel Publishing House, 1974.

Pearlman, Myer. *Knowing the Doctrines of the Bible*. Springfield, Mo.: Gospel Publishing House, 6th Ed. 1945.

Pinnock, Clark H. *The Grace of God and the Will of Man*. Grand Rapids: Zondervan Publishing House, 1989.

Pohle, Joseph. *The Sacraments,* Vol. 4. Ed. Arthur Preuss. St. Louis: B. Herder Book Co., 1945.

Pun, Pattle T. T. *Evolution, Nature and Scripture in Conflict?* Grand Rapids: Zondervan Publishing House, 1982.

Reddin, Opal L., ed. *Power Encounter: A Pentecostal Perspective*. Springfield, Mo.: Central Bible College Press, 1989.

Rogerson, John, and Philip Davies. *The Old Testament World*. Englewood Cliffs, N.J.: Prentice-Hall, 1989.

The Role of Women in Ministry as Described in Holy Scripture. Position Papers of the Assemblies of God. Springfield, Mo.: Gospel Publishing House, 1990.

Ryrie, Charles Caldwell. *Biblical Theology of the New Testament*. Chicago: The Moody Press, 1972.

_____. *What You Should Know About Inerrancy*. Chicago: The Moody Press, 1981.

Spittler, R. P. "Glossolaia." In *Dictionary of Pentecostal and Charismatic Movements,* eds. S. M. Burgess and G.

B. McGee. Regency Reference Library. Grand Rapids: Zondervan Publishing House, 1988.

Stamps, Donald C. ed. *The Full Life Study Bible.* Grand Rapids: Zondervan Bible Publishers, 1990.

Stronstad, Roger. *The Charismatic Theology of St. Luke.* Peabody, Mass.: Hendrickson, Publishers, 1984.

Tenney, Merrill C. *The Reality of the Resurrection.* New York: Harper and Row, 1963.

Thiele, Edwin R. *The Mysterious Numbers of the Hebrew Kings.* Grand Rapids: Zondervan Publishing House, 1983.

Thiessen, Henry C. *Introductory Lectures in Systematic Theology.* Grand Rapids: Wm. B. Eerdmans Pub. Co., 1949.

Utsey, J. Dalton. "Romans 7 and Sanctification." *Paraclete* 18, No. 2 (Spring 1984), 3–6.

Vermes, Geza. *The Dead Sea Scrolls in English.* 2d Ed. Harmondsworth, Middlesex, England: Penguin Books, Ltd., 1975.

Where We Stand. Springfield, Mo.: Gospel Publishing House, 1990.

Wigglesworth, Smith. *Ever Increasing Faith.* Rev. Ed. Springfield, Mo.: Gospel Publishing House, 1970.

Wiley, H. Orton. *Christian Theology.* Kansas City, Mo.: Beacon Hill Press, 1952.

Williams, Ernest Swing. *Systematic Theology.* 3 Vols. Springfield, Mo.: Gospel Publishing House, 1953.

Williams, J. Rodman. *Renewal Theology.* 3 Vols. Grand Rapids: Zondervan Publishing House, 1990, 1992.

Wright, Gordon. *In Quest of Healing.* Springfield, Mo.: Gospel Publishing House, 1984.

Wycoff, John Wesley. *The Doctrine of Sanctification As Taught By the Assemblies of God.* Unpublished Thesis, 1972.

Bible Doctrines: A Pentecostal Perspective

NEW TESTAMENT

Bible Doctrines: A Pentecostal Perspective

Blessings (*cont.*)
from the Lord's Supper, 119
millennial, 238–239
receiving, 200, 206
Blood of Jesus, 92, 98, 116, 251
justified by, 112, 113
purifies from all sin, 153
Body of Christ. *See* Church
Book of Life, 219, 250
Bride of Christ, 161, 214, 218, 259. *See also* Church

Calvary
Christ's work at, 101, 195–199, 216, 259
old covenant abolished at, 124, 158
Calvin, John, 26
Canon, 21, 28–30
Charismatic gifts. *See* Gifts of the Spirit
Chiliasts, 232. *See also* Premillennialism
Church, 264. *See also* Apostolic Church; Assembly
as Bride, 161, 214, 218, 259
Christ the Head of, 67, 175
erosion in, 9
foundation of, 160
as a new covenant body, 124, 158
normative patterns for, 25, 135, 138
predestined to be holy, 170
in relation to the Kingdom, 161–162
responsible for evangelism, 163–164, 180–181, 250–251
as a spiritual fellowship, 161, 182
Church Age, 25
Clergy, 184–185
Communication with God, 19, 85, 200
Communion with Christ, 154, 161
Compassion, 129, 152, 168
Confession
of sins, 72, 153, 200
that Jesus is Lord, 46
Conscience, 20–21, 88f.14, 112, 153

Consecration, 148–149, 151
Conversion, 103–104, 106, 107, 153
Creation, 20, 28, 50, 51, 54, 62, 78–85

Day of Atonement, 195–196
Day of the Lord, 224, 225
Deacons, 168, 180, 185
Dead Sea Scrolls, 30–31
Death, 243–244
author of, 192, 194
of Christ, 19, 28, 68–69, 97, 98, 101–102, 106, 112, 116, 124, 198, 259
fear of, 211
forces of, broken by Christ, 67
intermediate state of, 244–246
as the last enemy, 198
no second chance after, 250
second death, 91, 102, 219, 244, 251–252
spiritual, 91, 102, 106
as the wages of sin, 91, 98, 106, 191, 195
Dedication, 148, 149, 151
of infants, 114
Deliverance, 198, 205
from demons, 178, 203
from sin, 65, 101, 183
Demons, 202–203
Devil, 102, 192, 203, 234.
See also Satan
Dichotomists, 82
Dictation theory, 22
Disciples, 70, 158–159, 183, 199 248. *See also* Apostles
Discipleship, 183
Discipline, 83, 181
Dualism, 86
Dynamic theory, 22–23

Easy believism, 53
Edification, 139–141, 165–167, 178, 181
Ekklēsia, 157, 159
Elders, 176, 179, 200
'*Elohim*, 48–49, 77
Eternal
definition of, 251–252
life, 84, 102, 244, 246, 248, 252

Eternal (*cont.*)
punishment, 21, 91, 99, 102, 243–244, 248, 251–252
Evangelicalism, 9, 99, 213
Evangelism, 169. *See also* Church: responsible for evangelism; Great Commission
Evangelists, 177, 178
Evil, 52, 86–87, 116, 130, 150, 151, 216
Evolution, 79–81
Experience, 104, 127, 142, 205
Faith, 98, 104–105, 202, 206
Christ's resurrection, the ground for, 211
gift of, 166–167
Holy Spirit received by, 130, 137
prayer of, 200
sanctification by, 150, 152
shield of, 234
Faithfulness, 105, 161, 223
as a fruit of the Spirit, 169
rewarded, 183, 235–236
Fall of humankind, 87–89, 91, 97, 191, 192
Fellowship
with believers, 117, 127, 157–158, 261
55, 117, 127, 158, 259, 261
with God and Christ, 85, 92, 117, 153, 211, 252, 259
of the Trinity, 55
Forgiveness, 91, 113, 197
through Christ's sacrifice, 67, 112
through Old Testament sacrifices, 67, 98
Freedom, 51, 52, 85, 87, 88
Fundamentalist, 9

Gehenna. *See* Lake of fire
Geneva Bible, 33
Gentiles, 20, 136, 137, 163, 217
Gifts of the Spirit, 124, 164, 165–169, 170.
See also Administration; Interpretation; Prophecy